VALLEY CITY:
A CHINESE COMMUNITY IN AMERICA

VALLEY CITY:
A CHINESE COMMUNITY IN
AMERICA

Melford S. Weiss

SCHENKMAN PUBLISHING COMPANY
Cambridge, Massachusetts

Distributed by
General Learning Press
250 James Street
Morristown, New Jersey

for
Paula and Nicole

Acknowledgements

I wish to express my appreciation to the following persons who have both directly and indirectly contributed to this study. I am most grateful to Drs. Bernard Gallin and Iwao Ishino and to authoress Betty Lee Sung.

Additional appreciation is acknowledged to Drs. Robert and Ai-li Chin, Stanford Lyman, Francis L. K. Hsu, William E. Willmott, G. William Skinner, D. Y. Yuan, Isao Fujimoto and Lawrence Crissman.

I also wish to thank my University colleagues at the Department of Anthropology for their assistance. A note of special consideration goes to Ms. Brigitta Jordan, my friend and editor.

I am also grateful to my many Chinese friends and acquaintances and to my Asian students, whose patience and understanding made my fieldwork a pleasurable and rewarding experience.

I would like to express my deepest appreciation to my wife, Paula Helene Weiss, who not only helped frame the theoretical considerations of this research but who also participated in the fieldwork and encouraged me throughout the writing.

I am grateful to all my colleagues and friends who have helped to organize and critique this study. The analyses and or conclusions however are my own for which I take full responsibility.

CONTENTS

List of Figures   xi
List of Tables   xii
Preface   xv

PART ONE   INTRODUCTION   **1**

1. Introduction to the Research   **3**
    Framework for Analysis   4
    Social Organization and Community   5
    Historical Perspective   6
    Problem Orientation   7

2. The Assimilation Process   **9**
    Acculturation   10
    Structural Assimilation   12
    Marital Assimilation and Other Types   13
    Consequences of Assimilation   13
    Sequential Development of Majority-Minority Relations   14

3. Tradition and Structure in Southeastern China   **15**
    Chinese Familism   15
    Ascribed Identities and Voluntary Associations   17
    Supernatural and Philosophical Overview   19

4. Overseas Migrations   **23**

PART TWO   THE ERA OF THE TRADITIONAL CHINATOWN (1850–1900)   **29**

5. The Chinese Experience in America   **31**
    Early Chinese Family Life   32
    Chinatown   33
    Sojourners   35
    Chinese Social Organization   35
    Conflict and Control   39
    Chinese Religious Extensions   41
    Acculturation   42

6. Early Chinese Settlement in Valley City   **45**

History and Supposition   45
Valley City's Chinese Population   46
Chinatown   49
Economic Enterprises   51
Conflict and Control   53
Multiplex Relationships and Common Values   55
Social Organization   56
Chinese Inter-community Relationships   58
Prejudice and Discrimination   58
Chinese-American Religious Institutions   61
Acculturation   63
Summary   65

PART THREE   A TIME OF TRANSITION   (1900–1940)   67

7. The Changing Chinese Community   **69**

Population Trends   70
Demographic Characteristics and Social Organization   73
Conflict and Change   75
Acculturation   79
   Language   79
   Discrimination   81
   A Shifting Chinese-American Identity   83
Social Organization   87
   Family Associations   87
   Chinese Tongs   90
   The Chinese Benevolent Association   90
   The Chinese-American Church   92
   The Chinese Language School   93
Worlds in Transition   95
   The Old World   96
   The New World   96
Unity and Diversity: Prologue to the Contemporary
Community   97

**PART FOUR   THE CONTEMPORARY COMMUNITY
                  (1940–1970)   101**

8. Settlement Patterns   **103**

Chinatown   103
Contemporary Chinese Settlement in Valley City   107
Population Distribution and Ethnicity   113

Demographic Characteristics of Residential Areas   118
    The Central City   118
    The South Area   121
Ethnicity and Social Relationships   122
Residence and Social Class: Inner City and Suburb   127

9. **Contemporary Population Characteristics**   **131**
Demographic Profile   131
    Sex Ratio   131
    Age Distribution   133
    Nativity   133
    Education   134
    Family Income   136
    Employment   136
Demography, Social Organization, and Acculturation   137
    Population and Community Structure   138
    Nativity and Culture   138
    Males and Females   139
    Occupation and Organization   139
    Selective Migration   143

10. **Patterns of Social Organization in Overseas Chinese**
    Communities   **145**
The Segmentary System   145
Crissman's Model and Structure in Valley City   148
The Tripartite Model   151
Cultural Categories and Sociological Variables   155

11. **Traditionists**   **159**
Patterns and Processes of Traditionist Organizational Life 160
    Membership   161
    Association Officialdom   163
    Decision-making "Chinese-style"   166
    Profiles of Officials   170
    Overlap and Continuity   174
Functions of Traditionist Associations   178
    Chinese Historical-Cultural Continuity   178
    Provision of Physical Comforts and Social Support   183
    The Regulation of Disputes   187
Other Traditionist Organizations   190
    The Chinese Language School   190
    The Chinese Drum and Bugle Corps   194
    Traditionist Youth Organizations   199

The Tong 201
The Kuomintang 202
The Chinese Anti-Communist League 203
The Chinese Women's New Life Movement 203
Extension of the Traditionist Network 203
Summary 206

12. Modernist Associations **209**
The Civic Club 210
Recreational Groups 221
The Community Service Club 223
Organization and Identity 226
The Chinese-Christian Church 228
Modernist Youth Groups 231

13. Activists **233**
Conflict without Compromise 237
Activist Philosophy and the Search for Legitimacy 240

14. Understanding the Chinese Community **245**
The Assimilation Process as a Methodological Construct 245
The Present Status of Chinese Acculturation 247
The Chinese-American Community and the People's
  Republic of China 250
The Chinese: A Distinct Minority 251
Division and Unity 252

Epilogue **259**
List of References 263

List of Figures

1. Districts of Heaviest Chinese Emigration to America   26
2. Residential Concentration of Chinese in Valley City, 1968   109
3. Oriental Population Distribution, Valley City, by percent, 1964   110
4. Oriental Population Distribution, Valley City, 1964   111
5. Chinese Population Concentration, Chinese Community Center, and Chinese-American Churches, Valley City, 1968   117
6. Hypothetical Model I: Social Structure in Sacramento   149
7. Hypothetical Model II: Social Structure in Sacramento   150
8. Model for Social Structure in Sacramento   151

List of Tables

1. The Assimilation Variables 11
2. Chinese Labor in Valley County 1850–1880 47
3. Chinese Population, Valley City and County 1852–1900   47
4. Population Figures for Chinese and non-Chinese, Valley City, 1852–1900 48
5. Chinese Population for Valley and San Francisco Counties 1860–1900 57
6. Chinese Population for Valley City and the United States 1880 and 1930 70
7. Chinese Male/Female Ratio for United States 1880, 1930; and for Valley City, 1930 71
8. Marital Status of the Chinese in the United States 1890, 1930 71
9. Age Distribution of the Chinese in the United States by Sex, 1920 72
10. Nativity for Chinese in the United States for 1880 and 1930 72
11. Nativity for Chinese in Valley City, 1930 (approximate)   73
12. Distribution of Individuals over 21 Years of Age, Valley City 1930 73
13. Ethnic and Racial Distribution for Selected Census Tracts, Valley City 1964–1965 112
14. Demographic Characteristics for Selected Census Tracts, Valley City 1964–1965 112
15. Racial-Ethnic Distribution of Pupils in Elementary Schools with Largest Numbers and Percentages of Oriental Students 114
16. Number and Percentage of Oriental Students in Elementary Schools with High Concentrations of Negro and Mexican-American Students 115
17. Racial and Ethnic Student Movement in Valley City Elementary Schools 116
18. Ethnic Minorities in the Valley City Metropolitan Area   132
19. Chinese Age Distribution by Sex—California 1960   133
20. Chinese Age Distribution by Sex—U.S.A. 1960   134
21. Educational Attainment for Chinese, 14 Years and Over, in California 1960 135
22. Income for Chinese in America, 1959   136

23. Occupations of Chinese in Valley City, San Francisco, and
    Francisco, 1960 141
24. Industrial Distribution for Chinese in Valley City and San
    Nationally by Sex, 1960 142
25. Profile of Officials for One Family Association 171
26. Internal Overlap in Decision-making Committee 175
27. The Continuity in Titled and Advisory Offices 176
28. Overlap of Officials in One Family Association 177
29. Social-demographic Characteristics of Civic Club Mem-
    bers 212

Preface

I first arrived in Valley City, California, in September, 1967, having accepted a position as assistant professor in the Department of Anthropology at Valley State University. My previous knowledge of Chinese life in America was largely limited to written materials although my graduate specialization had been Chinese culture and society. My first meetings within the Chinese community were, not surprisingly, with local Chinese students attending the college. They invited me to meet their friends, parents, and other relatives and I gradually expanded my contacts. My strategy was to ask each new person I met who they thought were the five most important people in the Chinese community. When a name was mentioned several times, I made it a point to meet that person.

I took advantage of my academic position and, when questioned about my research, told my informants that I was a college professor who wanted to write a book about the Chinese people in Valley City. I explained that while there were many books written about the Chinese in San Francisco and New York, there was no material about Valley City's Chinese, even though they constituted a sizable and significant community. While a few persons worried that I might be a government spy sent to ferret out those Chinese who had illegally entered the country or that I was just another bothersome white man, most of the people I met accepted my book-writing objective at face value and were, for the most part, eager to help me with my research.

Before long I was attending major community events such as the Moon Festival, Double Ten Celebration, China Night, Confucius' Birthday, and the Lunar New Year. I also started to appear at Chinese weddings and funerals and began to spend Sunday afternoons and evenings at the Chinese-language movies. I often walked about the streets of Chinatown, occasionally chatting with people while drinking tea at a Chinese restaurant. On Tuesday or Thursday evenings I would sit in on classes at the Chinese language school or watch the Chinese community drum and bugle corps practice. Sunday mornings were spent attending services at one of the city's five Chinese-Christian churches. At first I was very much noticed, being one of the few or the only non-Chinese, and I was sometimes questioned about my intentions. Yet, and to my surprise, I was often greeted warmly and on occasion invited to a wedding or funeral banquet or to someone's home for lunch. By the end of my first year I was even ignored, regarded as a sort of permanent fixture at many Chinese events.

During my second year I was invited to speak at the Civic Club, where I presented a lecture on Chinese contributions to America. I soon found myself speaking to church groups, student clubs, and even to the ethnic studies class at a local high school. After speaking to the Chinese community service club, I was invited to become a member and thereafter attended their meetings, parties, and dances. It was not difficult to establish personal relationships with my new Chinese friends. I was not only invited to their official functions but into their homes. My wife and I would reciprocate. During the spring semester of my second year, I was actively engaged in the fledgling Asian-American studies program at Valley State University, and many of the Chinese student leaders were enrolled in my Chinese community field-work seminar.

My involvement with the immigrant and often poor Chinese families began when I was invited to a wedding. I asked if I could take slides and became the official photographer for the event. After the slides were developed, I brought a projector to the bride's parents' home, where friends and relatives had gathered. After this, I found myself being invited to family dinners.

It was necessary to actively seek out the elderly Chinese leaders; they were often more suspicious about my activities and reluctant to be interviewed. Although I had managed to appear at some family association functions, I felt I was regarded with some hostility, often ignored, and that it was out of either fear or courtesy that I was not asked to leave. The situation changed when I was invited to the New Year's banquet of the largest and best known family association. During the banquet I was even introduced along with visiting Chinese dignitaries. Members of other associations, perhaps jealous of my presumed relationship with this association, began to court my favor and I subsequently had little trouble being invited to their functions. It was as if I had come to be regarded as a status symbol and my presence at an event would accord them some prestige.

Most of my informants understand English and, while some had difficulty conversing fluently, I was usually able to understand them. When I spoke to non-English speakers, I would often use as an interpreter a relative or a mutual friend, often their son or daughter. I also utilized the interpretive services of one of my students, a native Cantonese speaker who was majoring in Asian-American studies. A prominent member of the Chinese Benevolent Association acted as my unofficial translator and would often explain the implied innuendos and colloquialisms of Cantonese speech.

As a college professor, I was respected as a scholar and many people were pleased that I sought their advice. They would often volunteer information and take the time to explain what they really meant. They seemed delighted to have me as a guest and were proud to introduce me to their friends.

Although not Chinese, both my wife and I are short of stature and have dark complexions. Perhaps we do not look as different at Chinese gatherings as we would if we were tall and blond. We are also of minority ancestry and, after I once mentioned this fact, I found some informants were most eager to tell me about their feelings as Chinese. They felt I could understand how minority people really felt about things and would know what it was like to experience prejudice and discrimination.

Because I am a Caucasian I no doubt was excluded from information that might be made available to a person of Chinese ancestry. But my informants also indicated that they would tell me certain things about their neighbors and families which they would not divulge to other Chinese because they did not want these stories spread within the Chinese community.

This research is an outsider's conception of Chinese social organization and community life and, as such, it lacks some of the feelings associated with a Chinese identity. Yet, if my perceptions have less depth and ethnic insight, they are also less subjective. Perhaps my objectivity helped me to question institutions and practices that a Chinese anthropologist might inadvertently overlook.

As an anthropologist, my major ethnographic technique was participant observation, emphasizing maximum interaction with the people of this Chinese community in both formal and informal settings. My research techniques also included the collection of data through questionnaires, life and case histories, and the utilization of contemporary and past documentary and statistical information. This study, which began in 1967 and ended in 1970, represents a four-year research period.

PART ONE

INTRODUCTION

Introduction to the Research

As OPPORTUNITIES FOR FIELD RESEARCH on mainland China are presently not available, the study of overseas Chinese as representatives of Chinese society and culture and, perhaps more important, as transplanted emigrants and minority groups in a foreign land, has assumed a new importance for anthropologists and sinologists alike. Although scholarly research has produced studies of villages in Taiwan, the New Territories of Hong Kong, and of Chinese enclaves across Southeast Asia, recent critical explorations of Chinese communities in the New World are less extensive and abundant. There is a definite need for more sociological investigations of Chinese communities in contemporary North America to provide additional comparative data on the organization of overseas Chinese social life. Such studies can contribute to present investigations of racial and ethnic groups, particularly to those dealing with the acculturation and assimilation of minority peoples.[1] At the same time, by focusing upon the processes of cultural change, they can add to the understanding of the patterns of Chinese adjustment to American society.

It is the intent of this researcher to explore the Chinese-American experience. The objective of this study is to examine critically the present community organization of the Chinese in Valley City, California, and to show how it emerged from experiences of the past.[2]

[1] The terms acculturation and assimilation are defined in Chapter 2.
[2] "Valley City" is a fictitious name, as are the names of many Valley City organizations. To protect their privacy I have changed the names of individuals, organiza-

Framework for Analysis

The changing structure of the social institutions of a racially and culturally different people in a foreign land is expressed in patterns of cultural adaptation which are based upon historical precedent and conditioned by local community practices.

Historical precedents focus upon the structure of the home community as it existed, or as it was thought to exist by the emigrants, prior to emigration. The diachronic approach is a necessary element of this study because traditional Chinese social structure in Kwangtung province became the institutional foundation for Chinese social life in the New World. Moreover, current organization is based upon past experiences, so that more recent developments are systematically related to previous ones.

Secondly, the process of cultural change is of paramount importance because the organization of the Chinese community today is related to the patterns of behavioral and structural assimilation of the Chinese minority in American society. The hierarchy and segmentation of organizations, the conflicting interests of modern and traditional associations, the extent to which these associations integrate and divide the community, and the nature of ethnic and racial relationships with other American minorities and society at large are determined by these processes of cultural change.

Finally, Chinese life in American cities is also a consequence of local community practices. These include both the specific social history of community growth and the strength of intercommunity relationships among the Chinese. The dynamics of a Chinese-American community must be approached within the context of the American community itself. Previous studies of minorities have been primarily concerned with the process by which the indigenous institutions of the minority group have been modified and changed when transplanted in a foreign setting. While this culture-change approach is a legitimate one, it has also been recognized that the specific nature of the community to which the minority group has immigrated plays a significant role in the structuring of the minority group itself. Chinese-American communities parallel each other in many respects, yet significant local differences exist. These ecological, demographic, and social forces are

tions and the city itself. I hope my readers will respect their privacy as well. I offer this book in the hope that it will help further greater understanding between the Chinese themselves and between the Chinese and non-Chinese peoples of America.

often responsible for specific institutional arrangements within a particular Chinese community.

Valley City's Chinese community is divided into a significant number of segments, often with conflicting goals. Yet, under certain circumstances, this community can function as an integrated and holistic entity. At the same time, it is tied to a network of economic, political, religious, and social relationships which extend beyond its physical boundaries to other Chinese centers in America and overseas. These ties to other areas are important to the community study, because these linkages not only influence the social organization of the Chinese community but also indicate the direction of change within the community.

Social Organization and Community

Social organization reflects the major social and cultural commitments of the community's members and diagrams the process by which these stated and unstated commitments are translated into behavior. For the purpose of this study the Chinese community will be treated as a social system composed of organizational and familial social relationships, and this investigation will focus upon the structure and function of those relationships. Community represents the images and identities that people hold. This study analyzes the changing institutional social relationships between groups, groups that are systematically arranged, interdependent and interrelated.

The Chinese community of Valley City, California was selected for this study because, although not a port of entry, it is nevertheless representative of the tradition of Chinese settlement and the changing character of Chinese life in America. As an urban center Valley City reflects both the historic and present pattern of Chinese immigration. The city has enjoyed a continuous and growing Chinese population from the gold rush days of the 1850's to the 1970's and promises to continue as a Chinese-American center. The Chinese community includes recently arrived immigrants as well as fourth generation Americans of Chinese descent, and their interests cover a wide range of occupational, educational, and social objectives. The community is composed of a number of organizations of varying orientations, organizations which can be grouped into three major categories—modernist, traditionist, and activist. A modernist organization is one whose primary concern is with establishing and maintaining an American as well as a Chinese identity; a traditionist organization is one whose objective is the preservation and continuation of the Chinese heritage;

and an activist organization is one that is oriented toward social action and concerned with developing a pan-Asian identity.

Valley City has never been an initial receiving station for Chinese newcomers, consequently, its Chinese community has never reached, either in population, complexity, or stability, the dimensions of the Chinatowns of San Francisco and New York. Moreover, the city's urban renewal projects have displaced the Chinese from their Chinatown ghettos, and the resulting increased exposure to, and fuller participation in, American life have precipitated significant changes in family and organizational structure. Thus, Valley City's Chinese community is an ideal testing ground for studies of social change and provides the opportunity to study directly institutional conflict.

Historical Perspective

This treatment of Chinese settlement in America is centered upon organizational and institutional adjustment to social and cultural change. The concern, therefore, is more with the processes of such adjustments and the dynamics of family and community life of the Chinese minority in America than with a detailed account of legislative actions or specific historical events. This concern is reflected in the decision to document the Chinese experience in America in three major stages: The Era of the Traditional Chinatown, A Time of Transition, and The Contemporary Community. During each stage certain features of Chinese adjustment to American life are highlighted and become a focal point for the organization of community structure.

The Era of the Traditional Chinatown begins with early Chinese emigration to America in the 1850's and concludes around the turn of the nineteenth century. Chinese social organization followed, in part, lineage-village principles. Male elders and successful merchants respectively dominated family and community affairs. A network of interrelated associations provided an atmosphere of institutional interdependency, assuring protection and security for Chinese in isolated ethnic enclaves called Chinatowns. The acculturation of the Chinese was limited to occupational and technological innovations and, for some, to a Christian religious life.

The Time of Transition ended with the repeal of Chinese exclusion in 1943. It was marked by gradual "liberating" changes. Women increasingly participated in economic affairs as wage earners and openly challenged their husbands' domination of family life. A new generation of American-born children expressed their American identity by demanding new freedoms in marital, economic, and social affairs and achieved minor successes in penetrating the outside community. Multiple revisions in both Chinese and American society created organizational strife as new problems demanded modern solutions, yet in both places elders continued their domination of community life.

The Contemporary Community of the 1940 to 1970 era witnessed large-scale Chinese participation in the dominant society surrounding its Chinese enclaves, ghettos which were rapidly losing their Chinese residents because of population movement into formerly restricted areas. This increased involvement in American occupational educational life, confusing yet exhilarating, demanded a new Chinese identity. As the ability of the traditional institutions to control community life waned, second generation Chinese adults created their own organizational structure. Moreover, intergenerational conflicts accelerated the breakdown of traditional family controls and restructured familial role relationships.

Problem Orientation

Because this study deals with the continuing relationship of social structure to culture and community, it will incorporate both synchronic and diachronic perspectives. This investigation is concerned primarily with the Chinese involvement in the assimilation process, as mirrored in the formal and informal social organization of the community. It will be guided by the following generalized findings:

1. In spite of the release of the Chinese from their Chinatown ghetto and their increased exposure to American life, Chinese are nevertheless able to maintain their cultural and communal identity.

2. The structure of the Chinese community is predicated upon the subcultural categories designated by the terms traditionist, modernist, and activist.

3. This organizational structure is directly related to the degree of behavioral and structural assimilation of the members of the Chinese community.

   a. As assimilation processes increase, the forms and functions of Chinese organizations will approach an American pattern. Where assimilation processes are retarded or restricted, the Chinese community will adopt isolationist and protective institutional measures.

   b. The acculturation of the Chinese in America does not necessarily lead to consequent structural and marital assimilation.

2

The Assimilation Process

IN THIS STUDY OF the changing social patterns of a Chinese community in America, the major objective is to focus upon community social organization, particularly the synchronic structure and function of institutions within the Chinese social system. However, this investigation is also based upon diachronic dimensions—an historical evaluation of Chinese social organization. Both approaches, synchronic and diachronic, are concerned with social and cultural change and demand a somewhat specialized vocabulary to discuss satisfactorily the dynamics of group social life.

The Chinese, as an American minority, are a subordinate segment of a complex society, are few in number, and are self-consciously aware of collective discrimination. Most important for this investigation, however, is the consideration of the Chinese as an ethnic group, a people more or less bound together by ties of cultural homogeneity with a "consciousness of kind." [Gordon defines ethnicity as the locus of a sense of intimate peoplehood (1964:38).] Ethnic groups exhibit distinctive folkways, mores, and customs and, more important, show a high degree of loyalty to certain basic social institutions, such as family, religion, and language. Ethnic groups do not, either willingly or unwillingly, embrace the totality of the host culture's cultural imperatives. The procedures by which they adapt to the dominant culture by changing their attitudes and behavior are therefore of particular interest to sociologists and anthropologists alike.

Social science literature abounds with definitions, labels, and typologies of these procedures. Many of these terms refer to specific sub-processes but are often used indiscriminately, resulting in confusion rather than clarification. Milton Gordon's assimilation variables (see Table 1) will be used in this study for two reasons. First, they stress the different "degrees" of assimilation (all sub-processes are not equal, nor can we use the same criteria), which are presented in an ordered if not sequential pattern. Secondly, these "variables" appear in the more recent literature about minority groups in America and offer us the opportunity for cross-ethnic comparison. (Prentice-Hall is presently publishing monographs on American racial-ethnic groups and M. Gordon is general editor of the series.) [1]

Acculturation

Acculturation (cultural or behavioral assimilation), defined by Gordon as a change of cultural patterns to those of the host society, may be the first type of assimilation to occur and may take place when no other type occurs either simultaneously or later (Gordon 1964:77). Acculturation varies inversely with discrimination and spatial-social segregation but may nevertheless occur in spite of these delaying phenomena.

Gordon claims there are basically two distinctive types of acculturation. Intrinsic changes are those affecting the vital ingredients of the ethnic group which are essential to their historical-cultural heritage; they include religious beliefs, religious practices (ritual), ethical values, musical tastes, literature, language, "sense of a common past," and folk recreation. Extrinsic changes are external to the core of the group's ethnic heritage; they include changes in dress, manner, patterns of emotional expression, and language pronunciation oddities. These changes do not usually directly threaten ethnic heritage and are most useful for social mobility within the dominant society (Gordon 1964:79). Prejudice and discrimination tend to be based upon differences in extrinsic rather than intrinsic cultural traits (Gordon 1964:81).

Changes, whether extrinsic or intrinsic, are likely to occur at both the conscious and unconscious levels. Changing styles of dress, establishing new residence patterns, learning new skills, and acquiring a new language are conscious processes. Changes in pronunciation, gestures, mannerisms, tastes, and sentiments are likely to take place gradually and in degrees so slight they may not be open to measure-

---

[1] Gordon's assimilation variables and sequences represent one attempt to understand the processes of majority-minority relationships. See chapter 14 for a more detailed discussion of the assimilation process.

Table 1

The Assimilation Variables

Subprocess or condition	Type or stage of assimilation	Special terms
Change of cultural patterns to those of host society	Cultural or behavioral assimilation	Acculturation
Large-scale entrance into cliques, clubs, and institutions of host society, on primary group level	Structural assimilation	None
Large-scale inter-marriage	Marital assimilation	Amalgamation
Development of sense of peoplehood based exclusively on host society	Identificational assimilation	None
Absence of prejudice	Attitude receptional assimilation	None
Absence of discrimination	Behavior receptional assimilation	None
Absence of value and power conflict	Civic assimilation	None

Source: Gordon (1964:71).

ment or observation. These are changes that occur at the unconscious level (Park 1925:281–83).

Tangible items (extrinsic) such as clothing and economic enterprise are more likely to be readily adopted while non-tangible (intrinsic) items such as religion and family organization are not readily adopted at first. But tangible items (the length of women's skirts) may have a direct relationship to non-tangible institutions (the proper role of women in the family). It is often difficult to separate these cultural items (Berry 1965:257).

Acculturation as a phenomenon involves the integration of new elements, and thus it is not merely the addition of the new and the subtraction of the old. These items may be intimately related to each other, but when, for example, the Christian religion is incorporated, it may not necessarily lead to the rejection of previously held supernatural beliefs (Fairchild 1947:109–12).

Although acculturation is most likely to occur in areas in which the cultures are similar, it is important to distinguish between behavioral and attitudinal similarity. These patterns may be quite different from those of the host culture although they express the same attitudes (Marden & Meyers 1968:437). For example, the American educational system differs from the Chinese scholarly tradition in both methodology and purpose, yet the attitudes are the same. Both stress the importance of formal education.

Contact between groups generally means that some degree of acculturation will occur, even when there is no expressed interest in adopting the other group's customs and when one's own culture is considered satisfactory. Acculturation then can be quite minimal (Berry 1965:250). Finally, acculturation is most likely to occur first among extrinsic traits, but the degree of acculturation will largely depend upon the kinds of contact and the frequency with which they occur.

Structural Assimilation

Structural assimilation is the entrance of the minority group into the primary institutions of the core (host) society at the primary group level. This process spans the life cycle of the individual, from children's play groups, through the college fraternity and the country club, to the grave. It involves the entrance of immigrants and their descendants into the social cliques, organizations, institutional activities, and civic life of the receiving (host) society (Gordon 1967:411). Once structural assimilation occurs, either simultaneously with or subsequent to acculturation, all the other "types" of assimilation will naturally follow. Thus structural assimilation is a keystone in the assimilation process (Gordon 1964:81).

At this level it is critical to distinguish between two kinds of relationships, the primary and the secondary. Primary relationships are created by personal friendship patterns, frequent inter-family visiting, communal worship, and communal recreation; primary relationships are warm, intimate, and personal. Secondary relationships are found in the general activities of civic life, involving earning a living, carrying out political responsibility, and engaging in the instrumental, rather than the expressive, affairs of the larger society; secondary relationships are relatively impersonal and segmental (Gordon 1967: 411).

It becomes necessary to distinguish clearly between the effects of acculturation and structural assimilation, for they occur at different levels of a group's social life. To paraphrase a social anthropological model (Beattie 1964:34–40; Parsons 1951a, 1951b), acculturation takes place at the level of meaning and its primary focus is the cultural system. Structural assimilation takes place at the level of action and centers upon the social system. Theoretically, we can isolate the processes and treat them separately. In this study, however, the primary concern is with institutionalized social relationships, those relationships which are stable and relatively enduring at the action level. Here the two processes must interact, for structural assimilation is dependent upon acculturation and intimately affects it.

Marital Assimilation and Other Types

Marital assimilation refers to large-scale intermarriage of the ethnic minority with the dominant (host) populace; there is an indissoluble connection in the time order between structural and marital assimilation, and all other types. Marital assimilation is an inevitable by-product of full-scale structural assimilation. Increasing intermarriage leads to a loss of ethnic identity for the minority group and identificational assimilation takes place. Descendants of the minority group soon become indistinguishable from the dominant group, and prejudice and discrimination are no longer a problem. Primary-group relationships are extended to all and civic assimilation follows.[2]

Consequences of Assimilation

The assimilation process varies among ethnic, racial, and religious groups. There are, however, some regularities which apply to all ethnic groups in America, including the Chinese:
1. A lack of intimate primary-group relationships between the minority and the dominant groups tends to promote ethnically hostile attitudes. Structural separation prevents the development of personal and intimate bonds and encourages the formation of disruptive stereotypes (Gordon 1964:236).
2. Structural separation aids in the retention of beliefs and historical symbols for the minority group. This structural pluralism is accompanied by a modest degree of cultural pluralism as well (Gordon 1964:237).

---

2 This sequence is a theoretical proposal. It is not a social fact, even for Caucasian Catholics (excluding Mexican-Americans) in American society. See paradigm for assimilation (Gordon 1964:76).

3. In most cases the structural assimilation of immigrants who enter the country in numbers substantial enough to establish a communal life is impossible. The newcomer needs the comfortable social and psychological milieu which his communal group provides (Gordon 1964:242).

4. The immigrant may adopt extrinsic cultural traits and engage in secondary social relationships but he will retain his primary-group communal life. The immigrant "sub-society" will mediate between his native culture and the "American" culture (Gordon 2964:243–44).

5. American-born children of immigrants are on their way to virtually complete acculturation, although not necessarily structural assimilation, at selected class levels. There will be a tendency for native-born children to become alienated from their parents and the culture they represent (Gordon 1964:244–45).

6. Desegregation (the process of eliminating racial discrimination) will not lead immediately or necessarily to integration or the dissolution of ethnic communality. It will lead to many secondary contacts but not necessarily to primary relationships within the dominant society. However, these secondary relationships, over a sufficiently extended period of time, will lead to an increase in personal, intimate contacts across ethnic lines (Gordon 1964:246–47).

Sequential Development of Majority-Minority Relations

Robert E. Park reached the conclusion that there is a cycle of events in race (ethnic) relations which tends everywhere to repeat itself. Underlying this assumption is the conviction that structural assimilation and amalgamation (marital assimilation) are the inevitable results of the meetings of peoples (Park 1949:150). At the other end of the assimilation spectrum, Lieberson (1961:902–10) insists that neither assimilation nor conflict is the inevitable outcome of race (ethnic) relations, and that there are wide variations between societies in the nature and processes of race and ethnic relations.

Not enough is known about the development of ethnic relationships to predict a casual and final sequence for the Chinese.

3

Tradition and Structure in Southeastern China

THE CHINESE EXPERIENCE in America is a syncretic and sometimes internally inconsistent blend of traditional prerogatives and American innovation. Although filled with conflict and compromise as well as institutional variation in both form and function, Chinese-American society still reflects a heritage where ancestral structural patterns prevail. The purpose of this chapter is to discuss the institutional principles of traditional society in Southeastern China which have played an important role in structuring Chinese life in overseas communities and which continue to influence Chinese social organization in American cities today.

Chinese Familism

The patrilineal, patrilocal, patriarchal, and patrimonial family was the social system of the Chinese Empire.

"The major characteristics of the Chinese family system are well known: subordination of the individual to the group, the young to the aged, the living to the ancestors, the wife to the husband, the daughter-in-law to the mother-in-law, emphasis on progeny, not romantic love, as the prime reason for marriage, with the resulting concomitants of arranged marriage and (for the wealthy, not the poor) concubinage? intense family solidarity, giving to the individual the psychological and economic security that came through membership in a tightly knit group. . . ." (Bodde 1957:44).

The average peasant family, rather than being an economically self-sufficient unit in regard to production and consumption, found itself tied to at least a local market which was "essential both as a source of necessary goods and services unavailable in the village community and as an outlet for local production." [1] (Skinner 1964:6).

The family, however, remained the basic unit for the allocation of power and responsibility. Decisions were made primarily with reference to family interests, the overriding focus for individual loyalties. Although friendship groups of various kinds tempered family relationships, when the interests of one's friends clearly contradicted those of one's family, the family interests ideally always took precedence (Levy 1967:69–71).

The family is pictured as a cohesive and stable unit of Chinese society, but the imbalance of intrafamilial relationships often made for internal conflicts. There was a tendency for households to split in each generation, for as sons matured and married they began to assert their independence as potential heads of domestic units. Married women in the household, by virtue of agnatic exogamy and patrilocality, remained "strangers" and often precipitated rivalry between brothers and between mother and son. The activities of women within the domestic unit were often as essential as those of men to the functioning of the family unit. They could handle the internal finances of the household and played an important role in the socialization of the children. Household division was seen by the Chinese themselves as a result of conflict initiated by women (Freedman 1958:21, 32). While Confucian ethics may have stressed the solidarity of brothers, the social options available exerted at least an equal pressure to force them apart (Freedman 1958:22). The effects of the conflicts within the family were not as strong in the gentry as they were to peasant families. Fragmentation occurred earlier in the lower socioeconomic peasant units than in gentry families, whose economic position enabled them to resist this trend for a longer period of time (Freedman 1958:26–31). Many households did separate, but because they were at least potentially members of a single ancestor worship unit, some forms of economic cooperation might be initiated. Indeed, the creation of new household units did not preclude the possibility of such cooperative ventures (Freedman 1958:25). The importance of the family as a basic unit is further validated by the extension of kinship terms to

---

[1] The dependency of local villages upon a market network is documented by Skinner (1964:3–43) and also noted by Kulp (1925:343), Hsiao (1960:11), and Wolf 1966:43–44).

non-kin friends, thus bringing "strangers" within the context of family relations (Levy 1967:71).

Family relationships were firmly ordered in a system of superordination and subordination, focusing upon the domination by male elders. This family system functioned best in a rural agricultural setting where the family could act as a self-perpetuating economic unit and where sons, daughters, and wives had little opportunity for outside employment. Women worked alongside their husbands and were usually dependent upon their husbands' positions for community status and economic well-being. Furthermore, the arrangement for and choice of marital mates reinforced the legitimacy of parental control over sons and daughters-in-law. To be sure, family conflicts occurred, but they were often resolved in terms of culturally prescribed alternatives.

Traditional family relationships continued in overseas families as long as social conditions were congruent with Chinese familism and where economic opportunities outside of the family were limited. Familial pressure was reinforced by community structure and, because the channels for social mobility were geared to family rather than individual accomplishments and merit, the fortunes of sons and daughters fell and rose with the family as a unit.

Ascribed Identities and Voluntary Associations

The Chinese lineage (*Tsu*) is an aggregation of male agnates and their children sharing a common ancestor and bound to each other by demonstrated descent. Such large-scale unilineal kinship organizations dominated Chinese life in Fukien and Kwangtung, the home "ports" for most overseas Chinese.

Although lineages are essentially local political organizations (Freedman 1958:2), with each unit usually occupying a distinct section or neighborhood (Hu 1948:173), they also perform economic, militaristic, religious, and governmental functions. Powerful lineages controlling the corporate property of their members not only exerted a strong influence upon the community but, by acting as tax collectors, became fiscal intermediaries between state and landowner (Freedman 1958:74–76). The lineage, socially and ritually differentiated, was organized so as to place considerable power in the hands of a controlling elite (Freedman 1958:69), and indeed one of the keys to the viability of Southeastern China's lineages was the interlocking of lineage elites with the national bureaucracy. Certainly many of the benefits of lineage membership accrued directly to the elites; yet even lowly members of power lineages, poor peasants, profited from membership through agnatic association with influential gentry (Freedman 1958:130).

Another basic societal unit was the nucleated village (Freedman 1958:1, 6) but, because so many villages consisted virtually of single lineages, lineage and village identities were often coincident—that is, many local communities consisted of male and unmarried female agnates and the wives and children of the men (Freedman 1958:3). Even the possession of a common surname might in certain circumstances lead to formal cooperation such as local lineages being grouped into wider agnatic units (clans). Lineages might be grouped not only upon similarity of surname, but also on the basis of certain traditional alliances of surnames (Freedman 1958:5). Furthermore, the prescriptions for marriage demanded lineage and surname exogamy and usually marriage outside the village, so that marriage partners, by crossing lineage and village boundaries, created inter-lineage and inter-village ties (Freedman 1958:104).

Where several lineages were found within a single village, the different lineages might cooperate, yet turbulence was also common among such groups, most specifically brought about by the subjugation of a poor by a rich lineage. Recourse to physical violence as a means of settling disputes was as common as the use of legal machinery (Freedman 1958:105, 111).

Other lineage functions were the compilation and revision of geneological records; ancestor worship and the establishment of ancestral halls, ritual land, and graveyards; material assistance to members in times of need; the education of the young; punishment of misconduct; and self-defense (Chuan 1967:36). The lineage was unmistakably a well-established and fundamental institution of rural, agrarian China.

Agnatic groupings were flexible, but the localized lineage limited the range and nature of relations (Freedman 1958:92), so there was also room for ad hoc groupings which might undertake tasks not provided for, or poorly provided for, within the lineage structure. Naturally, where the lineage was strong, other groupings could not assume as important a structural position, yet their influence could still be considerable (Freedman 1958:92). Thus, for example, the money lending clubs enabled poor villagers to borrow money when their rich relatives refused loans (Kulp 1925:189–91). Moreover, non-kin voluntary associations also gave individuals opportunities to exercise leadership and to gain prestige (Freedman 1958:93). Secret societies, also voluntary groups, were originally organized in opposition to the State (Ching Dynasty). They ranged from purely religious and contemplative sects to groups which practiced political violence (Freedman 1958:117), and some, particularly the Triad Societies, became key forces in community affairs. Most voluntary associations cut across class and kin lines, truly integrating the diverse elements of the villages (Freedman 1959:121–23); some, specifically the secret societies, developed ties of ritual brotherhood, thus assuming some of the obligations and prescriptions of agnatic kin groups.

Skinner (1964:33) further reports that even the standard marketing area involving several villages and lineages was a culturally, economically, and socially defined area; marital, voluntary, and kin ties tended to become inclusive within this territory.

While this treatment of village-lineage organization is admittedly cursory, the traditional social organizations of Southeastern China stressed certain structural features which functioned to order and preserve the continuity of community life. These features included: ascription as a basis for organization, competition, and cooperation between diverse groups; social and political differentiation within lineages; the ability of association leaders to act as intermediaries with governmental officials and as mediators in local disputes; corporate economic enterprises; the frequent use of violence to settle differences; and a local sense of community identity within a well-established system of linked organizations.

Supernatural and Philosophical Overview

In China "religion" was represented by such major universal religions as Buddhism, Taoism, and Confucian philosophy (Yang 1961:294–95); the "cult of the ancestors," in terms of which lineages and sub-lineages defined themselves (Freedman 1958:81) and which contributed substantially to the integration and perpetuation of the family as a basic unit of Chinese society (Yang 1961:29); and a highly eclectic or popular "folk" religion, whose moral and magical functions dominated the people's consciousness (Yang 1961:25).

Religion functioned to reinforce the organizational foundation of a family weakened by death and to reassert the status of the family by demonstrating its wealth and influence with funeral processions, impressive mourning arches, and elaborate decorations. Religion also provided the integrating force for reaffirming relations within the wider social circle beyond the immediate family at other life crisis events such as birth and marriage (Yang 1961:37, 54, 58). A supernatural belief system permeated the relationships between man and nature (Freedman 1966:118–26) and aided the peasant in his desire to appease the supernatural powers that influenced his fortunes by both customary observances and special invocations of a specific diety with regard to some particular need (Chen 1939:228–29). Moreover, most occupations and trades in China had patron gods, as did specific agricultural pursuits (Yang 1961:66, 71). One found temples, shrines, altars, and other places of worship in every corner of the countryside (Yang 1961:6).

At all levels of the lineage the sentiments required by the kinship system were both expressed and reinforced in the course of religious acts (Freedman 1958:91). Ancestor rites performed in the ancestral halls were conducted by and in the presence of men. Daughters and wives played no direct part in the public proceedings. Yet, although the women may have been theoretically inferior in the sphere of formal ancestor worship, they occupied a central position in its performance in the home by caring for domestic shrines and probably carrying out the ordinary daily rites of lighting incense (Freedman 1958:85). The Chinese woman hardly passed a day or faced a crisis without resorting to religious assistance (Yang 1961:339–40).

The pervasiveness of magico-religious phenomena in Southeastern China is well documented, and the nature of the "dogmas"—polytheistic, supernatural, and eclectic—has historically allowed for the diffusion into Chinese society of diverse belief systems which could be wholly or partially accepted. As a result the early Chinese emigrants had little difficulty adapting, at least superficially, to divergent religious beliefs, such as Christianity and Islam, by way of incorporating even opposing elements in a pan-religious panorama. Religions emphasizing traditional ceremonialism and colorful festivals with a pantheon of gods and saints proved particularly attractive.

Men were the major participants in institutionalized ancestor worship cults. They controlled overseas religious activities, which were invariably linked to other social and economic enterprises, while women continued their domination of home-and-family-centered practices. Since supernatural referents were infused in the daily activities of both men and women, adherence to supernatural principles continued to play an important part in the political, economic, and social life of the early emigrants, although the traditional occupations and pastimes had changed.

"Religion," whatever the form, played an integrating role in Chinese social and, in particular, familial life as long as it was functionally related to other institutions governing Chinese life. The continuance of ancestor worship and the desire to send the bones of the deceased back to China for proper burial still serve as an indication of the strength of Chinese-centered, home-village ties. "Religion" and magical experiences in traditional China were not isolated activities. Quite the contrary, they were inextricably interwoven with lineage, clan, family, and community patterns and functioned primarily to strengthen these institutions through supernatural sanctions.

4

Overseas Migrations

HISTORICALLY, CHINESE EMIGRATION has followed the routes of overseas Chinese trade and appears to be an extension of that early trading process. Vessels were sailing from southern China to Indonesia and the Malay peninsula as early as two thousand years ago. During the T'ang Dynasty (A.D. 618–906) the Chinese traders carried their wares into Southeast Asia, and by Sung Dynasty times (A.D. 960–1279) the South Seas trade was so profitable that Chinese rulers tried to make it a government monopoly (Heyer 1953:10; Kung 1962:5). Trade continued into the Ming Dynasty (A.D. 1368–1644), but during the fifteenth century the Ming Emperors, troubled by internal difficulties, abandoned plans for consolidating their position in the South Seas and Chinese shipping declined. By this time the Chinese had already established settlements through Southeast Asia (Heyer 1953:12).

Although there was migration during earlier dynasties, large-scale emigration to these regions did not begin until the middle of the nineteenth century. Moreover, the provinces of Kwangtung and Fukien, through which the overseas trade flowed from its earliest establishment, have always been the place of origin for most emigration (Kung 1962:7). This was particularly true after the Emperor restricted all foreign trade to the city of Canton in 1757 (Heyer 1953:14–15). Not only was emigration localized in Kwangtung and Fukien provinces, but it was also localized in certain districts and villages. Indeed, certain areas have been characterized by Chen (1940:59) as emigrant communities—communities in which the majority of the inhabitants depended for their living, in part, on remittances that

23

came from members of the family who were abroad. In such communities the sons of families ordinarily went overseas in each generation, usually to the same city in which the father, relatives, or other villagers worked.

A parallel to overseas migration may be found in internal Chinese rural-urban migration patterns. Chinese cities had long attracted a large number of people from the rural areas and from other cities, who came out of both necessity and choice to seek their livelihood in urban centers. Their living arrangements were similar to those in overseas communities. Their social ties remained to their community of origin, where their wives and children often remained, and they regularly sent home remittances to support their family. Their social organization in the cities was based upon commonalities of place of origin, language, or occupation. Even the internal organization of firms was modeled after the Chinese family, where the proprietor or manager filled the role of paterfamilias (Burgess 1928; Gamble 1921; Morse 1932). Thus it is apparent that localization and direction of emigration bind together a group of people with similar backgrounds. They provide a basis for cooperation and social organization in the new city as well as the new country that is based upon kinship, language, and territory. (The social organization of the overseas Chinese is more fully discussed in Chapter 10.)

Although emigration did weaken family ties to some extent, the typical life of the emigrant was arranged in such a way as to allow him to fulfill his familial obligations. The family would make the decision as to when a young man, usually between the ages of fifteen and thirty, was to go. He would join an overseas community where members of his localized lineage (*tzu*) were already established. Ideally, he would return to China several times—to be married; to beget children; and finally, when he was old or wealthy enough, to retire in China and be buried with his ancestors. During his sojourn abroad, he would continually send home remittances upon which his family depended for their subsistence. Generally speaking, emigrants came from an impoverished background, whether rural or urban, and the vast majority of them were illiterate and unskilled. Thus most remittances were from laborer's wages or the income from small shops or stores (Chen: 1940).

The Chinese in America come almost entirely from the *Sze-Yap* and *Sam-Yap* districts south of Canton [1] (see Figure 1) (Heyer 1953:16). This region is typed by Cressey (1963:154–55) as the Canton hinter-

---

[1] The Sam-Yap speaking districts in Kwangtung Province are Namhoi, Punyu, and Shuntak. The Sze-Yap speaking districts are Sunwei, Toishan, Hoiping, and Yanping.

land. Canton is situated in the Pearl River delta, yet the people living in the hinterland were easily able to reach this historical overseas port and had access to both Chinese and foreign merchants and traders.

The majority of early Chinese emigrants to America came from *Toishan* district, south west of Canton, and one of the ninety-eight districts in the Province of Kwangtung. This area is semitropical and the heat and humidity would be good for agricultural purposes, were it not for the excessively rocky, mountainous, and barren terrain. Toishan means "elevated mountain" and topographically it rises to a height of 800 to 1,000 feet while the surrounding regions drop like a cliff to sea level. The agricultural output is so poor that it can feed the densely packed populace only four months of the year. This made non-agricultural pursuits necessary; thus many Toishanese became traders and merchants, often traveling to cities and ports where their contact with foreign traders made them receptive to news of the discovery of gold in California in 1848 (Sung 1967:14).

Without a doubt, the California gold rush was an important stimulus for emigration to America, yet there were other factors that acted as impediments. Under the Manchus there was a repressive policy toward emigration, condemning emigrants living abroad. Section 225 of the Imperial legal code asserted that emigration was illegal and that Chinese emigrants were punishable as traitors. The penalty was death (Kung 1962:7). Secondly, there were strong cultural proscriptions against leaving. The Chinese are a people whose attachments to family, home, and ancestral place are proverbial, and Chinese thought and philosophy focus upon the family, the ancestral shrine, and the farm lands from which the family has earned its living for centuries.[2] Sung (1967:11) reminds us that "for a son to leave his ancestral home and aged parents for any protracted length of time was unfilial behavior, a cardinal sin." And Hu (1960:58) remarks: "Chinese have attachments to their ancestral homeland and family traditions that make them almost immobile." Finally, there were also monetary considerations. The price for passage to the United States was high, often necessitating borrowing against wages to be earned in the gold fields of California. Sung concludes:

"It took rare courage, grim determination, and a venturesome spirit for these men to circumvent the law, to buck society and to leave home and

---

2 For a discussion of the Chinese farmer's traditional sentiment for land and, to a lesser degree, his ancestral home, see Gallin (1967:367–75). Gallin suggests that this sentiment is frequently cast aside when there is an alternative way to earn a livelihood and accumulate status and wealth.

Source: Chinn (1969:3).

Figure 1. Districts of Heaviest Chinese Emigration to America.

loved ones for unknown destinations in the hopes of bettering their fortunes" (Sung 1967:11).

Yet, if the reasons for remaining were strong, the incentives for leaving were even stronger. The motive for the Chinese emigrant was primarily, if not exclusively, economic, for in Southeastern China's coastal regions the land cannot provide enough food or work for the dense population. In Chen's survey of 905 families in Kwangtung and Fukien provinces which had sent members overseas, almost 70 per cent claimed they left either because they were unemployed, saw little future opportunity for employment, or because the family income was insufficient even though all members were employed. About 20 per cent left because of previous connection with an overseas area (Chen 1940:260).

During the time of the California gold rush there were additional pressures in China that increased unemployment to a crisis level. One factor was the phenomenal increase in population. While toward the end of the seventeenth century the Chinese population had been over 100 million, it had reached over 300 million by the beginning of the nineteenth century, and by the 1850's had passed the 400 million mark (Hu 1960:24).

"With this rise the average per capita landholding dwindled from two acres to less than half an acre. The situation, aggravated by maldistribution and maladministration, was unrelieved by commerce and industry which the government disapproved of and made no effort to develop. Unemployment created discontent among the people and banditry was rife" (Hu 1960:24).

In addition, China demonstrated her increasing inability to defend her borders against western powers, and with the Treaty of Nanking in 1842 ceded Hong Kong to England. British influence in South China grew and added to the problems of a country already torn by civil strife and economic depression (Hu 1960:25).

But the reason deemed most directly responsible for massive emigration from the southern portions of China was the poverty resulting from the aftermath of the Taiping rebellion. This rebellion had its roots in widespread discontent. In the 1800's scholars seeking to free the Chinese mind from the shackles of neo-Confucianism stirred the nationalistic spirit of the people and provided an ideological basis for the movement against the Manchus. Rebellion began early in the nineteenth century and by mid-century had swept the country. The most formidable of all rebel forces were the Taipings in the south. Led

by a Christianized Chinese, Hung Hsio-ch'üan (1813-1864), the Taipings initiated drastic reforms and almost overthrew the Manchus, but
their reforming zeal degenerated and soon turned to terror. Eventually
their movement was crushed (Hu 1960:24-25). The horrors of war,
with its consequent devastation, plundering, and famine, had driven
many of the people to seek a livelihood elsewhere—beyond the waters
of the Pacific Ocean.

PART TWO

THE ERA OF
THE TRADITIONAL CHINATOWN

1850–1900

5

The Chinese Experience in America

THE FIRST CHINESE IMMIGRANTS to California, two men and a woman, sailed into San Francisco Bay aboard the American brig *Eagle* in 1848 (Bancroft 1890:336; Chu & Chu 1967:18). However, the first large-scale Chinese immigration of 13,100 to America occurred in 1852 (Kung 1962:65). By 1890 this population had increased to 107,488 (Sung 1967:111).

The Chinese, welcomed at first as cheap and hard-working laborers, were later excluded as "unassimilable aliens." In 1871 the largest and most spontaneous anti-Chinese riot occurred in Los Angeles when a feud between two rival Chinese companies resulted in the wounding of two police officers and the death of one civilian (Kung 1962:68). After 1870, with the rise of Kearneyism, the organization of the Working-man's Party in 1877, and the California constitutional convention of 1878, anit-Chinese fever reached a high point, and in 1882 an exclusion bill was voted, restricting Chinese immigration to America.[1] The bill became "permanent" with the Exclusion Act of 1904 and was not re-pealed until December 17, 1943 (Kung 1962:78–84).

[1] During the depression of the 1870's, there were various kinds of agitation and attacks against the Chinese. Dennis Kearney, the founder of the Workingman's Party, led the opposition against Chinese labor. His prejudicial rhetoric was based upon the premise that America was for the Americans and that all foreigners, particularly those of a different color, were interlopers and trespassers (Kung 1962:68). Kearney's speeches always ended with the slogan: "The Chinese must go" (Sung 1967:41–43).

The constitutional convention to frame the second constitution for the State of California met in an atmosphere overflowing with anti-Chinese feeling. Restrictive legislation was passed but was later declared unconstitutional by the Supreme Court of California (Kung 1962:73).

Early Chinese Family Life

"Whether or not an immigrant group established families in America has had a profound effect upon its subsequent community organization and acculturation" (Lyman 1968:321). There is little doubt that the majority of the early Chinese immigrants did not lead normal family lives. More than half of the arriving men were single and, of those who were not, many were separated from their wives and continued to live a good portion of their lives in this condition (Wu 1928:233). The absence of a wife in America caused many men to desire an early return to their homeland, making their voyage to America a sojourner's visit rather than a permanent commitment.

Remittances to families in China, periodic return trips to get married, produce children, and finally to retire and die produced a continuing flow of letters, monies, and personnel across the Pacific Ocean. In this manner a constant "cultural exchange" was maintained so that even poor and unlucky sojourners, unable to afford a trip home, could still comfort themselves with news and gossip of family and village affairs as well as retain their "Chinese-centered identity." Those who were later able to bring their brides and children to America or to send for "picture brides" increasingly tended to establish American roots.

By 1890 there were only 3,868 Chinese women registered in America for some 102,620 men (Lyman 1968:322). This early sexual imbalance meant that the birth and growth to maturity of a substantial American-born population would be delayed (Lyman 1968:328). It was not until after 1930 that most Chinese men in America could afford both the blessings and problems of living in conjugal family units. Moreover, the opportunities for intermarriage with Americans were extremely limited. The mutual peculiarities of dress, habit, language, and custom, as well as racial distinctiveness, segregation, and the anti-miscegenation laws prevailing in some states discouraged such unions (Lyman 1968: 326).

For those fortunate enough to have resident wives and children, the old patriarchal Chinese family system still dominant in the villages and cities of Kwangtung continued. The father expected to be and was obeyed; obedience to the patriarch was a prime virtue and was often exhibited by children long after maturity. This filial piety functioned to minimize intergenerational conflicts and the family remained a cohesive social unit.

The wife, her feet often bound, would rarely leave her home (Hayner and Reynolds 1937:633). She was kept in seclusion by her husband and seldom ventured out alone even within the Chinese community. Indeed, it was not uncommon for a woman to make a trip of a single block to a female relative in a closed carriage (Lyman 1968:325). Marriages were always arranged, either by relatives living in China or, in less favorable circumstances, between or within Chinatown settlements in America. In any case, women born in China were always preferred choices (Lee 1960:190). Success in marriage for a Chinese woman depended upon the number of sons she produced, a common belief being that large families led to less husband-wife strain; thriftness and the accumulation of jewelry, geared to an eventual return to China; tolerance of, and courtesy to, her husband's kinsmen (almost a necessity since few Chinese women had relatives nearby to depend upon for support); and, of course, faithfulness (Lee 1960:198–99). Nevertheless, according to Lee (1960:193), re-marriages and other familial violations occurred, but they usually remained well hidden. Thus, patriarchal dominance and the consequent submission of women and children to the father's will, established and continued by both economic and social circumstances, characterized the early Chinese family life in America.

But the adaptation of the Chinese family to America was not the same for all of its members. Often the father's occupation and participation in community life brought him into greater direct contact with American persons and indirect contact with American institutions, while the mother remained isolated at home. American-born children began to establish a new identity as they participated in Chinese-American life and came to regard themselves as at least more "acculturated" or less "old-fashioned" than their parents. While these youngsters were usually kept in line by familial and community pressures, they were already planting the seeds of discontent for familial revolt which would continue to increase in intensity as they matured and became more involved with their American experience.

Chinatown

The overseas Chinese have long maintained a distinct social, economic, and political system within segregated quarters of cities known as Chinatowns (Lyman 1961:1a). These Chinese enclaves are organized primarily upon an extended kinship structure but one which extends agnatic responsibilities and privileges to non-kin as well and is similar to that of the home counties from which the sojourners emigrated

(Lee 1960:429). Chinatowns, functioning as a defensive mechanism, protected the Chinese from American hostilities and discrimination (Yuan 1963:260). Thus the structure of a Chinatown enabled its residents to meet the problems of life crisis events—birth, marriage, old age, and death—and to find fellowship, social familiarity, and solace within its confines. It acted as a buffer against the prejudice and depredations of hostile whites (Lyman 1969:20) by forming an "invisible empire" containing a host of associations reflecting the traditional life of Kwangtung Province and fulfilling functions intimately associated with the personal view of Chinese relationships (Barth 1964:77). The lack of marriageable women and the inability to establish domestic ties in America increased the Chinese male's dependence upon these associations for assistance, protection, and companionship (Lyman 1968: 321–22).

Yuan (1963:260) portrays Chinatowns as an example of voluntary segregation involving involuntary factors. When anti-Chinese discrimination became intensive during the 1870's, the Chinese response included withdrawal from economic competition with the American world and the establishment of a segregated community. Thus, Chinatown provided a network of clan associations, secret societies, district companies, and occupational groups which flourished in an atmosphere of American hostility.

The development of a ghetto has been a common ethnic and racial minority response to American discriminatory practice, but its ability to maintain itself depends upon a host of concurrent cultural factors. The Chinese have always manifested a powerful sense of group feeling (Lyman 1969:20), a persuasive element of group solidarity and identity, so that even in a nation stressing "individualism" family and group cohesiveness survived. Moreover, the majority of immigrants were illiterate laborers burdened with linguistic and social difficulties; this easily contributed to the maintenance of a voluntarily segregated community (Yuan 1963:261). Voluntary segregation made it easier for both Chinese and American derogatory stereotypes to develop, images which invariably made any assimilation of the Chinese into American society more difficult. But by confining themselves in isolated colonies, the Chinese managed to lessen constant and, at times, competitive interaction with the majority and to minimize inter-group conflicts (Yuan 1963:262).

Lee (1949:422–23) claims that many Chinatowns were too small and too specialized to perform all the usual functions of a community, such as population reproduction and economic independence; this necessitated their forming symbiotic attachments to the larger American economic and social base. Nevertheless, Chinatowns produced and nourished a political-social system where people governed themselves, made their own laws, punished offenders, and led lives according to long standing traditions, ruled by their own "elites" (Lyman 1961: 72a). Americans helped to perpetuate and strengthen this internal control system by rarely interfering in Chinese disputes as long as they were limited to the streets and alleyways of Chinatown (Barth 1964:109). Barth further characterizes early Chinatown structure in California as an indigenous system of association control and oppression. However, in addition to fostering this system, Chinatown also functioned, through gambling, prostitution, feasting and periodic celebrations, to admit indentured immigrants temporarily to a life of affluence and a brief respite from a world of work.

Sojourners

The world of Chinatown nurtured a special kind of social personality, the sojourner. The sojourner is a stranger in a foreign land who clings to the culture of his own ethnic group and, although he spends much time in a foreign country, remains unassimilated (Siu 1952:24). The Chinese sojourner was motivated to cross the ocean to America for primarily economic reasons, to make his job a success and to return home a rich man. He did not participate in the greater American community, preferring to associate with his own countrymen in racial-cultural colonies. He maintained his cultural heritage while abroad, clung to his native language and sentiments, and constantly criticized life in America (Siu 1952:35–37). The sojourner mentality, characteristic of the early Chinese immigrant, was the life-blood of Chinatown; his outlook continuously supported Chinatown's institutions. The sojourner is both a product and a causative agent of the early social organization of the Chinese in America.

Chinese Social Organization

The large-scale Chinese emigration to America in the latter half of the nineteenth century was related to the discovery of gold at Sutter's mill in California but was substantially assisted, and in part governed, by the cultural and environmental conditions of the immigrant's homeland. The 1840's witnessed catastrophic flooding of Southeastern China, accompanied by political and social unrest (Lyman 1961:34). The Pearl River delta was also a quarrelsome region, with much fighting among government officials, villages, and lineages.

Chinese social organization in the New World bore the unmistakable stamp of these nineteenth century Chinese lineage and community conflicts (Lyman 1961:161). The social institutions of a society are usually formal systems whose functions reflect basic societal needs for control over its members. Associations usually concentrate upon only a few functions and generally supplement institutional controls. In Chinese immigration history, however, the development of associations preceded that of family and religious organizations (Lee 1960:143). Moreover, the nature of Chinese associations has converted them into at least pseudo-institutions, with controls as extensive as those of family or church. These early associations soon became viable Chinese-American institutions (Lee 1960:142).

The clan associations have their structural and historical origins in the lineage and clan organizations of Southeast China. Clan associations extended the benefits and privileges of agnatic lineage membership over a wider social and geographical base to include all members bearing the same surname. Their functions were originally political and economic. They settled internal disputes, protected their "brothers" from the harmful action of other Chinese, and attempted to ensure justice for members in disputes with non-member Chinese (Willmott 1964:36). By providing employment, housing, welfare, aid, and advice, enforcing the rules of propriety and incest, and in some instances obtaining a monopoly over some trades and professions— thus preventing other Chinese associations from encroachment in specific domains—they formed the basis for extensive social control (Lee 1960:174).

Clan associations could segment into smaller social units, often through fictive means, but could also combine into larger trans-family groupings, extending membership to other Chinese immigrants based upon blood brotherhood, traditional friendships, surname similarity (common Chinese language radicals), geographic proximity, and marriage ties (Lyman 1961:173). Primarily to counteract the powerful domination of large clan associations, smaller clan associations used these ties of historical, geographic, and social propinquity to band together and compete for some control over Chinatown activities (Lee 1960:174).

While clan association competition was characteristic of the larger Chinese centers in America, small Chinatowns were usually dominated by one clan association (Lee 1960:173). Although these associations were theoretically obedient to their national headquarters, usually located in San Francisco, it appears that local autonomy was the rule rather than the exception (Willmott 1964:34).

Clan associations functioned with other types of associations to form the "warp and woof of early overseas Chinese societies" (Willmott 1964:36) and further served, in the absence of original lineal authorities, to remind the sojourner of his ties to village and family in China by assuming a role in loco parentis (Lyman 1969:21).

Paralleling clan association in function, but different in structure, the hui kuan united all those who spoke a common subdialect or hailed from the same district of origin in China. These dialect and distinct associations primarily represented the Chinese from seven counties of heaviest Chinese emigration to America, the Sze-Yap and Sam-Yap speaking peoples of Kwangtung (see Figure 1, page 26). They played an important role in early Chinese history in America as immigrant receiving stations (Lee 1960:144–46); newcomers were welcomed by association representatives, fed, housed, outfitted, and, after thanking their village deities in a temple connected to the association building, were sent to their respective employers (Wu 1928:164–65). By controlling specific enterprises, settling disputes, and protecting the social and economic interests of their members, they competed with the clan associations for control of Chinatown life. Although both the clan associations and the dialect-district associations were theoretically based upon voluntary membership (membership in a lineage and village is involuntary), all new arriving immigrants meeting the minimum qualifications were summarily enrolled and counted as members Independent life in America was almost impossible for people belonging to racial, linguistic, and cultural minorities. Thus, the newcomers accepted the extension of the bonds of regional loyalty and familism, and the dialect-district associations were able to control their lives with little aid or interference from American institutions (Barth 1964:86).

Another facet of organizational life in American Chinatowns was the existence of secret societies, or "tongs" as they were often called. They began as American forms of old Chinese semi-political and semi-religious organizations, which for centuries had served as the principal association for protest, banditry, and rebellion (Lyman 1969:23). They often exhibited hostility toward the state and united persons who were otherwise divided by blood, local, and language ties (Lyman 1961: 222). They also functioned as a haven for those who, running afoul of the law, had been expunged from lineage and village identities (Lyman 1969:23).

Secret societies were established both in American cities and in the outlying areas, particularly in mining communities. They probably were formed in response to the needs of a primarily male society whose desire for rapid social advancement was blocked, and in which wealth, status, and the acquisition of women could not be achieved through legitimate activities (Lee 1960:162). In the mining regions these societies ran hostels, adjudicated disputes, and regulated claim boundaries (Lyman 1969:24). In the cities, however, they challenged other associations for control of gambling, prostitution, protection, and other activities on the borderline of social respectability (Barth 1964:102). They competed for the right to govern territories and control occupations with warfare and violence, a common way of establishing dominance (Lee 1960:163). They became best known in American folklore for their elaborate street skirmishes and for assassinations by "highbinders" and "hatchet men." The "clash" of 2,500 at Chinese Camp, California, in 1856 was perhaps the most famous and included white drill instructors, a magnificent weapons arsenal stocked with items from bamboo shields to rifles, much advance publicity, and some $20,000 to $40,000. However, street skirmishes seldom involved more than one hundred men and resulted in few deaths (Barth 1964:94-95). Americans tended to group all "tongs" together and to attribute their violent activities to rivalries within and between "tong" organizations. However, not all "tongs" were "fighting tongs" (Reynolds 1935:620) and violent fallings-out often involved clan associations and dialect-district groups (Lyman 1969:24).

The secret societies provided mutual aid for their members in a host of social and economic activities. Their political aspirations were limited to occasional interests in China, and they never interfered in the national politics of the United States of America (Lyman, Willmott, and Ho 1964:533). Although we know little about the secret memberships of such "societies," their activities indicate that membership was large and strong enough to rival other groups for Chinatown power (Lyman 1961:246).

In summary, these major points should be remembered: First, the organizational patterns upon which the secret societies were built had traditional Chinese antecedents. Second, there were similarities in form and function among clan associations, dialect-district associations, and secret societies (Reynolds 1935:613) because of overlapping activities and competition for members as well as their historical basis in traditional society. Third, because of this struggle for position and power, relationships between secret societies and other groups were complex and fraught with violence (Lyman 1961:251).

It was common practice for the dialect-district groups, clan associations, and secret societies to form a supra-community organization called the Chinese Benevolent Association (also known as *Chung wah hui kuan*, Chinese Public Association, and, in San Francisco, the Six Companies). It functioned primarily to provide Chinatown with a governmental superstructure. Furthermore, it served to represent the Chinese community vis-à-vis the larger society (Lyman 1969:22). In theory, the Chinese Benevolent Association ruled supreme over all activities because its membership was composed of representatives from all local Chinese organizations (Lee 1960:147). The association served as a self-appointed representative of all the Chinese in America and acquired quasi-judicial powers, particularly in matters of immigration and legal affairs (Lee 1960:148). In the absence of Chinese consular and diplomatic officials, it acted as a mediator between Chinese and American interests (Barth 1964:100).

By the 1860's the Chinese Benevolent Association had established its control over Chinatown where, through tight regimentation, it protected immigrants from the schemes of their own countrymen as well as from the wide range of American reactions. Its "rule," guaranteed by emotional ties to home, operated through an elaborate set of official rules and quasi-official pressures. It provided coffins for the poor; made provisions for invalids; arbitrated disputes among members; undertook community projects such as school financing, cemetery maintenance, and fund-raising; and controlled Chinese relations with the American world (Lee 1960:150; Barth 1964:90). The Benevolent Association generally commanded at least the grudging allegiance and obedience of Chinese, as well as the respect of many whites (Lyman 1969:22).

Conflict and Control

The early Chinese immigrants were wage laborers, sub-contracted and directed by a headman. Possessed of no special skills, these immigrants retreated to urban Chinatowns, which were large enough and diversified enough to support Chinese institutions. Their employment in restaurants and laundries, as factory workers and domestics, kept them dependent upon Chinatown associations for their livelihood (Lyman 1961:127).

The Chinese world in California was without gentry, scholars and officials, for their status in China kept them out of the main stream of emigration (Barth 1964:81). Thus merchant-creditors became community leaders with undisputed eminence, in contrast to their low position within Confucian traditions. In the absence of traditional village and governmental controls, these "self-constituted mandarins" often despotically ruled Chinese immigrant life in America through their leadership position in clan and district associations (Barth 1964:81–82).

Because many emigrants were unable to afford the price of passage to America, they depended upon monies advanced by relatives or associations which were to be repaid from wages earned; this credit-ticket system enforced the debt-bondage of the emigrants. Furthermore, the district-dialect associations often collected mandatory arrival and departure fees, often with interest. The collection of both Old and New World debts by association officials tightened association controls over immigrant life. Chinese newcomers, unsure of their rights under the American legal system or afraid to use such recourse, remained tied to Chinese solutions and generally accepted the extension of lineage-region bonds over their lives. When American courts were used, it was often to the advantage of the wealthy merchant-creditor. The immigrants' plight is well summarized by Lyman:

> "By the turn of the century, the Chinese were isolated, neglected and demoralized. Locked inside the Chinatowns of American cities they achieved some sense of cultural freedom, a relaxation of tensions and a precarious independence. . . . A few prospered as merchants and gained political and social power in the ghetto; but most remained homeless and trapped, too poor to return to China and too oppressed to enter fully into American society (Lyman 1969:43).

The interrelationships between secret societies, clan associations, dialect-district groups, and the Chinese benevolent associations reflected an organizational system laden with constant conflict (Lyman 1961:251). Associations were unequal in power and affluence (Lee 1960:147) and controlled their members by brute force and by hidden persuasion that went with regional loyalty and filial piety (Barth 1964:89). Village and lineage feuds found a new expression in these New World institutions (Barth 1964:93, 97). Dialect-district associations split as clan associations within them established priorities (Lyman 1961:274), and secret societies constantly challenged benevolent association rule (Barth 1964:100). Within individual organizations struggles for leadership also took place, and these internal conflicts were often settled with violence and assassination (Barth 1964:86). In spite of the struggle of individual associations for control, the overall effect of these conflicts was an extension of association dominance over all Chinatown activities.

We have already indicated that conflict became an endemic factor in Chinese overseas life in America. Yet its presence does not indicate community disorganization; instead internal conflict can best be described as "realistic" (Coser 1956:48–49). Individuals and groups engaged in struggles for wealth, power, status, and women; yet custom and tradition dictated how the conflict should be resolved (Lyman 1961:347). Conflicts were initiated, prolonged, and finally resolved by a shared set of sentiments common to all participants; American values and precepts rarely entered into Chinatown conflicts. The resolution of these often violent disputes reinforced cultural ties to one's own group and to Chinese society. Many rivalries were entered into according to rule and custom, from the declaration of war to the settlement of dispute at a peace banquet (Lyman 1961:367). Thus, although Chinatown disputes made for changes in leadership and power, the new victors continued to perpetuate the old institutions, whose legitimacy was rarely questioned. In addition, because the changes occurred within Chinatown society, the Chinese were able to present a united appearance to the bulk of American society.

Chinese Religious Extensions

Early Chinese temples in America, commonly called "joss houses," followed the pattern of Buddhist and lineage temples in the Chinese homeland and often fulfilled the same functions in much the same manner. Local "gods" were occasionally grouped together under one roof in a religious panorama which usually included both Kuan-Yin, the goddess of mercy, and Kuan-Kung, the god of war. Chinese celebrations and religious festivals centered upon the temples, allowing temple managers to earn income from the sale of fireworks, good luck symbols, and proper prayers. Donations were also made by businessmen and by association groups. Gods and goddesses were occasionally lent to other nearby communities and temple festivals were attended by Chinese both near and far. Temples were sometimes connected to company or association houses which incorporated religion and superstition in their set of controls.

But perhaps the two most important functions of the temples were the integration of the Chinese community (at least during festive occasions) and the provision of solace, comfort, and entertainment for Chinese immigrants. These latter found security in prayer and a host of other beliefs and religious practices which constantly reminded them of home. The Chinese temples remained an integral part of the Chinese enclaves in urban and rural areas and rarely had dealings, other than those necessary for their continuation, with the non-Chinese population of the larger American settlements (Eberhard 1962: 362–71; Barth 1964:91).

Acculturation

Acculturation, as defined by Redfield, Linton, and Herskovitz (1936: 139), includes those cultural changes which result when groups of individuals having different cultures come into continuous first-hand contact. The early history of the Chinese in America strongly suggests that acculturation, or behavioral assimilation into American life, rarely occurred. The goals of the Chinese immigrants to make and save money quickly, to pay off their debts, and to rejoin their families in China (Barth 1964:157) did not foster a permanent commitment to America, either as a place to settle and raise families or as a cultural system to emulate. They left their homes defending the tenets of their culture and rejected values opposed to those tenets. Siu (1952:41) describes the sojourner's pattern as accommodation, isolation, and unassimilation, and Lyman (1968:52) calls the early Chinese experience in America "an instance of unusually persistent social isolation and preservation of Old World values." Yuan (1963:259) further characterizes the adjustment of the Chinese to America as primarily economic.

Linguistic and cultural differences prevented all but the most minimal contacts with American institutions. Moreover, the immigrants' social environment, controlled through an overlapping Chinese associational system and aided by anti-Chinese discrimination and prejudice, maintained and perpetuated a closed cultural system.

Some adjustment and accommodation to the American scene, however, was inevitable, particularly in the mining counties, where long separation from countrymen and a specific economic pursuit meant a skillful adaptation to, and familiarity with, American technology. Many Chinese accepted such products of American culture as hats and shoes, particularly mining boots (Barth 1964:157), and western dress was not unknown among community leaders who constantly dealt with American officialdom. A few Chinese acted as translators for banking firms, merchant houses, and stage lines, and many were employed in American factories as domestic servants and as washermen (Barth 1964:171). But these occupations demanded only that they gain proficiency in technical and commercial enterprise and not a moral-religious and philosophical commitment to American life.

Perhaps the greatest force for acculturation was the church and mission movement of the late nineteenth century which, led by a few influential ministers, initiated programs for the conversion of the "heathen Chinese." The establishment of Chinese missions and regular mission work attracted Chinese as pupils, teachers, and translators.

Whenever the opportunity arose, Chinese flocked to Bible classes and mission schools to acquire the rudiments of English grammar but, to the consternation of the missionaries, no more. Barth (1964:169) writes that in dress and habit they evidenced their exposure to American values but the influence of the new culture could not substitute for the expected return to China. Nevertheless some Chinese, attracted to the American church in order to learn English, were gradually won over to Christianity; indeed, some had already been converted while in China. For these individuals there was at least a partial escape from the restricted life of the Chinese ghetto and emancipation from the constrictive forces of Chinatown life. Nevertheless, they would still remain somewhat responsive to Chinese community controls.

Thus, by 1900 the forces of acculturation were beginning to influence the external-extrinsic traits of the Chinese in America. But significant changes in Chinese social organization could not take place until a sufficient number of American-born sons and daughters could make their American experience felt as a group and could successfully challenge their immigrant generation of fathers.

6

Early Chinese Settlement
in Valley City

History and Supposition

HISTORICAL RECONSTRUCTIONS IDEALLY rely upon accurate and substantial documentation. Unfortunately, many of Valley City's Chinese merchants, gold miners, and laborers were illiterate in both English and Chinese and left few primary sources documenting their commercial or social activities.[1] Caucasian commentaries on the life style of Valley City Chinese are largely limited to western newspaper accounts. Thus our information is restricted to some general descriptive accounts of early Chinese life in America and to United States Census Bureau data.

Most historical writings specifically concerned with this early period of Chinese emigration to America focus upon San Francisco's Chinatown, the most populous and influential center for Chinese New World settlements. As a result, descriptions of the Chinese in Marysville, Stockton, and Valley City are generally incomplete. Moreover, most accounts tend to focus upon history and the legislative, legalistic, and

---

[1] The *Valley City Chinese Daily News* first appeared in December, 1856. Except for the heading and date, it was printed in Chinese. It was primarily a commercial bulletin suited to the particular needs of literate sojourners and contained few lofty editorial pronouncements. At first printed daily, it later appeared tri-weekly and then irregularly. It lasted for only two years and then disappeared without a trace. A report listed Ze Too Yune, alias Hung-Tai, as editor (Barth 1964:176). There is no known copy in existence today (Chinn 1969:70).

emotional reaction toward increasing Chinese immigration, rarely upon the social organization of the Chinese themselves.[2]

In spite of the paucity of reliable and documentary data, there is no reason to believe that the social organization of the Valley City Chinese community was significantly different from that in San Francisco and other west coast communities. All Chinese were aliens in a foreign and often hostile land and were largely subject to the same population pressures and cultural problems of adjustment. Their shared social, linguistic, and territorial backgrounds enabled them to perpetuate coincident institutions to regulate and control community life. The specific directions of the Valley City's community's history and growth cannot be denied, for local circumstances and leadership can lead to unique social arrangements; yet, even within the parameters of individual choice, Chinese organizational patterns throughout America seem to have remained similar and to have followed identical structural principles.

Valley City's Chinese Population

The Chinese first arrived in "Valley County" following Marshall's discovery of gold at Coloma in 1849 (Fang 1961:28). By 1860 Valley City was supporting a Chinese center large enough to supply groceries, equipment, and other wares to Chinese mining settlements in the "gold rush" country. It attracted Chinese miners, scattered in camps and settlements, to the California State Fair in September and to Chinese religious festivals in October (Barth 1964:111). While San Francisco served as the primary receiving center for Chinese immigrants, Valley City, Stockton, and Marysville were processing centers, where agents and collectors representing the Five District Companies contracted for and controlled the Chinese laborers who worked in mining camps (Barth 1964:90, 113).

Ping Chiu (1963:11) lists only six Chinese miners and two laundrymen as living in Valley County in 1850 (see Tables 2, 3, and 4 for Chinese labor and population figures in Valley City County and city). Expanded mining operations and the construction of the Central Pacific Railroad (1863–1869) facilitated community growth, and by

---

2 Some of these early historical sources are Mary R. Coolidge's *Chinese Immigration* (New York: Henry Holt and Company, 1909); Hubert Howe Bancroft's *History of California* (San Francisco: The History Company, and A. L. Bancroft Company, 1883–90); George M. Stephenson's *A History of American Immigration, 1820–1924* (Boston: Ginn and Company, 1926); and William S. Wells' *Chinese Immigration* (New York: Charles Scribner's Sons, 1879).

1880 Valley County claimed 4,893 Chinese, approximately one-third of whom lived within city boundaries. During the 1880's and 1890's spreading anti-Chinese feelings led to restrictive legislation and the number of Chinese declined appreciably. The 1900 U.S. census lists only 1,065 Chinese living in Valley City, a loss since 1880 of over 700 Chinese residents.

Table 2

Chinese Labor in Valley County 1850–1880

Year	Chinese Miners	Chinese Farmers	Gardeners Chinese	Farm Laborers Chinese
1850	6	*	*	*
1860	*	3	120	*
1870	892	37	72	668
1880	1,165	558	184	218

*Information not available.
Source: Ping Chiu's *Chinese Labor in California*, University of Wisconsin Press, 1963.

Table 3

Chinese Population, Valley City and County 1852–1900

Year	Chinese population Valley County	Chinese population Valley City	Population increase (+) and decrease (−) of non-city Chinese	
			Number	Increase/Decrease
1852	804	600*	204*	
1860	1,731	988	743	+ 539*
1870	3,596	1,371	2,225	+1,482
1880	4,893	1,781	3,112	+ 887
1890	4,371	1,753	2,618	− 494
1900	3,254	1,065	2,189	− 429

*Estimate.
Source: U.S. Census.
Note: On August 3, 1882, Congress passed the Chinese Restriction Act, which brought to an end the free immigration of Chinese laborers and began an era of Chinese exclusion from American shores (Kung 1962:80). This accounts in part for the decrease in Chinese population in 1890 and 1900.

Table 4

Population Figures for Chinese and non-Chinese, Valley City, 1852–1900

Year	Total population Valley City	Chinese population Valley City	Percentage Chinese Valley City	Chinese city population increase (+) and decrease (−)
1852	6,820	600*	8.8*	
1860	13,785	988	7.2	+388*
1870	16,283	1,371	8.4	+383
1880	21,420	1,781	8.3	+410
1890	26,386	1,753	7.0	− 28
1900	29,282	1,065	3.6	−688

*Estimate.
Source: U.S. Census.
Note: After 1880, the Chinese population started to decrease while the total population of the city continued to expand. Thus the Chinese percentage of the overall city population became increasingly smaller. Despite the increase in the actual numbers of Chinese in Valley City, particularly after 1940, the Chinese percentage declined to 1.3 by 1960.

Valley City's early Chinese settlers were primarily young adult males. The shortage of females becomes apparent in the 1860 census, which records only 180 females for 808 males. Over 70 per cent of all Chinese immigrants were between 20 and 39 years of age at that time. By 1900, 913 persons of the total Chinese city population of 1,065 were males over 21 years old. Furthermore, one of the outstanding characteristics of the Chinese population was the fact that they were overwhelmingly foreign-born. For example, in 1870 only 31 of Valley County's 3,598 Chinese were American-born; this figure rose only to 36 in 1880 and by 1890 had dropped to 29.

These early immigrants were predominantly Sze-Yap speaking peoples,[3] by virtue of their dialect nominal members of the Ning Yuen, Hop Wo, Kong Chow, and Shui Hing territorial associations. These "district-dialect" associations were well established in San Francisco (Barth 1964). However, although they may have had representatives in Valley County, it is doubtful that they controlled local politics.

3 Sze-Yap, a dialect of Cantonese, is a variant of that language and is primarily spoken in a district southwest of Canton. There is no linguistic breakdown for Valley City's Chinese during this early period; however, by 1876, 82 per cent of all Chinese in California were Sze-Yap speakers (Chinn 1969:20).

Not only was this early population largely composed of single males, but a good proportion of the single females of marriageable age were engaged in prostitution and were therefore unavailable as prospective brides. As was customary, many of the married men had left their wives and families in China (Farwell 1885:97). The majority of Valley City's Chinese population were denied the mixed blessings of conjugal family life and were therefore increasingly dependent upon extra-family groupings for their primary social and sexual needs. Thus, family associations, guilds, tongs, and other fraternal and familial organizations, modeled after structurally similar institutions in Southeastern China, were able to command the allegiance of the Chinese and control the patterns of work and leisure in American Chinatowns.

Chinatown

One particularly vivid description of life in Valley City's Chinatown was published in an 1873 newspaper account:

"Before the dawn of day the Chinese quarter is alive and the inmates may be seen moving to their various places of business. Saloons, hotels and many private houses require attention. Fires must be made and carpets swept. At this early hour it is interesting to observe the Chinese vegetable dealers with their immense baskets on their shoulders congregating at the intersection of the city streets and purchasing from the producers the esculents which they afterwards peddle out in the confines of the city. The Chinese vegetable peddlers travel a great deal on foot each day for a small remuneration.

"It is morning and now the Chinese quarter itself re-echos the sounds of trade and traffic. From above and below the sidewalks appear the hucksters stands, bearing everything edible from varnished pork down. Then the drug stores throw open their doors, the pastry cooks and fruit dealers lay out their inducements, the cobbler and carpenter have their work benches in order, fish swim and flounder in artificial ponds, ducks quack in the gutter and chickens complacently await their doom. By late morning one hears the actual hum of business and everyone is working very hard. The dens of infamy open their doors.

"It is night time. The Chinese who have been engaged on the outskirts of the city congregate on city streets and the district becomes lively. Gambling is carried out among discordant music, the smells of offensive oils and the rattle of apparatus used in gambling games" (*Valley City Daily Union*, January 11, 1873).

Valley City's Chinatown was established at least as early as 1854[4] and evidences a geographic-historical continuity. The Chinese community had expanded only slightly by the 1870's, and in 1885 particular streets were still referred to as the center for Chinese activities in the city (Farwell 1885:102). By the turn of the century, "the Chinese quarter still remained as the population center for the city's Chinese residents" (*Valley City Union*, June 6, 1900).

The newspaper's picturesque rendition suggests three important structural features of Chinatown life. First, Valley City's Chinatown was a specific geographic district with rather well-defined boundaries and corresponded to the classic enclave, a segregated community called a "ghetto" (Wirth 1928:283–85). Within this area there was a wide variety of business enterprises which included: 125 prostitutes, 25 cigarmakers, 10 grocery stores, two large-size food wholesale establishments, one pawnbroker shop, three eating houses, six drug stores, six barber shops employing a total of 12 barbers, seven physicians, two shoe and slipper manufacturers, two fruit stands, and four butcher shops (*Valley City Daily Union*, January 11, 1873).

Chinese economic enterprise, however, was not limited to Chinatown. The Chinese were also engaged in mining, farming, and various types of gardening in the nearby rural areas. Large numbers of Chinese were employed in mining and railroad construction, 15,000 in the building of the Central Pacific Railroad alone. By 1869, however, rural occupations shifted to farming and truck gardening (Fang 1961:17).[5] Moreover, the Chinese "peddled their wares," "set up their laundries," and worked for Caucasian employers throughout the city. These activities all involved constant Chinese-Caucasian interaction. The Chinese played subservient roles in these social relationships but were also becoming familiar with the English language and the American monetary system. Thus, the "ghetto enclave" was not in all aspects a closed system.

---

4 Barth (1964:95) refers to a "melee" involving some 600 Chinese in September, 1854.

5 In the 1880's there was a total of 64 Chinese-owned farms in Valley County. Forty-eight were owned and operated on a partnership basis with two to thirteen partners each. The three largest farms employed eleven laborers each (Chiu 1962:73). Market and truck gardens were generally small, with up to five persons working in each garden. Annual garden income rarely exceeded $4,000 and most gardens had assessed value at $500 or less (Chiu 1963:75).

The majority of Chinese-operated fruit orchards were valued at less than $800, but four had a value of over $1,000. They were usually rented from Caucasian landowners. The larger ones employed fifteen to twenty men who were paid $10 to $16 per month plus board, while whites averaged about $22 to $25 per month in addition to board. Several Chinese storekeepers, in order to diversify their holdings, invested as partners in orchards and farms (Chiu 1963:77).

Secondly, Chinatown was both a commercial and a residential district, so that living quarters and business enterprises, including gambling and prostitution, were spatially coincident. Finally, Chinatown was, in an economic sense as well as in a political, religious, and social sense, a self-sufficient unit that provided most of the goods and services necessary for the effective maintenance of community life.

If Chinatown was the hub of the legitimate Chinese business-marketing complex, it was also the center of a formal Chinese organizational network. Since a function of this associational complex was to provide recreational activities for its members, Chinatown also served as a center for many illicit ventures, such as prostitution and gambling. The fact that these activities were conducted in the public eye no doubt served as a point of friction between the white community and Chinatown and perhaps explains the preoccupation with vice and moralizing found in early Caucasian accounts of Chinese life.

Economic Enterprises

In the 1870's Valley City boasted 55 Chinese wash-houses (laundries) employing some 300 men. The laundries were scattered throughout the city but were controlled by a central headquarters in the heart of Chinatown. The *Valley City Daily Union* reported that: "It is here that the washermen's guild fixes prices, regulates transactions, and sets forth the rules to which all members are obligated to conform. Business is cooperative and each man is payed in proportion to profits" (*Valley City Daily Union*, January 11, 1873). The guild appeared strong enough to enforce its decisions, even when its policies were opposed by Caucasians, as is illustrated by the following account:

"In 1877 a Valley City resident had rented the basement of his hotel to a Chinese for a laundry. The Laundrymen's guild, however, had determined that this laundry was located too close to an already existing laundry and that the new Chinese proprietor must leave. The hotel owner guaranteed him legal protection. However, the prospective laundryman was subsequently approached by three members of the guild who, brandishing pistols and knives, threatened him with death and demanded that he pay the guild $110 as a fine. He gave them all the money he had" (Wu 1928:167–68).

Valley City's Chinese also engaged in illicit enterprises, primarily gambling, opium smoking, and prostitution. In 1876 the *Union* reported:

"There are some 16 opium dens within the city. Most of them are below street level. One which is high-toned and private is located next door to the schoolhouse. The chief one is beneath the rickety [wooden] sidewalk on the south side of the street" (*Valley City Daily Union*, February 23, 1876).

Another newspaper article vividly described the inside of an opium den.[6]

"You descend a narrow flight of stairs, the ceiling is low and at head level. It has earthen floors and walls of rough board and measures 8 × 10 feet. It is always filled with smoke and the men recline on mat-covered low platforms using blocks of wood for pillows. It is lighted by burning tapers floating in oil. The opium is smoked through a bamboo pipe two feet long" (*Valley City Daily Union*, February 23, 1876).

One street was reported to have been lined with sixteen to eighteen gambling houses. Both Chinese and Caucasians would play the "lotteries," tickets for which were drawn at night, their price ranging from ten cents to one dollar with prizes varying from twenty-five cents to five dollars.[7]

In the 1880's, police officers reported approximately 200 Chinese women (probably exaggerated) engaged in prostitution. Their function was to serve the social-sexual needs of the city's unmarried or lonely Chinese men.[8] The women were owned by Chinese men and were reported to be as young as fourteen years of age (Farwell 1885: 104). One police officer testified that he was called into a Chinese house to be a witness to a transaction. He was later informed that he had indeed been witness to the sale of a woman for $400. The woman soon afterwards committed suicide (Farwell 1885:98). Prostitutes had little chance of escaping from their owners, should they so desire, and it was

---

6 Opium dens were primarily frequented by Chinese males but the smoking of opium was not confined to these quarters. Opium was smoked in laundries, in the back room of shops, and in men's lodginghouses. Caucasians, particularly women and men of "undoubted reputations," were also known to patronize opium dens. Caucasian names such as "Minnie," "Bessie," and "Alfred" were reported to have been scrawled on the walls of such establishments (*Valley City Daily Union*, February 23, 1876).

7 A lottery ticket measured four inches square with a total of eighty Chinese characters arranged in two sections of forty each. The player crossed out ten of the characters. Drawings were held in secret and the winners were announced twice daily. Many Caucasians apparently trusted the Chinese policy makers. These Chinese lotteries are the forerunners of KENO, a game popular in Nevada's gambling casinos and frequently played by Chinese gamblers. One casino in Reno provides KENO tickets with instructions in Chinese.

8 Some police officers testified that occasionally young boys, 14 and under, were enticed into these houses of prostitution, but it was not a usual practice. Caucasian men, however, did frequent such establishments (Farwell 1885:103–104).

common for Chinese owners to report runaways to the Caucasian police, claiming they had stolen household goods. The courts usually returned the women to their "owners" (Farwell 1885:111).

Conflict and Control

Although the Chinese residents of Valley City were subject to many of the laws of the American nation, including specific municipal and state ordinances, they were usually able to circumvent the American legal system and dispense justice "Chinese style." This type of justice was based upon traditional Chinese prerogatives and was manipulated by a system of community controls, a blend of transplanted and local features. The system was effective primarily because most Chinese were dependent for their life and livelihood upon the leaders of the Chinese community. Recalcitrant individuals who violated community "laws" were punished and served notice that errant Chinese would, in the final analysis, be properly disposed of.[9] Moreover, most Chinese, unfamiliar with the English language and suspicious of American legal practices, preferred the familiarity of the Chinese judicial system.

That the Chinese in Valley City had their own judicial system is evidenced by testimony in the Report of the Special Committee of the Board of Supervisors of San Francisco, which included in the appendix the testimony of Valley City civil employees. Police officers insisted that:

"The great number of offenses committed by Chinese are among themselves and are settled long before they can come to issue in our courts. They use threats and intimidation among themselves but never towards whites. It is common that when several men are arrested, one will be offered whom we may convict if we let the others go. Chinese leaders offered to furnish me with the necessary evidence if I would let the others go. The Chinese have their own tribunals where they try their own cases; they settle everything within their own counsels" (Farwell 1885:105–14).

The social and economic life of Valley City's Chinese rested upon the leadership of the various Chinese associations. These groups controlled both legal and illicit enterprises and acted as courts of justice for the Chinese community. Control over members was facilitated by

[9] The offer of rewards for the murder of individuals was reported to be posted openly on a wall. The notices were reputedly translated for the benefit of Caucasian police officers.

the use of physical force through "highbinders" and "hatchet men" working in the employ of the organizations.

"It is estimated that there are about 100 to 150 highbinders within the city. They are young toughs who travel about in groups and raid the gambling houses. These groups of assassins are regularly organized into rival groups who constantly patrol the Chinatown streets" (Valley City Daily Record Union, November 12, 1883).

"The leader of the Tong had an organization of 30 highbinders. Clothed in bullet-proof armor and heavily armed they were hired solely for waging war, murder, and for defense at the bidding of the 'Lodge.' They are paid from $3.50 to $10.00 per day for this occupation. The more desperate the character the more money he receives. The leader of the Tong imported an additional 15 fighting men from San Francisco at $300 each to do bloody battle" (Valley City Daily Record Union, November 12, 1883).

The actual use of physical force, however, was not always necessary; the threat of retaliation often proved sufficient.

"The Chinese refused to talk to the police about the shooting between two groups, but later in the evening a merchant went into a back room with some officers, barricaded the doors, and after he was sure he could not be seen or heard said: 'If the Chinese knew I would divulge anything I would be killed before tomorrow night. I have a family in China and I don't want to die in California'" (Valley City Daily Record Union, November 12, 1883).

"A Chinese was arrested for stealing from the congregational church school room. Three Chinese and a white teacher were present. The Chinese begged the white teacher not to go to court, for if they had to go they were sure they would be killed by order of their own countrymen. At the trial two of the Chinese witnesses had disappeared and the one remaining had perjured himself saying he knew nothing about the crime. Later I was informed that he was very much scared and doubtless acted under orders" (Farwell 1885:112).

Actual battles were uncommon and were short-lived occurrences, but some cases were reported in the Valley City press.

"On September 9, 1854 at 10:00 p.m. some 500 Chinese gathered to do battle. Some were armed and wore tin hats and carried bamboo shields. After a one-half hour melee police broke it up and twenty leaders were taken to the Station house" (Daily Alta Californian, September 10, 1854).

"On November 11, 1883, at 7:00 p.m. the discharge of firearms attracted attention in Chinatown. Four people were shot and hundreds filled the streets. The police later found one wounded Chinaman at a lodging house nearby who later died. It was rumored that several others who had been wounded were hidden away in Chinatown" (*Valley City Daily Record Union*, November 12, 1883).

Encounters between rival "companies" and "associations" involved competition for control over commercial enterprises, and the regulation of prostitution, gambling, and opium, and for political ascendancy. They also grew out of antagonisms and traditional rivalries brought over from the counties of the Pearl River Delta (Barth 1965:95).

Multiplex Relationships and Common Values

As was mentioned earlier, Valley City's Chinese community (1850–1900) existed within a well-defined geographic district which contained both entrepreneurial and residential dwellings; it was relatively self-sufficient with regard to its political, economic, religious, educational, and social needs; and it was "home" to primarily young adult male immigrants who shared a similar cultural background. These facts have important structural implications for inter- and intra-community role relationships. Given this demographic structure, it can be expected that roles within the community will be multiplex.[10] The multiplexity of roles means that people tend to have many relationships in different spheres of social activity with the same individuals. Thus, if two individuals interact not only in business but also attend the same religious festivities, are members of the same association, share common dwellings at night, participate in similar activities such as gambling, buy their vegetables from the same vendor, and send remittances home to the same village area, their relationship may be said to be multiplex. Life in Chinatown constantly reinforces these multiplex relationships, binding residents together and strengthening their feelings of common Chinese community and identity.

On the other hand, simplex or single-interest relationships dominate Chinese interaction with the outside world. A Chinese in legal diffi-

---

[10] The terms "multiplex" and "simplex" were originally used by Max Gluckman. My usage of these terms corresponds to Gluckman's definition in *The Judicial Process Among the Barotse of Northern Rhodesia* (Free Press of Glencoe), pp. 17–19.

culties may deal with a policeman; the only interest he shares with him pertains to these legal matters. He does not meet him in church as a fellow parishioner, nor does he invite him to Chinese festivals or to his home as a friend. Moreover, simplex relationships tend to be divisive while multiplex relationships encourage community interdependence and promote group solidarity. Each individual is dependent upon the web of relationships for his psychological and spiritual, as well as his physical, well-being. He can ill afford to antagonize his employer, because doing so may jeopardize more than an employer-employee relationship. It may threaten his position in other social and economic fields as well. If a man transcends the codes and mores of the Chinatown community, he can no longer function within it.

Activities in Chinatown were basically multiplex, shared by people who also shared a common set of values. Moreover, these values were applicable to any one of a given number of roles a resident may have played throughout his life. Though role playing is to some extent flexible and different situations may emphasize one aspect of a role at the expense of another, shared community values act as a restraining parameter. The outcome is an integrated network of activities. In particular, the roles of father, son, husband, employer, employee, leader, or follower were to a large degree complementary and consistent because they were mediated by the Chinese respect for tradition, filial piety, and familism.

Chinese did not usually participate in the social-political activities of the outside world. They were unlikely to adopt foreign values which could contradict those of the community. Those members who incorporated American individualism and self-sufficiency into their value system participated less and less in the Chinese community. There were some individuals, however, usually leaders, who made contact with police and politicians. By representing the Chinese community, particularly as mediators in conflict situations, they facilitated the peaceful coexistence of the two communities.

The majority of the Chinese thus remained faithful to their old-country traditions and institutions. Although they lived in cramped and crowded quarters, which often led to quarrelsome and disruptive activities, multiplex relationships and shared values helped to resolve these difficulties.

Social Organization

It is difficult to exact a clear picture of the Chinese organizational network in early Valley City (1860–1900), for Chinese sources are not available and the local American newspaper adds to the confusion by frequently misspelling names of Chinese organizations and by not distinguishing between "tongs," "guilds," "lodges," "companies," and "associations." Nevertheless, inductive generalizations can be made.

The presence of highly paid 'highbinders" indicates the existence of at least two large competing organizations wealthy enough to hire "professional protectors." Such men, moreover, are usually connected with such illegal and quasi-legal activities as gambling and prostitution, which apparently flourished in Valley City's Chinatown. Furthermore, such activities are usually dominated and controlled by tongs rather than family or business associations. Their violent activities would be most likely to be reported in the American newspapers and in police reports.

But other organizations, less flamboyant, were also a part of Chinatown. By 1873 the Chinese had established "wash houses" throughout the city, employing at least 300 men. These laundries were controlled by the Washermen's Guild (*Valley City Union*, January 11, 1873). It was also a common practice for other commercial activities to be organized, so we might assume that waiters and grocery and factory workers had similar organizations (Wu 1928:166–70).

Valley City's Chinese were primarily Sze-Yap dialect speakers, making competing organizations based on language and territorial differences improbable. However, both family associations and tongs could flourish in a relatively small Chinese community. Lee (1960:173–74) further suggests that small Chinatowns are usually dominated by one family association; this was probably the situation in Valley City.

Valley City's Chinese population was, indeed, relatively small, less than 2,000 at its height in 1880, as compared to almost 22,000 at that

Table 5

Chinese Population for Valley City and
San Francisco Counties 1860–1900

Year	Chinese population, Valley County	Chinese population, San Francisco County
1860	1,731	2,719
1870	3,595	12,022
1880	4,892	21,745
1890	4,371	25,833
1900	3,254	13,925

Source: *A History of the Chinese in California*, Chinese Historical Society, San Francisco, California, 1969, p. 19.

time in San Francisco (see Table 5). It is therefore doubtful that
Valley City's Chinatown could support as diversified an organizational
system as that which prevailed in San Francisco.

Chinese Intercommunity Relationships

The Chinese community was, to some degree, a holistic entity, an internally integrated system; cooperative activities between communities
and the exchange of personnel as visitors were quite common. For
example, ceremonies held in Valley City were attended by Chinese
visitors from San Francisco; it will be seen that even religious objects
"visited" many communities. Moreover, there was a constant flow of
people from San Francisco to Valley City and back to San Francisco
for the return trip to China.

Chinese organizations, be they "tongs," "family associations," or
"district associations," had branches in many west coast cities and visiting between dignitaries and members often occurred, particularly during festive occasions. At such times Chinese miners would flock from
their camps to enjoy fellowship and feasting at their respective associations. The constant flow of personnel, monies, and letters kept the
Chinese sojourners aware of happenings in the home villages in China
and no doubt helped them overcome their loneliness in America, the
"Gold Mountain Country."

In summary, guilds, associations, and tongs dominated the social
and economic life of the early Chinese settlements in America. These
surname and occupational groupings regulated the social life of individuals, set economic standards within specific enterprises, and, often
using threats and violence, regulated internal competition. By also
providing their members with food, lodgings, recreational, religious,
and social security benefits, they strengthened their hold over intransigent individuals so that virtually no Chinese could remain outside
the system. Although organizational conflicts frequently occurred, cooperation and harmony endured and linked divergent associations into
an interdependent institutional network.

Prejudice and Discrimination

The Chinese, easily identifiable racially and culturally, became the
unwilling victims of derogatory stereotyping. In addition to racial
and cultural distinctiveness, the mutually reinforcing factors of spatial
and social isolation provided the ingredients for discrimination and
prejudice.

Alien and non-white, the Chinese were subjected to legal discrimination at the local, state, and national levels. Laws were passed, for example, forbidding Chinese to own property, to vote, or to testify against white men; many of these were later found to be unconstitutional.[11] The attitudes upon which these laws were predicted were certainly a part of American community life and tended to reinforce social discrimination.

Derogatory stereotyping was infectious and rapidly spread to include all aspects of the Chinese character. The exclusion of Chinese from the labor force, based on the claim that Chinese would work for wages unsuitable for a white living standard, was the first link in a chain of discriminatory attitudes and practices which, at its end, maligned Chinese moral, philosophical, and intellectual abilities .

The literature of this period was resplendent in its anti-Chinese characterizations. Newspaper and magazine stories about Chinatown dealt with "Bootlegging in Humanity," "Whys and Wherefores of Tongs," "Opium Empire," and other lurid and sensational Chinese episodes (Lee 1960:359). Anti-Chinese sentiment is well illustrated in an 1895 Butte Chamber of Commerce bulletin:

". . . Anyone in favor of home industries cannot consistently patronize Chinese. Every dollar given to him is lost to America. He buys nothing from us except that which is not convenient for him to have sent from China. . . . With the million idle men in this land the claim that no other help can be secured to displace the Chinese is false. We call upon everyone to assist us in our efforts to remove an evil which should not be tolerated" (Lee 1960:358) .

These damaging racial invectives were fed by the opinions of those who had actual contact with Chinatown residents. The following statements are from citizens of Valley City who were interviewed by a commission investigating Chinatown conditions:

11 One of the first actions taken against the Chinese in California was the California Legislature's 1852 "Miners' Tax Law." In 1862, the "police" tax required the payment of $2.50 by each Mongolian over eighteen who had not paid the miners' tax. Another law passed by the California Legislature in 1860 required Chinese engaged in fishing to pay a tax of $4.00 per month.

There was also a variety of laws and statutes designed to harass the Chinese and other minorities. The California school laws provided separate schools for whites, the San Francisco cubic air ordinance required a lodginghouse to provide 500 feet of clear atmosphere per adult, and the so-called "queue ordinance" required every male in the San Francisco city jail to have his hair cut to one inch of his scalp. One of the most burdensome of these was a California state law which intentionally excluded all persons of color from testifying in court against white people.

These laws were eventually declared unconstitutional by the Supreme Court of California (Kung 1962:70–73).

"They [the Chinese] disregard the fire and health ordinances. They build fires in their rooms on the floor, under the sidewalks and on the sidewalks. The Chinese live together 15 or 20 in a small room and do their cooking there and sleep there. This enables them to live on probably 10 cents a day or 70 cents a week, while a white laborer would be under an expense, at the very least, of twelve dollars per week. He (the Chinese laborer) has usurped the place of the white girl maid in families. He has driven white labor from the factories, the fields and the ordinary work of laborers" (Farwell 1885:109).

"I have seen small boys visit their houses of prostitution. In one instance, I saw a woman entice a boy of about 11 into her room.
"Question: 'Have you ever known of any Christian (Chinese) here (in Valley City) ?' "
"Answer: 'No Sir, nor do I believe there was ever one made in California' " (Farwell 1885:99).

Anti-Chinese sentiments were encouraged by newspapers and magazines but were also expressed in public demonstrations and anti-Chinese rallies and meetings:

"A meeting of the opponents of Chinese labor was held in Turum Verein Hall where addresses were delivered by ex-governor Bigler, Dr. Clapp, and Deputy Sheriff Sherman. Resolutions were adopted taking ground against Chinese employment in any Department of Labor" (*Valley City Union*, February 27, 1867).

"At the Democrats' rally held at the Metropolitan theatre, Democrats presented to packed crowds why their party could successfully handle the Chinese question. Governor Irwin was applauded when he claimed that Chinese immigration is detrimental to our civilization" (*Valley City Daily Record Union*, March 4, 1895).

Yet not all Caucasian sentiments and published opinions were anti-Chinese. Judge N. G. Curtis of Valley City made the following remark about a young Chinese man:

". . . I found him devout, honest, upright and true. I have been looking for a model Christian life and have found it in the Chinese lad from across the seas" (Wu 1928:172).

"The Chinese quarter may appear squalid but there is no epidemic there, even for smallpox which took a toll of the whites. . . . Chinese merchants and businessmen . . . possess sterling integrity and their word is their bond" (*Valley City Daily Union*, January 11, 1873).

These voices testifying to Chinese integrity for the most part went unheeded. The major exception was a growing number of Caucasian missionaries intent upon the conversion of the Chinese to Christianity, who thereby provided one way in which Chinese could convince the Caucasian world of their desire to become "good Americans."

Chinese-American Religious Institutions

While Chinese immigrants continued to practice their ancestral religious traditions, including the construction of temple edifices, a small but continually increasing minority was attracted to the Christian church. As early as 1854 the Reverend Jehu Lewis Shuck purchased a lot for the construction of a Chinese church (Barth 1964:163). He was able to raise the needed funds, and in June, 1855, he established his 200-seat chapel. Many Chinese crowded the aisles to hear Reverend Shuck deliver the first service in Cantonese. After the service was over, the Chinese parishioners quietly departed (*Valley City Daily Union,* June 11, 1855; January 11, 1873). Reverend Shuck continued to preach in both English and Chinese every Sabbath until 1861. His successor, Reverend Frederick Charlton, was less successful, however. Chinese community interest waned, attendance dropped off, and the chapel remained deserted for many years until it was destroyed by fire in 1872. It is doubtful that Reverend Charlton spoke Chinese, which probably accounts for waning Chinese interest (*Valley City Daily Union*, September 7, 1872).

Missionary work continued, nevertheless, with the establishment of the Congregational Chinese Mission in 1880. Forty Chinese members attended the first anniversary of the mission, where they recited scripture and sang psalms in both Chinese and English. The highlight of the service was a recital by Lem Chung, a mission helper, on the evils of Chinese "superstitious" and "spirit worshipping" practices, in which he proclaimed his love for God and Christ (*Valley City Union,* May 23, 1881). By 1885 the Chinese mission in the heart of Chinatown, was reported to be still functioning and was apparently run by the Chinese themselves. Sunday attendance was reported to include from fifteen to twenty parishioners (Farwell 1885:100).

Chinese residents attended Sunday school, but particularly evening classes conducted by young ladies. By 1873 a class for English language instruction was held daily in the lecture room of the Congregational Church with an average evening attendance of twenty students, all males (*Valley City Daily Union,* January 11, 1873).

Although some Chinese became at least nominal Christians, many others continued to perpetuate their indigenous religious practices. The *Valley City Daily Union* (January 11, 1873) reports that a Chinese "Joss House" across from the China slough "has its votaries and would seem to be in a flourishing condition, and that pagan rites are performed in the public streets." The Chinese "joss house" or temple is an Old World institution. According to belief, the idols protect the worshippers from misfortune and their good will must be solicited by periodic offerings. The offerings consist of food, wine, and the burning of incense or paper. The wine and food are consumed by the worshippers afterwards (Wu 1928:175).

In 1869 the *Valley City Union* reported that:

"The Chinese residents commence today their annual ceremonies, having for their object the driving out of devils from the community which have lately been extensively making much sickness."

On October 19, 1869, the ceremony commenced:
". . . the driving out the devil ceremony begins. Musicians went after the cloven footed gentry straight from the word go, creating racket sufficient to drive out the biggest devil in the city. The ceremony continued for five days and nights closing with the burning of the bamboo figures that ornament the temple."

In 1890 the "Joss House" was still an important community concern and was described by a traveling artist, B. Kroupa (1890:32):

"In the Chinese quarter I arrived at a joss house. On either side of the entrance stood two large figures twelve feet in height, tinselled and painted in true celestial art. The inside of the place looked very much like a curiosity shop, being filled with bronzes and china. Groups of wood carvings were suspended from the ceiling and about six feet from the floor were large glass cases arranged upon shelves in which all sorts of Chinese figurines, ten to fifteen inches in height, were displayed. . . . The great Joss (apparently from the description, a figure of Confucius) had an immense flowing beard and mustache. On a table in front of the idol was a spread of what looked like roast chicken, pork and tea, and wax candles burning, mingled their fumes with odor from numerous smoldering tapers and pastilles."

Chinese temples of this early period were self-sufficient and were supported by the local community and by contributions from home villages in China. It was not uncommon for Chinese to travel to attend religious services in communities which supported a Chinese temple.

For example, Chinese visitors from San Francisco were reported at festivities in Valley City (*Daily Union*, October 19, 1869), and Eberhard (1962:366), discussing the tax ledgers from a temple in Marysville, attests to entries which indicate that Chinese deities, referred to as "the one in the silk dress," customarily were lent out to other Chinese communities, including Valley City.

Chinese Christian religious centers were established and run by Caucasian missionary personnel with the help of Chinese assistants. These churches, as well as Chinese religious institutions, were all located within Chinatown. There is no mention of a Chinese religious edifice outside of this area nor is there mention of Chinese churchgoers attending predominantly Caucasian churches. Many Chinese, however, participated in both Chinese and Christian services. This attitude, which strives to accommodate both religions, is well exemplified by the following account: Lem Chung, a sincere convert to Christianity, was approached by people from his home town in China who wanted him to make a contribution toward building a temple over there. He was informed that he would have his name engraved if he would contribute. He adamantly refused. He was rebuked and told that his parents would feel sorrow and disgrace if they did not find his name, and that no one would tell his Christian friends about it (*Valley City Union*, May 23, 1881).

Acculturation

It may make little difference to a resident of Chinatown which god he worships, but it is of vital importance to him that he be able to speak English. The church provided him with just that opportunity. Although many Chinese became eager converts to Christianity, attendance at church services and particularly at church schools offered the convert secular benefits as well. The following statements are testimony to this fact:

> "They go to these schools solely to learn English. I have heard Chinamen frequently say that they went to these places simply to 'catchee English.' They laugh at the idea of being converted to Christianity" (Farwell 1885:100).

> ". . . There was an old Chinaman there, Billie Holung, who has been around here for twenty years, and turning to him I asked what the performance was. He said it was a Christian church. I asked him what he (a Chinese preacher) was saying and he said: 'He is talking about Jesus Christ; he is damn fool, he never sees Jesus Christ' " (Farwell 1885:100).

From the testimony of Charles T. Jones, District Attorney from Valley City:

"They go (to the Christian Sunday school) to learn English. I have had Chinamen who pretend to be very devout Christians tell me that the only reason they go to Sunday school and church was to learn English without any expense to themselves" (Farwell 1885:101).

The polytheistic and syncretic nature of Chinese religious beliefs may have allowed the immigrants to America to adapt to Christian practices and to incorporate the Christian deity into a Chinese religious panorama. This did not necessarily mean, however, that a Chinese Christian had privately to repudiate his native religious identity. Christianity may have provided religious security, but the tangential benefits from congregation membership enabled one to learn the English language, an obvious help in securing better employment and a direct way of acquiring the necessary funds to return to China.

This approach toward the "advantages of Christianity" is also reflected in the Chinese utilization of the American courts. The Chinese used some processes of the American legal system to their advantage, although they may have cared little for American jurisprudence.

"They use the machinery of the American courts to enforce their own contracts. When a woman escapes, they swear out a warrant for her arrest for grand larceny or some felony. Sometimes it is sworn out against the man who has her and sometimes against both. As soon as they get possession of the woman, they trifle with the cases until they fall through. . . ." (Farwell 1885:111).

"Sometimes when several men are arrested one will be offered whom we may convict if we let the others go. Several men were arrested for robbing Harpers shoe store, these fellows put up a man who admitted he was guilty but I did not believe he had anything to do with it. These Chinese leaders offered to furnish me with all the evidence I wanted if I would have a nolle pros, (a formal notice by the prosecutor that prosecution in a criminal case will be partly or entirely ended), entered in other cases" (Farwell 1885:105).

It is not the intention herein to disclaim all Chinese sincerity toward American religion and law and order. However, those areas in American life to which the early immigrants seemed most adaptable are precisely the areas in which adoption of American practices permitted retention of a fundamentally Chinese way of life. Valley City's Chinese residents were accommodating themselves to some American institutions; they were utilizing American religious and judicial processes, but primarily to further Chinese ends. This type of accommodation does not demand shifts in value orientation, nor does it signify a desire to embrace the ideology of the host nation.

Acculturation can be viewed as the process by which a minority group changes its cultural patterns and incorporates new norms and values in an effort to become accepted members of the new society. This process is dependent upon a change in attitudes and values, the receptivity to new ideas, and the ability to accept the institutions of the host society. Acculturation, therefore, did not occur in Valley City.

Summary

Chinese merchants and farmers brought their wares into the greater Valley City community, and Caucasians visited Chinatown for commercial, recreational, religious, and gastronomical reasons. The church missions taught the English language and converted some Chinese to the professed ideals of Christianity. Chinese eagerly adopted miners' boots and improvised on Caucasian technology. A few, acting as spokesmen for the Chinese community, visited city, state, and federal officials. On the surface they may have accepted selective portions of the "American Dream," but they rarely rejected the basic tenets of Chinese tradition.

The Chinese resided within a segregated community where contact with Caucasian individuals and institutions was infrequent. Isolation encouraged stereotyping, and many Americans, eager to find scapegoats to explain the ills of a changing society, readily blamed the Chinese. Prejudice and discrimination helped to keep social relationships between these groups at a minimum. The majority of Chinatown residents spoke little English, believed in a foreign philosophy, worshipped Oriental deities, and had as their primary concern a desire to return to their homes on the Chinese mainland. They were economically and politically bound to internal Chinese institutions which sometimes, through terror and violence, but more commonly by persuasion, locked them into a Chinese world. Chinatown spawned an interdependent and interrelated social system that was reinforced at every turn by common values and multiplex relationships. The Chinese associations, tongs, guilds, and clans expanded their functions and modified their traditional structures to better fit the American setting, thereby dominating both the spiritual and physical life of their members, who depended upon their respective associations for their primary needs.

PART THREE

A TIME OF TRANSITION

1900–1940

7

The Changing Chinese Community

FROM APPROXIMATELY 1910 TO 1940 Chinese communities began to experience important changes in social, structural, and cultural orientation. This transitional period was the start of a significant era for the acculturation and assimilation of the Chinese into American life. During this time a new generation of American-born Chinese began to question the traditional principles of community leadership; although their successes were limited, they were nevertheless setting the stage for the dramatic changes which followed World War II. Educational and occupational mobility, accentuated by urban renewal projects, changed the geographic boundaries of many Chinese communities. As the Chinese moved into formerly restricted areas, they faced discrimination and prejudice and, although their efforts to penetrate an American wall of intolerance were not immediately successful, they did not create new Chinatown ghettos.

Changes were most evident in family life when the conflict of generations was underscored by a change in cultural orientation. The authoritarian role of the parents, particularly the father, was challenged as growing children demanded independence and freedom from some traditional restrictions. Women were kept less and less in domestic servitude and began to participate in activities beyond the home. Chinese, both young and old, but especially the young, started to reassess their identity both as Chinese and Americans.

At the same time, images of the Chinese became more favorable. Community organization was still firmly rooted in traditional associations and based upon principles already established in early Chinatowns. Yet the ability of these associations to dominate and control Chinese-American life was beginning to decline.

The primary focus of this chapter is on the changing demographic, familial, and organizational life of the Chinese community of the 1930's, a period representative of this historical phase. In order to make the nature of these changes more obvious, comparisons will be made when appropriate with the life of the Chinese community of the 1880's, a period representative of the more traditional era.

Population Trends

The Chinese-American world of the 1880's was overwhelmingly male; men made up 95 per cent of the population. In 1890 the proportion of males to females reached the fantastic ratio of 27 males for each female (Kung 1962:32). Chinese overseas emigration had always been a male venture. Rose Hum Lee (1960:23) states:

"The Chinese were inclined to bring in their sons rather than daughters. Not only had the expense of bringing the children been a consideration, but the daughter remained home to keep the mother from being too lonely. Women had fewer opportunities for emigrating because Chinese social custom opposed it (women were supposed to remain close to the ancestral hearth) and because fewer overseas occupations were open to them" (Lee 1960:23).

Moreover, after the Chinese exclusion acts first enacted in 1882, China-born women rarely qualified for entrance into the country (Lee 1960:23).

Table 6

Chinese Population for Valley City and the
United States 1880 and 1930

	U.S. Chinese population	Valley City Chinese population
Year		
1880	105,465	1,781
1930	74,954	1,366
Population Decline	30,611 (29%)	415 (18%)

Source: U.S. Census 1880, 1930.

By 1930 the total Chinese population in America had declined 29 per cent (about 18% in Valley City, see Table 6).

However, the male/female sex ratio had begun to shift significantly. In 1930 Valley City's Chinese population was still predominantly male, but the female population had risen to 30 per cent, which was slightly higher than the national figure at 20 per cent. While there were about four males to every female nationally, the ratio in Valley City was only two to one (see Table 7).

The increase in the number of women during the early decades of the twentieth century is primarily due to an increase in female Chinese children born in the United States. Furthermore, the excess of males was reduced by the return to China of a large number of single males, and the exclusion acts prevented a further influx.

The growing number of available females no doubt affected the number of families. In 1890 only 26 per cent of the Chinese males in

Table 7

Chinese Male/Female Ratio for United States
1880, 1930; and for Valley City, 1930

Year	Chinese males #	%	Chinese females #	%	Excess of males	Males/100 females
			Chinese in America			
1880	100,686	95.5	4,779	4.5	95,907	2,106.8
1930	59,802	79.8	15,152	20.2	44,650	394.7
			Chinese in Valley City			
1930	957	70	409	30	546	234.0

Source: U.S. Census 1880, 1930.

Table 8

Marital Status of the Chinese in
the United States 1890, 1930

Year	SINGLE Male	Female	MARRIED Male	Female	WIDOWED Male	Female	DIVORCED Male	Female
1890	69%	32.3%	26.1%	63.5%	.5%	2.8%	.1%	.1%
1930	48.7%	23.3%	46.3%	68.2%	2.6%	7.7%	.3%	.5%

Source: U.S. Census, 1890, 1930.

America were reported as married. This figure probably also includes men who had wives living in China and lived a bachelor life while in this country. By 1930 the number of Chinese married men had increased some 20 per cent to 46.3 per cent of the total number of Chinese men in the United States. Because of economic necessity and because of the Chinese tradition of marrying at an early age, Chinese women of marriageable age rarely remained single (Kung 1962:34) (see Table 8).

While the overall sex ratio was in the process of becoming more equitable, however, the number of Chinese males and females in similar age brackets remained very unequal. In 1920 only 7.6 per cent of the males were under 14 years of age, as compared to over 43 per cent for women. In the age group over 45, which roughly accounts for almost half (46.7%) of the male population, there were few (10.3%) females (see Table 9).

During the 1880's, 98 per cent of the Chinese in America were foreign-born. By 1930 the foreign/native-born ratios were changing

Table 9

Age Distribution of the Chinese in the
United States by Sex, 1920

Age	Males	Females
1–14	7.6%	43.1%
15–44	45.7%	46.6%
Over 45	46.7%	10.3%

Source: U.S. Census 1930.

Table 10

Nativity for Chinese in the United
States for 1880 and 1930

	MALES			FEMALES			BOTH SEXES	
Year	Total	Foreign-born	Native-born	Total	Foreign-born	Native-born	Foreign-born	Native-born
1880	95%	94%	1%	5%	4%	1%	98%	2%
1930	80%	52%	28%	20%	7%	13%	59%	41%

Source: U.S. Census 1880, 1930.

Table 11

Nativity for Chinese in Valley City, 1930
(approximate)

MALES		FEMALES	
Foreign-born	Native-born	Foreign-born	Native-born
588 (60%)	369 (40%)	143 (35%)	266 (65%)

Source: U.S. Census, 1930.

Table 12

Distribution of Individuals over 21
Years of Age, Valley City, 1930

	Males over 21	Females over 21	Total	Per cent of total
Foreign-born	487	122	609	83%
Native-born	142	50	192	30%

Source: U.S. Census, 1930.

significantly. Although females accounted for only 20 per cent of the total population, nearly two-thirds were native-born. The male native-born increased to 28 per cent, one-third of the total male population.

In 1880 Valley County claimed 4,893 Chinese, of whom only 36 (less than .01%) were native-born, yet by 1930, 369 of the 957 males, and 266 females, over one-half the total female population, were native-born and therefore United States citizens. Furthermore, the total foreign-born population was less than 100 persons more than the native-born. The number of the foreign-born over 21 in Valley City, however, was 609, as compared to only 192 for the native-born (see Tables 10, 11, 12).

Demographic Characteristics and Social Organization

Although the population characteristics for both Valley City and the nation changed dramatically after World War II, the trend was already evident in 1930. The Chinese population was shifting from a foreign-born, older, and single-male profile to a younger, native-born populace with a more equal sex ratio for all ages. It appears that Valley

City enjoyed both a more favorable sex ratio among the Chinese and a more equal representation of native- to foreign-born than other Chinese settlements, a fact which helped to accelerate the forces of change.

These population shifts affected the basic structure of both family and community organization:

1. The predominantly single male Chinatown population, living without the benefits of family life, was dependent upon traditionist groups for their social-sexual needs. The increase in the number of available women of marriageable age released many of these men from what Lee termed "rooming-house culture" (Lee 1960: 45). The dependence of married men upon the traditionist organizations not only decreased, but their chances as family men, for integration into the mainstream of American life increased. While the network of Chinese associations continued to provide many services, their domination of their members' social and economic life was declining. The expanded economic opportunities which were offered by small businesses, run by families living in quarters behind or above their shops, led to a decrease in dependence upon services provided by the associations.

2. In spite of the increase of married couples, there still remained a large number of elderly men who did not marry. Those men remained dependent upon the associational network for their livelihood and recreation. They often functioned as organizational leaders and continued to act as representative spokesmen for the entire Chinese community.

3. The increasing numbers of native-born sons and daughters presented a problem to the continuation of associational control by the predominantly foreign-born because these "American natives" began to challenge the intellectual and cultural foundations upon which that control was established.

"The shift toward youthfulness has its implications. Youth is more adaptable, more pliable and more receptive to change. Children under 14 will attend school in this country and be brought up in an American environment in their most formative years. Their outlook cannot help being different from the outlook of those who came to this country fully grown, already imbued with the ways of the old country" (Sung 1967:121).

Chinese youth were not quite ready to threaten directly the traditional organizational institutions which were still controlled by the foreign-born adults, but they began to challenge the foundations of Chinese familism in their homes. Since the principles of filial piety and propriety served both family and society, changes in one would necessarily lead to changes in the other.

4. Marginal men (and women) are the products of parents who remove themselves from their native country and settle in a foreign land. Born and reared in America, yet raised by Chinese parents, these individuals are bound both to their traditional legacy and to their new cultural heritage.

"Hence they vacillate between two ways of life, two cultural heritages, and two racial groups, each of which is diametrically opposed to the other. As marginal men they keenly experience the prejudices and discriminations because they cannot effectively isolate themselves from either the dominant or Chinese groups" (Lee 1960:144).

As Wirth (1928:290) has pointed out, marginal men are social hybrids, oscillating between the strange and fascinating world outside and the restricted secretarianism of a group into which they happened to be born but of which they are not fully a member. They may rush head-long into the activities of the outer world or bound back to their old familiar primary group.

Marginality did not originate with the native-born sons of Chinese immigrants. Yet these men born in the early years of the twentieth century are the leaders in many Chinese community activities and often the parents of today's Chinese youth. In order to understand the social organization of the contemporary community, it is necessary to examine the conflicts and compromises in both the familial and organizational structure of this transitional time.

Conflict and Change

Institutional and role conflicts are natural processes of social life and do not always threaten the stability of social relationships. There are, however, different types of conflict which should be categorically distinguished from each other. Traditional conflict is built into the social system and challenges neither role performance nor values. Transitional conflict may result in a shift in roles, yet the shift does not undermine the traditional system. Radical conflict, on the other hand, which is often a by-product of acculturation, challenges the traditional social life and can often result in a major structural realignment.

There are certain kinds of conflict which have always been a normal part of Chinese family and community living. Some of these conflicts are an inheritance from the homes of the Chinese emigrants in Southeast China, where powerful lineages vied for political and economic control of local areas. Government officials often clashed with lineage elders, rich lineages dominated poor ones, and secret societies attempted to establish hegemony over territorial and occupational spheres. Quarrels over land, family, and marital arrangements, both within and outside of lineage and village boundaries, were often violent and frequently continued for years. An example of such conflicts is well documented and perhaps best commented upon by Freedman:

> ". . . I discussed what evidence I had managed to find on hostile relationships between lineages in Fukien and Kwangtung. It seemed to me then, and now seems even more certain, that fighting between lineages, governed by rules, was an important characteristic of social life in Southeastern China" (Freedman 1966:104).

Within the Chinese family, mothers clashed with daughters-in-law, who, often in an attempt to improve their position in the family, turned son against parent and brother against brother. When the patriarch died, sons fought over the rights to property and authority in the "new" family. Parents and matchmakers argued over marriage arrangements and dowries, and consanguines did not always come to terms with their affinal relatives. Lin Yueh-hwa's *The Golden Wing* presents a good description and analysis of such family feuding.

Even in the New World, divergent associations based upon territorial, linguistic, and surname identities constantly vied for power and often controlled dissenters by intimidation and violence. Associations fought over real and imagined social and economic injustices and political competition within American Chinatowns was fierce. Men argued over access to women, and parents frequently squabbled over the internal affairs of family life.

These conflicts were part and parcel of everyday community life and were eventually resolved by socially approved methods. One might argue over access to scarce resources, but the goals were often identical, as were the means of reaching them. Differences could be reconciled within a traditional set of values, mores, sentiments, and beliefs common to all. For example, Mr. W. claimed:

> The L. Family Association was the largest and they always had the most elaborate dinners. During the New Year, all the poor people would come to their Association for a free dinner. One day, our Association invited on

the second day, many poor people. Some of them were not even of our clan. The L. Family was ashamed. They who were so rich were not as generous as we were. We made them lose face and some still do not forgive that.

Mrs. T. reported:

My husband was a stubborn man. He wanted a smart girl for the wife of our eldest son. I wanted someone who was strong and could work hard. I told him that girls who think too much make poor mothers but he kept on saying that smart girls make better mothers. I told him you don't have to be so smart to have children.

These conflicts—over "saving face" at the institutional level and the best mate for a son at the familial level—involved arguments over propriety and marriage. However, both associations were in apparent agreement that sharing food wtih the indigent was desirable, and both parents agreed that being a good mother is a prime consideration in choosing a daughter-in-law. Thus, these conflicts did not overtly challenge the innate righteousness of traditional Chinese values, nor did they directly threaten the foundations of either family or community life. We will be less concerned with these types of conflict because they do not involve changes in either cultural orientations or social structure.

We know that the mother has always been instrumental in the mate-selection process, particularly because she would have direct control over a daughter-in-law. We suspect, however, that traditionally she achieved her goals by means of persuasion and subtle pressure. But changing economic conditions in the New World frequently resulted in the father's absence from the home since he usually had to spend twelve to fourteen hours a day at his employ. Thus, the mother often found herself more and more responsible for the disciplining of the children, their schooling, and the economic affairs of the household. It was natural for her to assume some of the decision-making functions of the father and even to publicly override her husband's demands in such matters as mate-selection.

The slowly changing roles of the parents do not, however, impair the transfer of traditional values such as filial piety and respect for elders from old to young. The children are still socialized according to Chinese custom and Chinese values. Firth calls this type of change "organizational change," changes in the way of doing things that do not directly threaten the social order (Beattie 1964:247).

Nevertheless, this "organizational change," a product of transitional conflict, can be seen as a forerunner of radical change; a change in familial roles will eventually lead to changes in basic social structure. Firth's construct is useful as a half-way measure between the resolution of traditional conflict, which maintains the status quo, and the resolution of radical conflict, which leads to structural change.

In the 1930's, as an increasing number of Chinese were prepared to enter into the larger society, the acculturation process intensified. Individuals were increasingly caught up in conflict situations, the resolution of which inevitably led to fundamental readjustments in behavior and attitudes. This situation is effectively illustrated by the dilemma of Calvin G., a perceptive and sensitive first-generation native-born Chinese.

> I was always a good son. I respected my parents' wishes and dutifully went to Chinese language school. While I went to college I worked in my father's shop. I held a minor post in my family association and used to help with banquet preparations and the welcoming of dignitaries. I understood my parents and even though they seemed a little old fashioned, particularly my mother, I respected them just the same.
>
> But I knew I could never do things their way. How could I, an engineer, work in a laundry shop? I read American novels and really understood American thought. I had very American tastes. I liked some Chinese customs but also American ones. I was confused being American and Chinese.
>
> Sometimes, then, it's so hard to be right. When I brought my Chinese fiancée home to meet my parents I thought they would be pleased, but my mother wanted me to go to China to marry, as she put it, "a real Chinese girl." My mother was hurt and called me a disrespectful son. My fiancée felt awful, but I love her very much. How can I possibly please everybody?

Calvin was involved in two distinct relationships; he was a son to his parents and a prospective husband to his fiancée. His relationship to his parents was based upon traditional filial piety, while his commitment to his fiancée was characterized by love. He found it impossible to solve his dilemma because traditional and emergent individual values clashed. His ideas about marriage no longer fit the ideals of familial social relationships, nor could this conflict of interests be solved in terms of a traditional value system. This type of conflict—one that will lead to structural changes for the individual and the society—has been termed "radical opposition" by M. Wilson (Beattie 1964:248). It describes a situation in which two different but related areas of social action vary widely and in which the individual is involved in both at once. It involves ways of thinking and acting that are basically incompatible.

An individual can hold different and conflicting values but only as long as he can effectively isolate them from each other. For example, Calvin can accept a subordinate position in his family association be-because he can conform to Chinese priorities that stress age over youth. Yet he would not accept the same position as an engineer, where ability is more important than age or generation. However, in the realm of interpersonal and familial relationships, the two distinct value systems collide. His decision, should he decide to marry the girl in spite of his parents' wishes, will lead not only to a modification of his value system but to a structural change of traditional relation-ships within the family. The right of parents to arrange marriage has been challenged, mutual obligations and expectations have shifted, and the fundamental assumptions concerning the authority of parents have been redefined. The result is a reassessment of personal values as well as a basic change in family structure.

Acculturation

Language. One of the most important factors influencing integration of the Chinese into American society was the increasing use of English as the primary language. The 1930's witnessed an increase in the num-ber of American-born Chinese; these youngsters attended the public schools, where the language of instruction was English. Chinese boys had attended the public schools since the turn of the century when compulsory education laws were enforced. Schooling for girls was at first resisted, but after World War I parents found it too difficult to disregard the law and to keep the girls at home (Lee 1960:120). As a result, by the 1920's the number of non-English speaking Chinese had decreased from 33,498 in 1900 to only 10,030 (Wu 1928:277).

Although many of Valley City's Chinese could speak "a little English," English was still not the primary language of communication and the more personal intra-family business was more often than not conducted in Chinese. However, in the public school system and in the world outside of Chinatown, the Chinese language was inadequate for conversing with teachers, businessmen, and non-Chinese peers. One informant states:

> I was taught that going to school was important and in order to do well and make my family proud I had to master the English language. How could I talk to my teacher if I knew only Chinese? Even my friends pre-ferred to speak in English. The teacher got mad when she didn't understand me. For a while I was ashamed of speaking Chinese.

Thus, success in school often meant discarding the Chinese language (Wu 1928:280), while this established better relationships with teachers and peers, it often led to troubles at home. Many American-born Chinese youths refused to converse in Chinese at home, angering their parents, who in turn would retaliate by refusing to speak English at all. This led to alienation and conflict for young and old alike. Although some youths refused to study the Chinese language, most acceded to the wishes of their parents and attended the Chinese language schools in the community.

Language is more than merely a way of communicating facts and events. It is the way to express one's most intimate experiences, hopes, desires, and goals. Inadequate communication facility on the part of parents and children leads to social barriers such that, although the family lives under one roof, they are virtually linguistic strangers (Lee 1960:127).

Although most Chinese living in Valley City in the 1930's were Chinese speakers to at least some degree, the shift to the English language as a primary means of communication had already begun. This shift has an importance beyond the family and can be directly related to acculturation and social structure. First, the English language serves as *the* primary means of induction into the mainstream of American social and economic life. It not only exposes the user to American thought and perspective but greatly facilitates social contacts, if only at the secondary level. It is the *only* path to educational mobility in America and thus indirectly affects both income and occupation, the determinants of a class-based social system. Secondly, the shift to English leads to parent-youth alienation and underwrites the social gap between immigrant and native-born generations. Because non-English speaking parents have great difficulty understanding the immediate problems as well as the eventual goals of their children, the children become more self-sufficient and depend more on their peers and less on their parents for emotional stability and intellectual adventure. Once parental authority and control are weakened, other areas of family life may be affected.

Finally, if English is used as the primary means of communication at the expense of forgetting "one's Chinese," it significantly cuts the English speakers off from the non-English speaking members of the Chinese community. Not only were the associations controlled by many non-English speaking immigrants, but entry into the decision-making circles and participation in association affairs demanded at least a working familiarity with Chinese; these associations were major clearinghouses for employment within the Chinese community and many young men were dependent upon them for their economic livelihood.

In conclusion, it is not so much that American ideas are sometimes poorly explained in Chinese but that it is easier to express American thoughts in the English idiom. Being able to converse in the same language can more readily lead to intimacy, trust, and cooperation. For many Chinese just starting to leave the Chinese quarter and, with it, their dependence upon the Chinese organizational network, the ability to converse easily in English was a necessary precondition for success.

Discrimination. One of the greatest impediments to Chinese assimilation was prejudice and discrimination. By 1924 Chinese immigration had been severely curtailed. The Chinese had, for the most part, withdrawn from open competition with organized labor and were becoming small entrepreneurs (Lee 1960:361). Yuan (1969:160) reports that at this time the majority of Chinese were employed in such low-prestige occupations as laundry and restaurant work, although they would soon shift occupational categories and become the managers and owners. During this period the Chinese "image" also started to change. Originally ridiculed as coolie laborers, they were now characterized as evil, opium-eating Dr. Fu Manchus; this adverse imagery was sustained in popular magazines.

After World War I, increasing Chinese participation in American life led to a decline in derogatory stereotyping, which in turn facilitated further participation. Public sympathy for those Chinese who wanted to leave Chinatown increased (Hayner and Reynolds 1937: 633), while the mutual aid and protective functions of the associations were emphasized, as opposed to the earlier emphasis upon opium dens, tong wars, and houses of prostitution. Chinatowns began to become popular as tourist attractions (Lee 1960:362–63).

Yet the problem of assimilation remained. The American-born Chinese were becoming "Americanized," but American groups were unwilling to accept them. C. C. Wu, writing in 1928, states: "If there is an obstacle that keeps the native-born Chinese from feeling completely at home in America it is color" (Wu 1928:287). And Hayner and Reynolds (1937:637) report that ". . . racial and cultural barriers cut off young people from full membership in American society and throw them back upon their own people."

Chinese high school and college graduates found themselves restricted from prestigious occupations, and one young man who was accepted at a local Y.M.C.A. as a basketball player on a church team was still denied individual membership in the "Y" (Smith 1925:165). Chinese finding gainful employment outside of Chinatown extremely difficult respectfully deferred to the wishes of their elders and became economically dependent upon the Chinese associations for their livelihood. Sons and daughters readily became workers in their families' laundries, restaurants, and small grocery stores. The divergence between children and parents and between youth and the heads of the family associations might have been greater if it were not for this consciousness of being members of a small racial minority (Hayner and Reynolds 1937:637).

During this period Valley City's Chinese generally solved their problems, but it was rarely by outwardly challenging the social dictates of the community. This does not mean that there was no discontent and dissatisfaction over existing social arrangements. But in spite of disagreement, children tended more often than not to accede to parental demands, youth resigned themselves to the advice of their elders, and Chinese adults chose to participate in a Chinese political-economic world.

Mr. L., presently a restauranteur, states:

> I needed a bank loan to start my business. I went to three banks but they all wanted collateral that I could not offer them. Their interest was too high also. I talked the matter over with my two brothers and we went to the family association. They agreed to a loan with plenty high interest too. I was bound to them for a long time of my life.

Mr. G. remembers:

> I had just graduated from Berkeley and was an accountant. We moved to Valley City but I could not find a job. I was even willing to be a bookkeeper but no one would hire me. Finally, with the help of my wife's brother, I became a waiter in her cousin's restaurant.

Mr. L. reports:

> We knew that the streets south of Broadway were not open to us Chinese people. The men would call us "Charley Chinamen" and would beat us up. Although my house is too small, I feel safe living with my Chinese neighbors.

Attempts to move outside the Chinese community often resulted in social and economic embarrassment. Chinese could not participate as equals with Caucasians, nor could they overcome the barriers of discrimination and prejudice. The Chinese family and Chinatown social system continued to dominate Chinese life in America and, although many young people were dissatisfied with their leaders, internal rebellion was limited because there were few realistic alternatives.

A Shifting Chinese-American Identity. During the earlier traditional era of Chinese settlement in America (1850–1900), it was easy to develop and maintain a Chinese social and geographic ethnic boundary, separating the Chinese population from the larger, predominantly Caucasian world. American society was generally hostile to the Chinese and except for a few individuals, primarily missionary personnel, little effort was made to welcome the Chinese as equals into the American social system. To be sure, the Chinese were well aware of discrimination and prejudice; but as long as they could find economic, social, and ideological security, based upon adherence to Chinese tradition, they remained within Chinatown walls. Some Chinese strayed beyond ghetto confines for their livelihood, but the majority of Chinese in Valley City lived their lives, from cradle to grave, within a Chinese social world. American doors remained closed to Chinese visitors and the Chinese made little attempt to open them.

The transitional era (1910–1940) witnessed a change in the Chinese acceptance of their status as second-class citizens. Although they had few successes and many failures in breaching the fence of Caucasian intolerance, they began to make the attempt to move into social and economic Caucasian activities. Dressed like other Americans and equipped with an American education and a native command of the English language, they attempted to enter into Caucasian employ. Many of their attempts led to failure and a retreat back to the Chinese enclave. But the rebuff had a different effect upon older, non-English speaking and uneducated Chinese as compared to the native-born and English-speaking children, whereas the parents resigned themselves to accepting realistically the discriminatory and unequal system, the children were outwardly outraged.

A foreign-born gentleman tells the following anecdote:

> Once I remember I go to barber shop. I sit one hour. No one ask me what I want. Pretty soon barber say: "What you want?" I tell him I want haircut; how much? He say $3.00. That make me mad but I make him cut my hair just the same. He give me good haircut. When he through I pay him $3.50. He very surprised. He tell me come again. I never go to white bastard again.

> We were at the Lake (Lake Tahoe). My family went into a restaurant but they refused to serve us. I didn't want to cause any trouble so we left. The next time we go out to eat we will go to a Chinese restaurant.

The native-born also suffered from discrimination but their attitudes were different.

We needed a bigger home and wanted to move to the ——— neighborhood. I knew they wouldn't sell a home to a Chinese family so we had a white man buy it for us. Our neighbors didn't accept us at first. We had to prove that we were as good as they are. We kept our street (front yard) clean and always gave a generous contribution to community fund drives. I even would cut my lawn wearing a clean white shirt. Our children were always scrubbed, well dressed, and polite.

The ——— movie house at first refused to let Chinese in. Later they made us sit upstairs with the Negroes and Mexicans. Maybe it was because they thought we were dirty and uneducated, too. Once I went there with my white schoolmates. I sat with them and no one told us to leave. But I was always hesitant about going alone.

When the attempt by the young Chinese to penetrate anti-Chinese barriers was unsuccessful, many residents blamed their failures on themselves, rather than on the dominant society. They believed that if they went to school and worked harder, they too would be accepted. This attitude still persists today.

The differential attitudes toward discrimination can be attributed partially to the degree to which the Chinese were assimilated into American life. The older Chinese found security with Chinatown's social system. They were annoyed with discriminatory practices but resigned themselves to them and retreated from further unnecessary contacts with the outside world. Their "behavioral assimilation" to American ways had been slight and limited mostly to outward changes in clothing, hair styles, and the adoption of some English phrases. But the young people had attended American schools and often thought of themselves as Americans. The traditional world of Chinatown was foreign and strange to them, as were the mannerisms and dress of newly arrived immigrants. They could not and would not give up their newly acquired American heritage.

The exposure of a new generation of Chinese-Americans to American institutions and ideas could not help but result in a challenge to traditional ways. United States citizens by birth, yet culturally tied to their immigrant parents, this group experienced a desire to fit into an American world yet to remain faithful and dutiful sons and daughters. At first the changes were superficial, limited to extrinsic traits, primarily dress and style. Young women bobbed and frizzed their hair, wore makeup, and enjoyed keeping up with American fashions. The men sported American-style jackets; indeed, the new Chinese uniform consisted of a dark blue suit with wide lapels and a white shirt and tie. Young men and women walked down the street holding hands and went for walks in nearby parks in the day and to American movies at night (Wu 1928:282–83). Baseball, ice cream cones, and frankfurters became acceptable parts of the new way of life.

Even China-born parents were changing. Although mothers rarely left the house and spoke but little English, Christmas became a family celebration complete with a big tree and gifts from Santa Claus. Father, wearing a tailor-made dark suit, carved the Thanksgiving turkey and the family ate with knives and forks. Horns blared on New Year's Eve and the firework displays of Chinese homes on the fourth of July were every bit as splendid as those of other Americans (Leung 1942:100).

Although many of the outward manifestations of Americana were clearly visible, Chinese custom did not disappear. Gai-chuk (chicken porridge) was served and rice was almost always present at the evening meal. Chinese dominoes and mah-jong were played by women in the afternoon and by the men at night. Children still respectfully served tea to their elders with two hands, took small steps in the home, and made sure to use certain "phrases of respect" to make their parents proud. Traditional Chinese holidays (New Year's, Moon Festival, etc.) were celebrated with large feasts and special delicacies both at home and at the association hall or restaurant. Although some youngsters expressed the desire to be elsewhere, they nevertheless dutifully accompanied their parents to these dinners and festivities. Sons might be named after American presidents, but their birth was still marked by a family celebration in the traditional manner. Father remained formal and reserved and mother was often the de facto ruler of the domestic scene.

Nevertheless, changes were occurring, changes that challenged the traditional parent-child and husband-wife relationship and undermined the structural stability of the Chinese family. Chinese youth started to attend dances and parties and, as was the custom of the time, girls took singing lessons. Future brides and grooms demanded western weddings complete with white wedding gown and church service and wore the traditional "red dress" only at the celebration afterwards. Couples at times even embraced in public, laughed at the thought of getting married, discussed divorce and remarriage, and equated courtship with romantic love and physical attraction, often to the consternation of their parents. These attitudes and behavior, particularly in inter-sex relationships and the use of leisure time, were anathema to their parents' ideas of Chinese propriety and often led to family conflicts. Girls resented the fact that they were often forbidden to go to socials as the Americans did and abhorred their parents' attempts to arrange a suitable marriage. Young men demanded a more equal voice in family affairs and valued freedom and independence from parental dominance, the right to choose their own careers, and the right to raise their children as they saw fit. The ideal family was one that was to be based upon love and equality.

Chinese women were breaking away from the tradition of staying inside the home. They visited their friends, shopped in neighborhood stores, and attended Chinese community functions such as concerts given by the Chinese schools. Their husbands often appeared helpless as their wives demanded education, the right to appear in public places, and the discarding of traditional behavior in relations with other men. Chinese men expressed their dismay, particularly with regard to American-born Chinese women who seemed to spend money, go to shows, buy pretty clothes, and raise a small family. If a woman was born in America, her position approximated that of other American women. With the father away at work for long hours of the day and night, the mother raised and disciplined the children and often became the adjudicator of disputes, acting as the intermediary between husband and children.

Extrinsic changes were soon followed by intrinsic ones, often resulting in conflict between two widely divergent ideals, Chinese and American. The importance of the family as a cohesive social unit decreased when it conflicted with the rights of its individual members. Paternal authority in matters of occupation, education, and marriage was challenged by children and young adults. There was a tendency to solve problems "American-style," by attention to the specifics of particular situations and by the evaluation of personalities of individuals, rather than by the traditional dictates of familism. Chinese were no longer indifferent to strange American mannerisms as they tried to picture themselves as Americans, too. Sometimes, however, these new ideas conflicted with what they thought right and proper and often shocked youngster as well as parent. Many parents realized that the traditions they had brought with them did not function efficiently in the new environment, but they were often at a loss as to what should be done.[1]

Yet, in spite of all the demands of youth, most sons and daughters

[1] Similar changes were occurring at this time in Chinese settlements all over the United States and are discussed by Haynor and Reynolds (1937), Wu (1928), Smith (1925), and Leung (1942).

remained somewhat obedient to their parents; regardless of differences in ideology and behavior and the conflicts these differences generated, the new native-born Americans of Chinese descent did not stray too far from the ancestral hearth. They were not completely at ease in the American world and could not make the break from family and community. In the final analysis, they were still dependent upon their "Chinese world" for financial and spiritual security.

Social Organization

The formal social organization of Valley City's Chinese community will be more fully discussed in Chapter 10. However, it is necessary at this time to present a summarizing sketch of its organizational structure, primarily to serve as historical background and to set the scene for a more detailed analysis.

Chinese overseas social organization is basically hierarchical and segmentary, which means that there are progressive levels of community leadership and an established pattern for organizational fragmentations. Valley City's Chinese population, however, did not exhibit the organizational diversity of larger Chinatowns because of its relatively small size. Thus, the principles of hierarchy and segmentation could not be implemented fully. Nevertheless, the basic organizational unit was, and remains today, the family name association.

Family Associations. Family associations, referred to as "clan associations" by Lee (1960:174) and "surname associations" by Crissman (1967:196), were of two kinds—those based upon a single surname and those that included two or more surnames but which functioned as a single organization. Single surname associations are based upon stipulated descent: The possession of a common surname automatically entitles the holder to membership regardless of his ability to demonstrate his genealogical relationship to the founder of the association or to fellow members. It was also common for smaller surname groups to combine in a single association. These mergers were justified on the basis of historical commonalities and "blood-brotherhood," usually dating back to the early days of Chinese civilization. Smaller surname groups often found it advantageous to recognize these sometimes historical, sometimes fictive, connections because their increased actual and potential numbers allowed them to compete more favorably with the larger associations. In Valley City family associations were established during the early decades of the twentieth century and by the 1930's there were eight family associations in existence. Four were single surname family associations; the remainder were combined groups.[2]

Generally, and for Valley City in particular, these associations were indispensable for the welfare and integration of the Chinese community. Their functions included the establishment of a headquarters for single and unattached males, where they could live, cook, sleep, socialize, and conduct meetings. Often the rooms were located above or adjacent to a store operated by a member. The association purchased their food and other necessities from the proprietor and he in turn would take care of their mail, write letters to their families in China, and act as an intermediary in financial transactions.[3] The association helped in finding work for unemployed members,[4] lent money to the needy, arranged funerals for the impoverished, and provided for the shipment of their bones back to China. The association would provide recreational facilities for its members, as well as celebrations and feasts commemorating major and minor Chinese holidays such as New Year's, Moon Festival, Ching Ming, Dragon Boat Festival, etc. As the family associations increased in size and wealth, they would purchase property and erect a headquarters separate from a commercial establishment. By 1930 all of the association headquarters were located in the prime Chinatown area.

When discussing the makeup of family associations, membership must be distinguished from participation in association affairs. Many Chinese who possessed the requisite ascribed qualifications for membership did not pay dues, nor did they participate in any associational activities. Yet the association nevertheless represented all members in community functions and readily enlisted their aid, particularly for numerous fund-raising projects. These nonparticipating members also had the rights to services that the association provided. Most major events attracted not only participants and officers but a good percentage of the total surname community. For example, an association official estimated that some 75 per cent of the total membership attended the annual New Year's celebration and dinner. The association

2 The family associations were formally incorporated from 1900 to 1920. There were formerly no family association branches in Valley City; those who participated in their family association activities would often travel to San Francisco to attend meetings and to celebrate holidays. The increase in the number of families aided and accelerated the founding of local branches in Valley City.

3 The "hui" was one informal banking institution for family association members. It served to pool financial resources to meet immediate needs for funds. See Sung (1967:141–42) for a detailed discussion of this procedure.

4 Certain families had virtual monopolies over specific businesses and could control employment in these enterprises.

officers and participating members were primarily older, China-born, single, male residents. Women did not hold office in family associations.

Most Chinese were reluctant to bring their problems before the family association. Every attempt to resolve differences was made at the lesser and more personal family level, so that only serious, irreconcilable cases were aired in association chambers. These arguments were primarily concerned with financial matters but occasionally would involve other difficulties. A typical case study from the ——— association follows:

> A member had lent another member the sum of $3,000. After waiting for a year he wanted his money back. The other man claimed he could not afford to pay back the money. They decided to go before the family association. They gathered in a meeting room in front of three officers. The first party agreed that he had lent the money to Mr. I. but he now needed to make payments on his rented shop and had lost his own money at the gambling house. He admitted that there had been no date set for payment. The second party claimed he had invested the borrowed money in some property and that he had no reserve cash and was unable to make repayment. The president and the officers conferred and presented a solution to the two men. They stated that it was a bad thing to owe money to a "cousin" and be unable to pay it back. They felt it was foolish to lose rent money in the gambling house. They suggested that the second party pay back part of the money as an act of good faith and that perhaps the former could wait a time for the final payment. Both parties agreed that this was an equitable solution.

The case illustrates some basic principles of conflict resolution. First, it is the disputants who must bring their case before the family association since the association does not have the right to discuss a case that is not specifically referred to it. Secondly, the association elders have no legitimate means to enforce a decision. The decision is really a suggestion and is not legally binding upon the disputants. Should one party be dissatisfied with the suggestion, he could not be forced to comply. Although the decision has no legal force, it is based upon traditional authority and carries a strong moral force. A disputant who disagrees with a decision which is supported by the Chinese community will lose face and be shamed. Moreover, because the Chinese community was still characterized by a web of multiplex relationships, such social sanctions could effectively bring intransigent individuals into line. Noncompliance could threaten future success in other social, economic, and political dealings. The success of such social sanctions is inversely related to the opportunity to operate outside of the Chinese community. Most disputants were older, foreign-born, and, in many instances, uneducated in both English and Chinese. Their dependency upon this Chinese judicial system was great and they often complied with the elders' suggestions. The younger, native-born, English-speaking, educated Chinese rarely brought their troubles to the family association. Their financial problems were more often handled in the American courts.

The association elders usually decided upon a solution that would allow both parties to "save face." Each disputant was viewed as having "just demands," thus enabling them to resolve their difficulties. There were cases, however, where powerful individuals used the family association conflict-resolution mechanism to further their own concerns.

Chinese Tongs. Tongs were originally organized to control gambling, prostitution, and other clandestine activities. They also performed many of the functions of the family associations, and individuals who did not have a local family association often joined a tong for social and economic security. Furthermore, it was possible for individuals to hold dual membership; but in cases of conflict, loyalty to the family association took precedence over ties to the tong. Only large Chinatowns could support more than one tong. When a tong is located in a city with small Chinese population, a rival tong cannot establish a branch without the consent of the first tong.

During the 1920's and 1930's the only tong in Valley City, a local branch of a well-established West Coast tong, was quite active and functioned as a protective association for anyone involved in gambling. It offered protection to operators of gaming houses for a fee. It was reported that almost all heavy gamblers were also tong members; moreover, anyone whose income was primarily derived from such activities was almost certain to be a tong member.

The establishment of a single tong meant that the violence that had characterized an earlier era of Chinese settlement had decreased significantly. By the 1930's tongs were also losing their ability to coerce and control American-born Chinese, who provided less demand for gambling and prostitution. Tong wars were rare after 1921 (Reynolds 1935:622).

The Chinese Benevolent Association. All Chinese communities have a local benevolent association which draws its members from the established organizations in that community. It may appear under various names in different cities, but its most important function is to represent all Chinese residents in a given locale. Valley City's Chinese Benevolent Association was composed of representatives from the eight family associations, the single tong, and the local branch of the

Kuomintang, a politically oriented organization founded by Dr. Sun Yat-sen around 1912.

The Chinese Benevolent Association sponsored and coordinated all community-wide activities, but particularly Chinese festivals and the official welcoming of dignitaries. For example, the Chinese Benevolent Association acted as sponsor for Dr. Sun, and later for Madame Chiang, when they visited Valley City. It also supported the Confucius Church, less a religious establishment than a hall for social activities, a local Chinese cemetery, and one of the Chinese language schools. The leaders of Valley City's Chinese Benevolent Association were invariably chosen from leaders of its representative organizations, exemplifying the hierarchical and segmentary structure of formal Chinese organizations.

During the 1930's the Chinese Benevolent Association acted as spokesman for the entire Chinese community, particularly when dealing with the Caucasian superstructure. Its officers cooperated with Valley City's officials and lent financial support to fund-raising and other patriotic and social city events. It was the unofficial court for disputes that involved members of different associations and its judicial procedures paralleled those of the family associations.

The "Six Companies" in San Francisco considered themselves the legitimate representatives for all the Chinese in America and the official headquarters for all the local benevolent associations. Yet, in spite of these public claims, local autonomy for the Chinese benevolent associations and the family associations was the rule rather than the exception. This autonomy did not preclude cooperative ventures, particularly fund-raising activities, but each local association preferred to solve its internal conflicts with a minimum of outside interference and jealously guarded its independence. The following is a case in point:

A girl attending one of the Chinese language schools claimed she had been sexually attacked by one of the school teachers, a married man. The girl's family association demanded restitution. The school teacher's family association rejected the demands. The conflict worsened and spread to the family association's national headquarters in San Francisco. The conflict had become so bitter that the school teacher feared for his life. He would closely watch the classroom door at all times and was prepared to dive behind his desk to avoid the bullets of a hired assassin. Finally the local Chinese benevolent association was invited to attempt a resolution. It was apparently successful for the furor died down. The school teacher paid for the girl's hospitalization and the girl went to live with a relative in Hawaii.

The Chinese benevolent association did not enter a dispute until it was invited by the aggrieved party's family association. Moreover, in this case it was brought in only after the conflict had spread across community boundaries and had reached the stage where violent confrontations were expected. The accepted solution was also nonpunitive; although the school teacher paid the hospital bills, he was not convicted of the charge and continued teaching in the school. Theoretically, both the school teacher and the girl had "saved face," and the credit for an equitable solution went to the local Chinese benevolent association.

The Chinese-American Church. Chinese missions had first been established in Valley City during the 1850's. Missionary activities expanded, and by the mid-1930's Valley City had three Chinese churchmissions: Baptist, Methodist, and Church of Christ. These churches, preaching a Protestant Christian doctrine, catered to an exclusively Chinese congregation.

From the Methodist Chinese pastor's personal records, we can surmise the following: In 1926 his church counted 93 Chinese parishioners, 52 of whom (41 males and 11 females) were resident. Of the listed members who were no longer resident, 9 had returned to China, 10 were living in other cities on the West Coast, 3 had moved to the east, and 19 had moved away with unknown addresses. Half of the resident congregation had Chinese first names, as did 38 of the 41 nonresident members. Sixteen children, nine males and seven females, were enrolled in the church school. Only four of these students had Chinese first names.

By the 1930's each church maintained a Chinese language school attended by youngsters and an English language school in the evenings for adults. The church school taught classes in English while services were primarily in Chinese, with the readings of the scriptures in both languages. The school staff in the Methodist church consisted of seven teachers: four Chinese females, two Caucasian females, and one Caucasian male. By 1939 their church school enrollment rose to 100 students with an average attendance of 80; there were six grades, with 50 students in the junior and senior divisions. All churches supported a choir, choral club, a band and drum corps. They were administered by Caucasian supervisory personnel who were assisted by Chinese preachers and Chinese staff. Sermons and services adhered strictly to scripture and doctrine, with an occasional reference to the Chinese Republic in East Asia. In 1930 the total resident church membership in Valley City listed some 100 Chinese persons, about 10 per cent of the total Chinese population.

Generally, church congregations consisted of older males, although the percentage of women steadily increased. As the general population shifted from foreign-born to native-born during this time, so did the church membership. Religion, usually considered a family affair by Americans, was an individual endeavor for the Chinese. Most Chinese little understood or cared about doctrinal differences and children were free to choose their own church should they so desire (Lee 1957). It is also difficult to assess the commitment to a specific church or doctrine or to Christianity in general, since many of the church's functions were of a secular and social nature—particularly the English and Chinese classes. Church affairs provided a legitimate social outlet for women who otherwise might have been restricted to more domestic activities. Churches were also probably important as a place for young people to meet and establish dating as an important way to form marriages.

Finally, church membership did not preclude membership in other traditional Chinese associations. While Christian doctrine might have conflicted with traditional practices, many churchgoers appeared to be little disturbed about the contradictions and were also quite active in other associational affairs. In Valley City, however, Chinese churches did not have representation in the Chinese Benevolent Association.

The Chinese Language School. By 1900, Chinese children were enrolled in American schools, but the Chinese, feeling a need to instill and perpetuate a Chinese heritage in their sons, established the first Chinese Overseas School in Valley City in 1908 in the heart of Chinatown. It was sponsored by the Chinese Benevolent Association, the tong, and all of the family associations. Contributions were also accepted from family associations and benevolent associations in other Chinese communities, particularly the Six Companies in San Francisco. Each sponsor informed its members of the establishment of the school and encouraged its families to send their children.

The first class consisted of only twenty-five boys, but enrollment steadily increased, reaching 50 to 75 during the 1920's, 120 to 125 during the 1930's, and finally a high of about 175 in the 1940's. In 1935 females were admitted to classes. In grades one, two, and three, the primary emphasis was on reading, writing, and speaking the Cantonese language. As the student body increased in numbers, upper grades were added, in which subjects included Chinese history and literature, classical philosophy, Tang poetry, calligraphy, and some of the writings of Sun Yat-sen, in particular his "Three People's Principles." Instruction was in the traditional manner and learning was done by rote and repetition of lessons. The teacher would read the lesson, and the students would repeat it after him a line at a time.

This was followed by class reading, and writing the lesson on the blackboard, character by character, up to 100 times. Students were forbidden to write English words next to Chinese characters. Then came oral reading to the teacher. It was not uncommon to have as many as three grades in one room, two grades writing while the third read. Examinations consisted of copying a lesson by page number.

All texts were printed by the Chinese Nationalist government; thus all material was subject to its approval. Students purchased books and writing equipment and paid a small monthly tuition, about $2.50. The pupils were generally serious and worked hard, as their parents reproached them over a poor report and encouraged them to attain high grades. Report cards were not issued until 1940, but parents were constantly informed, either directly by the teacher or indirectly through word-of-mouth, of their children's progress. Classes were held from 5:00 until 8:00 P.M. on week days, and from 9:00 A.M. until noon on Saturdays. The teachers were educated in mainland Chinese schools, were usually men, at least in the upper grades, and were strict disciplinarians, with corporal punishment not uncommon. Yet the pupils were often delighted by legends and tales of ancient China and considered their teachers to be good and competent instructors. Filial piety, traditional morality, and "good character" were a significant part of the learning experience. Members of the school board, as well as the teachers, were highly respected within the Chinese community and were often influential members of their respective family associations.[5]

Apart from actual instruction, the nonacademic aspects of these schools were also important. The school run by the Benevolent Association had a drum and bugle corps, the Methodist Church Chinese school had a band, and both provided for outings and social activities for their students. One former student states:

> School was o.k., but the real fun was going to picnics and outings with our classmates. Sometimes the school would rent a bus and take us to Yosemite or up to the snow line. We all wore white uniforms with sailor caps and when Mr. Y., a rich philanthropist who had contributed much money to the school, died the entire class came to his funeral. It was quite a procession.

The drum and bugle corps played at Chinese holiday functions, at school graduations, and was called upon to help welcome dignitaries from other Chinese communities and from China. They also played at

5 This information was obtained from a former teacher and several students.

American holiday celebrations, as for the Fourth of July. Graduation exercises and school concerts were well attended by the parents and, amidst food and laughter, celebrations lasted for many hours and were fondly remembered.

The three churches also ran Chinese schools, although the Chinese Benevolent Association school seems to have been the best attended and most prestigious. The schools functioned to unite rather than divide the community and were highly regarded by Valley City's Chinese residents. Aside from transmitting Chinese language skills, they were also responsible for keeping alive a Chinese heritage for the sons and later for the daughters of the foreign-born. Not only did they attempt to instill traditional virtues in their pupils but they provided a social life for their students, an important attraction in a society where Chinese were often excluded from such activities. As a result, students continued their studies for an average of from five to eight years. Many obtained the Chinese public school diploma and, not a few, a Chinese high school certificate. These schools kept alive a sense of Chinese tradition and history which was being threatened by the new generation's increasing involvement in other areas of American life. Chinese language training enabled children to continue to communicate with parents, and particularly with grandparents, in their native tongue and was a positive force for family cohesiveness.

School friendships continued after class hours and graduation ceremonies and became an important part of an informal network of social and economic ties (Weiss 1969:12). Moreover, most of the Chinese school children were either native-born or had been brought to America at an early age, for the foreign-born and foreign-raised already had a command of the language and a Chinese education and did not need the benefits of the Chinese school in America. These informal friendships, established among Chinese school classmates and among Chinese classmates in the American high schools, may well have functioned to separate native- from foreign-born and to provide the basis for a dual community structure.

Worlds in Transition

A standardized sociological presentation of structure and function is a necessary part of academic discipline. Such a presentation does not always catch, however, "the flavor and sentiment" of the Chinese perspective. The following is a composite picture-image of Chinese community life in Valley City circa 1930, gathered from the reports of living informants, which will perhaps reveal more clearly those "feelings" which are an important part of the community experience. *The Old World.* Chinatown remains the geographic and social center of Valley City's Chinese community. Amidst the smells and sounds of the Orient, one can hear familiar voices speak Cantonese during the day and the click of the mah-jong and domino tiles emanating from behind the closed doors of gambling houses at night. Family association halls are filled with the activities of busy officials and permanent residents. Funeral processions, complete with a hired American fire department band and Chinese mourners, wind their way through the Chinatown streets and alleyways, and wedding banquets held at one of the four larger restaurants last for many hours. During the Lunar New Year the streets are alive, and young and old alike stand listening as the sounds of firecrackers accompany the Dragon's March through the brightly lit streets. On one street a father admonishes a son for his impropriety and is in turn later admonished by the president of the Benevolent Association for his public display of anger. On another a woman with bound feet shuffles four paces behind her husband, ignoring the laughing youngsters dressed in white uniforms on their way to the Confucius Chinese School. In the basement of a family association, an old man shares with his friends the news of his second eldest daughter's marriage to a wealthy farmer in Toishan, China, a marriage made possible by his monthly remittances to his family; he promises to visit their families when he returns to China once again.

A New World. Chinatown can no longer house the entire population and the Chinese have spread to other areas of the city. They live in an area which overlaps with "Japantown," and the small Filipino colony. People no longer live above the store, and their new homes are filled with American furniture and magazines.

There are "Asian faces" at the High School senior dance and the girls are attractive with their bobbed hair and new dresses. The boys, spiffed up in their dark blue suits, look forward to graduation and college careers as mathematicians and engineers. They are secretly ashamed of their parents, who cannot speak English well and who toil for long hours as bus boys and kitchen help or, worse, as gamblers. A young lady, her lipstick slightly smeared, walks hand in hand with her beau to join their Chinese friends seated in the corner of the dance hall. A boy looks forward to impressing his date with a ride in his brother's new car, which will be all paid for in just three months. Another thinks of what will happen when he tells his father he wants to quit Chinese school so that he can concentrate on his increasingly time-consuming algebra classes and his new position on the debating team. After the dance three boys walk past a theater, which does not admit Orientals, and curse the owner in English.

Calvin Mar does not believe in "silly dances." He is also too shy to ask for a date. He ate his hamburger dinner early and his books are now spread out on the dining room table. His grandmother is listening to her "Chinese records" and the notes, discordant to his ears, distract him. He does not want to hurt her feelings, so he says nothing. She doesn't understand English and his Chinese is not very good. He must rise at 6:00 A.M. to help his father open his laundry shop, but it is difficult to concentrate because his older sister is crying and shouting at their mother, "I'll get married when I am ready, so don't try to fix it up with Mrs. F.'s son."

Unity and Diversity: Prologue to the Contemporary Community

These descriptive renditions of Chinese life in Valley City portray the Chinese social worlds of the 1930's and dramatize the qualitative differences between foreign-born parents and their native-American children. During this transitional period, both representations are valid expressions of family and community life. They exist side by side and frequently overlap, so that the individual actors in this ethnographic scene must constantly shift their perspectives and live in both worlds at the same time.

Conflict between the traditional and transitional approaches was frequent and continues today. But in the 1930's it was more readily held in check, and, for several reasons, the Chinese community appeared more united than divided. First, although Chinatown boundaries were becoming more diffuse, the Chinese were still geographically restricted to certain areas of the city. Their residences coincided with those of other Oriental groups but were discrete from those of other minorities and the majority of the Caucasian population. Their churches, schools, and association headquarters were well within the major population clusters, and this spatial-social propinquity aided the sense of community solidarity.

There was little occupational and social mobility for most Chinese, particularly during the Depression years. Last to be hired and first to be fired, the Chinese, like other minorities, turned to their own community for economic resources and security. Prejudice, discrimination, and the fear of being deported for illegal entry into the country [6] enhanced a general distrust of American legal and financial institutions and kept most Chinese dependent upon the traditional associations which continued to dominate community life.[7]

It is true that children challenged their parents in family decision-making matters, that enthusiasm of youth clashed with experience of age, and that modern innovation threatened traditional stability. But because the challengers themselves were products of "Chinese" households and had to function within a social world controlled by traditional organizations, they were often unable or unwilling to break completely from the world of their ancestors.

America was rapidly becoming a cultural melting pot for the Chinese immigrant as well as his sons and daughters, although the degree of acculturation was dependent upon age, sex, generation, education, and occupation. Yet this country still remained structurally

[6] United States immigration laws and procedures have restricted and controlled the flow of Chinese immigrants into America. There were, however, two major exceptions. First, any person born in America is a United States citizen, as are his children, regardless of their birthplace. Secondly, although officials, teachers, students, travelers, and merchants were exempted from restrictive legislation, only merchants could remain for extended periods.

But if a man had sons in China he would send for them. Sometimes the sons had died, or the father had reported extra sons (presumably conceived when he last visited his China home). Such "slots" were available for sale to boys with no family connections and were known as "paper sons." Merchants could buy into business enterprises and qualify for admission and it was common that many Chinese firms had an unusually large number of partners. Both ruses were moderately successful and many Chinese entered this country contrary to legal procedures Sung (1967:99).

One cannot claim that Valley City's Chinese Benevolent Association, family associations, and tong were involved in such maneuvers. Illegal immigration was considered a personal matter between two individuals and their nuclear families. However, given the close-knit and multiplex nature of Chinese society, it was inevitable that many leaders would know about such transactions and this knowledge could be used to coerce, threaten, and blackmail the illegal entrants and their families.

[7] Leadership in traditionist associations was overlapping and more or less continuous. Leaders could hold official positions in the Chinese benevolent society, the family associations, the tong, and the Kuomintang. Moreover, once elected to an office, most men continued to serve in similar offices although their titles might be changed from year to year.

Rose Hum Lee (1960:152–60) has chastised the traditional leaders as being selfish, self-seeking, vindictive, and of amassing personal power and wealth because of their positions. This statement was not altogether untrue for Valley City's Chinese; however, traditional leaders were also known for their generosity, sacrifice, and service to the community. In any case, these leaders were quite influential in community affairs and dominated political and economic life. Thus they had vested interests in maintaining an exclusively "Chinese" community and looked upon acculturation and assimilation of the Chinese into American life as a threat to their continuing control.

a pluralist society, where Chinese maintained institutional separation from American society.

The "accepting," and "tolerant" nature of the Chinese in America has long been considered a part of the personality make-up of the Chinese populace and has been likened to their child-rearing practices (Sollenbarger 1968; Hsu 1949:261–84). "Passivity" was thought to be a Chinese social fact of the 1930's. In Chinese homes throughout the country the ideals of the ancient and classical Chinese tradition of forbearance were taught to youngsters. It was a matter of pride to "grin and bear it" and wait patiently for a better opportunity. Yet it also made many Chinese, particularly men, feel rather inadequate when competing in an aggressive and turbulent Caucasian social-economic world, a fact which led to a retreat from involvement in Caucasian society. In recent times this ideal has been criticized by the more aggressive and more militant Chinese. They have suggested that Chinese acceptance of their social status and willingness to jeopardize their gains have resulted in the inability to challenge social injustice.

During the following years acculturation, both intrinsic and extrinsic, would become a social fact for most American-born Chinese and would intensify the conflicts at both the familial and associational levels. Structural assimilation would increase in secondary contacts but inter-personal contacts remain ethnocentric in primary areas. For the majority of Chinese assimilation through intermarriage would be unlikely. The principles upon which family life was based would be drastically modified and the internal structure of the Chinese community would be threatened by the growth of new organizations which would be challenged in turn.

PART FOUR

THE CONTEMPORARY COMMUNITY

1940–1970

8

Settlement Patterns

SETTLEMENT PATTERNS REFLECT, and have important consequences for, (1) the internal structure of the Chinese community, (2) the acculturation and assimilation of the Chinese into American life, and (3) the spatial-social relationships of the Chinese both to the Caucasian majority and to minority peoples. This does not mean to suggest that these settlement patterns are causative agents of social change, although, once established, they may speed or retard organizational and assimilation processes. It suggests, instead, that residential realities are intricately linked to both social organization and assimilation, that these three dependent variables are interrelated, and that changes in one are very likely to generate changes in the others.

Chinatown

"Ghetto" is a term commonly used to designate a specific geographic area usually populated by persons with different racial, ethnic, linguistic, or political backgrounds from those of the dominant group (Lee 1960:55). Such areas are associated with the residential pattern of persons of Chinese ancestry, particularly immigrants, and are referred to as "Chinatowns." These areas exhibit the classical characteristics of ghettos as defined by Wirth (1928). They are still a prominent aspect of Chinese settlement in America and an important feature of the Chinese communities of San Francisco (Dare 1959), New York (Heyer 1953; Barnett 1952), Los Angeles (Chen 1952), and, to a lesser extent, Philadelphia (Loh 1945), Boston (Murphey 1952), and Chicago (Lee

1960). However, Chinatowns, particularly those in the smaller cities, have been continually losing their Chinese population as well as their demographic specificity.

The decline of Chinatowns in American cities is a complex process and varies with individual urban centers. Yet the overall process entails certain recurring events applicable to the logical order of decline of any Chinatown in this country. These factors include (1) a decline in the number and a change in the kinds of Chinese occupations and services catering to a strictly Chinese clientele; (2) a loss of population attributed to the departure of sojourners and families; (3) social changes precipitated by wars and depressions, which weaken the economic structure and redistribute the population; and (4) ecological invasion, which not only changes land use patterns and land values but brings in new residents who change the racial composition of the neighborhood (Lee 1949:429–31). These factors are largely responsible for obliterating the geographic identity of the community. Once the configuration of a community is so altered, it rarely resumes its former characteristics.[1] Moreover,

> ". . . all available evidence points to the fact that no new Chinatowns will be created. It appears that the number of Chinatowns in this country will decrease almost to the vanishing point" (Lee 1949:432).

Valley City's Chinatown, although already rapidly losing its Chinese population, was still a definable area in the late 1920's. An old-time resident reports:

> When I first arrived in Valley City in 1928, I lived at a Caucasian banker's home. My grandfather was his family cook. I liked the smells in the shops of Chinatown and it reminded me of my village (Toishan) back home. I remember I used to come back from the shop and go to the ——— place and lose my income at mah-jong. In Chinatown there were many small homes and there were three Chinese language schools and the churches, and I played in their drum and bugle corps.

Yet by 1937 the Chinese population had spread to other areas of the city and by 1939 old Chinatown had so changed that the once numerous Chinese shops were reduced to a mere handful of qaint old-fashioned stores (*Guide Book* 1939:79).

---

[1] For an analysis of the changing geographic scene of a particular American Chinatown, see Rhodes Murphey's "Boston's Chinatown," *Economic Geography*, pp. 244–55, 1952.

During World War II the Japanese, who shared the same residential area, were taken to relocation camps and other minorities started moving into the area, prompting many Chinese to leave. However, it was the large-scale urban renewal projects of the post-war years, when residential and business sections were disrupted by stepped-up expansion of the city hall and office building complex, that accelerated the breakup of the Chinese residential community. Private residences were dismantled as business and government enterprises expanded south and westward. Along the Valley River properties deteriorated as a new population of male transients and drifters started to occupy multi-story hotels and apartments. As rent decreased, private homes were turned into multiple family dwellings and Mexican-American and Negro families infiltrated the area.

When the Chinese Exclusion Act was repealed in 1943 and the Chinese were the first foreigners to become eligible for immigration and naturalization, the flow of Chinese immigrants into America increased.[2] While most immigrants settled in the San Francisco Bay area, some made their way up-river to Valley City. These new immigrants, combined with American-born newcomers, increased Valley City's Chinese population from 1,508 in 1940 to 6,770 in 1960 (U.S. Census, 1960). Chinatown could no longer provide adequate housing for these people and they were forced to locate in other areas. Many chose to reside in the Central City, which already had a sizeable Chinese population.

Before the 1940's the Chinese had been restricted from owning property in certain areas of the city, particularly because of the discriminating practices of real estate agents and individual home owners. One informant summarizes:

> Everyone knew we Chinese could never own land in the South Area, the former home of the big-shots. Back in the '30's, P.Y. built a house, and was threatened by the whites. My grandfather had to purchase this lot here by having a Caucasian represent him and sign all the papers. When we moved in, the neighborhood was sure surprised at our yellow faces. We were the only Chinese family on this block for fifteen years.

But after the war the attitude toward Chinese, who were, after all, our allies, had changed. Anti-discrimination codes were enforced by

---

[2] The repeal of the Chinese Exclusion Act in 1943 was followed by the War Brides Act (1945), the Displaced Persons Act (1948, 1950), the McCarren-Walters Act (1952), and the Refugee Relief Act (1953), all measures that opened the doors to Chinese immigration (Kung 1962:103–31).

federal officials and the south area was opened up to Chinese families. These families were increasingly successful in business and the professions. They were opening up supermarkets and restaurants in non-Chinese areas, abandoning smaller neighborhood stores, and the hand laundries were giving way to dry cleaning establishments.

The adventurous Chinese entrepreneurs looked for new and better neighborhoods to increase their earnings and to validate their achieved social and financial gains. If not openly welcomed, they were at least tolerated by their new Caucasian neighbors.

By the 1950's the end of old Chinatown was a demographic fact. An elderly informant comments:

> There isn't any real Chinatown any more. Oh, sure, there are still some shops and restaurants and all the family buildings, but many of them are already closed and so run down that no one comes there any more. There are lots of Chinese families here but no real sense of unity. I have to go to San Francisco to find a real Chinese community.

In 1961 the Chinese community leaders could claim that although Chinatown was the spiritual home of the Chinese community, most of the Chinese had moved out of the area (Fang 1961:29).

In 1967 the old Chinatown consisted of little more than five restaurants, two of which had permanently closed their doors, some living quarters primarily in basements, and the somewhat dilapidated headquarters for the Chinese associations in the city. The only recent new construction had been the Confucian Church (Chinese Community Center), completed in 1959. In the summer and fall of 1969 the wrecking cranes had completed their job and, except for the Confucian Church, had obliterated old Chinatown. Thus, the most strikingly obvious, as well as perhaps the most important, feature for the Chinese in Valley City is that there presently does not exist a Chinese ghetto, a "traditional Chinatown." [3]

Although the social organization in terms of social structure of traditional Chinatowns were previously discussed, generally in Chapter 5 and specifically for Valley City in Chapter 6, a few findings bear repetition.

[3] Traditional Chinatowns are categorically distinguished from "new Chinatowns." New Chinatowns are primarily commercial and associational centers rather than residential areas. They are designed to attract tourists and often provide a contrived Oriental atmosphere.

"But the new Chinatowns are not like the old. Nor will they ever be unless we turn back the clock of history and re-create the conditions of yesteryears. The bonds that held the early Chinese together in Chinatowns are gone. Communal organizations have lost their leadership anl their functions" (Sung 1967:150).

First, because Chinatown provided for the functional prerequisites of community life, its residents could find social and economic security within its boundaries and could live out the major part of their lives with little contact with the outside world. Since this practice fostered "ghetto" solidarity by preventing and discouraging outside contacts, it decreased both behavioral and structural assimilation processes. It has also been concluded that:

> "Persons who work, sleep, eat, worship and socialize within the ghetto confines have to make fewer adjustments. They can insulate themselves sufficiently to ignore the surrounding society" (Lee 1960:62).

Secondly, it has been seen that the power of community leaders, usually elders, to control the varied facets of Chinatown social life was, originally, quite extensive. Once the ghetto population is dispersed, the internal social organization of the community is affected. Institutional organizations die out and the control which these community leaders had over the former ghetto dwellers weakens and finally grows altogether ineffective.

Finally, Chinese racial visibility, enhanced by few actual contacts, led to the development of stereotypes, discriminatory with implications. Behavior was often predicated upon such stereotyped images. Furthermore, large numbers of a minority group who cluster in a given area of the city are not only visible as individuals but visible as a segment of the community (Marden and Meyer 1968:27).

In summary, three distinguishing features of Chinatown life are: the restriction of Chinese assimilation, control over community life by traditional leaders, and the development of derogatory stereotypes by non-Chinese. Thus, a change in residence pattern, destroying the boundaries of the Chinese ghetto, leads to concomitant changes in attitudinal and behavioral characteristics for both groups. These changes will be discussed in this chapter.

Contemporary Chinese Settlement in Valley City

The following information is drawn from two sources: the Valley City Census (1964–1965) and the ethnic composition of the pupil population of the Valley City Unified School District (1963–1968).

Valley City's Oriental populations may be found in almost all of the city's census and enumeration tracts except in those which are either sparsely populated or zoned as industrial-commercial. Oriental students are enrolled in all of the city's fifty-seven elementary schools.

However, there are no census tracts in which the resident Oriental population exceeds 40 per cent of the total population, and only two tracts in which the Oriental population is over 30 per cent. No elementary school district has more than a 49 per cent total Oriental enrollment.[4]

Although the Chinese reside and attend school in almost every area of the city, Valley City's Chinese are significantly concentrated in specific city districts[5] (see Figure 2). There are only eight census tracts or enumeration districts in which the Oriental population exceeds 11 per cent (see Figure 3), and only seven tracts in which the total Oriental population is over 600 persons (see Figure 4). In 1968 there were 2,164 Oriental elementary pupils, 7.4 per cent of the total enrollment in the Valley City Unified School District. Sixty-six per cent, or 1,245, of these students were concentrated in only eleven of the city's fifty-seven schools.

It is apparent, then, that while Valley City's Chinese are no longer restricted to a ghetto, they are nevertheless concentrated as an ethnic group in specific residential areas of the city. Moreover, the areas of high Oriental concentration are not homogeneous; each area exhibits distinct characteristics. These districts can be further divided into three city areas—Central City, Southgate, and Southland. Sample

---

[4] Population figures for Chinese are submerged because they are included with "Orientals" in the Valley City Unified School District bulletins (1963–1969) and grouped as "others" in city census tract reports (1964–1965). However, by utilizing a 1.3 per cent ratio of Chinese in the total population and by applying a simple formula,

$$\frac{\% \text{ Chinese} \times \text{number of Orientals or others}}{\text{combined } \% \text{ of Orientals or others}} \quad \text{number of Chinese,}$$

one can arrive at the approximate number of Chinese in a given census tract or school district. To estimate the number of Chinese in a given tract, consider the following example: City Census Tract 21 has the greatest number of Oriental residents. The combined Indian and Oriental (others) population for this area is 1,459. Applying the formula,

$$\frac{1.3 \times 1,459}{3.5} \quad 542 \text{ (number of Chinese persons),}$$

it can be assumed that there are approximately 542 Chinese persons in this tract.

[5] The 1968 Valley City Metropolitan Area telephone directory served as the primary source for defining Chinese residence clustering. The major (Fong, Wong, Yee) and some minor (Chow, Chan, Louie) Chinese surnames listed in the directory were located on a 4' × 8' map, which was later reduced to standard paper proportions.

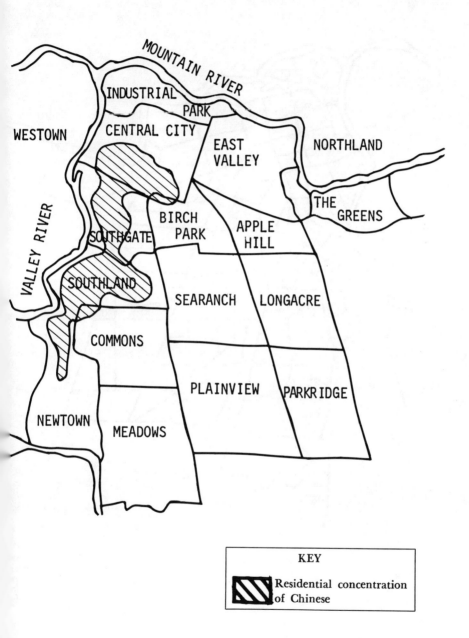

Figure 2. Residential Concentration of Chinese in Valley City, 1968.

Figure 3. Oriental Population Distribution, Valley City, by percent, 1968.

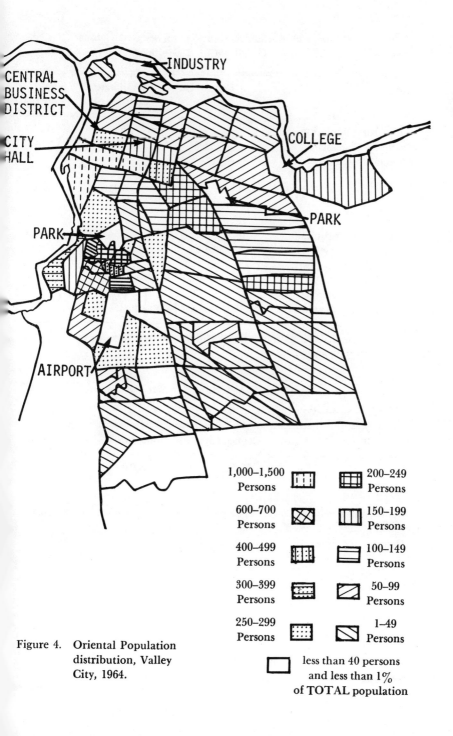

1,000–1,500 Persons	200–249 Persons
600–700 Persons	150–199 Persons
400–499 Persons	100–149 Persons
300–399 Persons	50–99 Persons
250–299 Persons	1–49 Persons

less than 40 persons
and less than 1%
of TOTAL population

Figure 4. Oriental Population
distribution, Valley
City, 1964.

Table 13

Ethnic and Racial Distribution for Selected Census
Tracts, Valley City 1964–1965*

	Central City (3 districts)	Southgate (2 districts)	Southland (8 districts)
Caucasian population (includes Caucasians of Spanish surname)	2,167 (62%)	4,658 (81%)	1,833 (86%)
Negro population	620 (14%)	297 (5%)	75 (2%)
Other races (includes Chinese, Japanese, and other non-whites)	996 (24%)	834 (14%)	268 (12%)
Chinese population (estimated by formula)	[370 (8.9%)]	[310 (5.2%)]	[100 (5.5%)]

*Based upon city census tracts for 1964–1965, Valley City.

Table 14

Demographic Characteristics for Selected Census
Tracts, Valley City 1964–1965*

	Central City	Southgate	Southland
Median family income	$5,647	$8,043	$8,952
Median gross rent	$73/mo.	$76/mo.	$95/mo.**
Deteriorated units	201 (12%)	48 (2%)	4 (.86%)
Dilapidated units	22 (1.3%)	8 (less than 1%)	1 (less than 1%)
Renter/owner ratio	191/109	65/113	87/673

*Based upon city census tracts for 1964–1965, Valley City.
**Estimate.

census tracts were selected for each of the three areas[6] and the following variables compared:

1. Number and percentage of Chinese residing in the area
2. Number and percentage of other ethnic groups in the area
3. Median family income
4. Median gross rent
5. Number and percentage of deteriorated housing units
6. Number and percentage of dilapidated housing units
7. Owner/renter ratio.

The results are presented in Tables 13 and 14.

Population Distribution and Ethnicity

Pupil enrollment is based primarily upon home address, since students attending specific schools generally reside within that school neighborhood. Using the Valley City Unified School District reports for 1968, those school districts with the largest numbers and percentages of minority group people can be identified, and the conclusion reached that Oriental pupils do not generally attend school with either Negroes or Mexican-Americans. Of the ten elementary schools with the highest numbers and percentages of Oriental students, there is only one school in which the combined percentage of Orientals and whites falls below 65 per cent. In three schools the percentage is over 70 per cent, in five schools over 80 per cent, and in one school over 90 per cent (Table 15). Conversely, schools with large proportions of Negroes and Mexican-Americans have relatively few Oriental students (Table 16). Most Chinese elementary school children in Valley City attend schools with Caucasians rather than with members of other minority groups. Because school attendance reflects residence, these same data are useful in establishing residence patterns and spatial-social relationships with majority and minority people for the adult Chinese community.

The movements of minority peoples within and without the city are an indication of the degree of discrimination against the group as well as of the economic status of the mobile members. Information provided by three Chinese realtors explicates the 1963–1968 population shifts for Oriental students. The Chinese are primarily moving

---

6 Census tracts were selected for their relatively dense Oriental population and include: for the Central City area, tracts 19, 20, and 21; for Southgate, tracts 22 and 24; and for Southland, census tracts 34 and 38 and enumeration districts 163N, 148, 149B, 150, 154, and 156A.

Table 15

Racial-Ethnic Distribution of Pupils in Elementary Schools with
Largest Numbers and Percentages of Oriental Students

School	Orientals		Mexican-Americans		Negroes		Whites		Oriental and white
	#	%	#	%	#	%	#	%	%
Riverside	173	48.5	20	5.6	10	2.8	151	42.3	90.8
William Land	182	45.2	91	22.6	54	13.4	74	18.4	63.6
Sutterville	227	36.9	26	4.2	47	7.6	306	49.7	86.6
John Cabrillo	180	31.4	20	3.5	71	12.4	300	52.4	83.8
Alice Birney	114	20.1	11	1.9	111	19.6	321	56.8	76.9
Collis P. Huntingdon	85	18.6	58	12.7	10	2.2	305	66.5	85.1
Pony Express	120	18.2	61	9.3	18	2.7	459	69.8	88.0
Bear Flag	87	16.8	24	4.6	60	11.6	344	66.6	83.4
Hollywood Park	93	16.6	58	10.4	77	13.8	316	56.5	73.1
H. W. Harkness	99	11.4	55	6.3	186	21.4	517	59.4	70.8
Total	1,360	263.7							
Average	136	26.4							

Source: Table 1, Valley City Unified School District Pupil Population Report for 1968.

Table 16

Number and Percentage of Oriental Students in Elementary
Schools with High Concentrations of Negro and
Mexican-American Students

School	Negroes #	%	Orientals #	%
Camellia	259	82.5	0	0
Donner	248	61.5	6	1.5
Oak Ridge	198	38.7	9	1.8
Elder Creek	115	35.7	3	.9
Bret Harte	180	35.7	12	2.4
Ethel Phillips	193	32.5	11	1.9
Fruitridge	239	32.5	30	4.1
John D. Sloat	114	21.6	16	3.0
Jedediah Smith	115	21.5	23	4.3
Total	1,661	362.2	110	19.9
Average	184.5	40.2	12	2.2

School	Mexican-Americans #	%	Orientals #	%
Washington	99	46.9	3	1.4
Jedediah Smith	206	38.6	23	4.3
Maple	112	36.0	11	3.5
Lincoln	56	34.6	20	12.3
Elder Creek	109	33.9	3	.9
Ethel Phillips	190	32.0	11	1.9
Woodbine	105	30.2	1	.3
Oak Ridge	145	28.3	9	1.8
Early Warren	111	24.2	13	2.8
Joseph Bonnheim	123	13.1	57	6.1
Total	1,256	317.8	151	35.3
Average	125.6	31.8	15	3.5

Source: Table 1, Valley City Unified School District Pupil Population Report
for 1968.

from north to south, away from the Central City downtown area to
the southern suburbs of Commons and Newtown. As new areas open
for housing developments south of the city limits, continued Oriental

Table 17

Racial and Ethnic Student Movement in Valley
City Elementary Schools

Ethnic Racial Group	1964	1965	1966	1967	1968	1969	Percentage change
Caucasians	19,222	19,387	19,391	19,328	18,970	18,626	−4.8%
	68.8%	67.5%	65.3%	65.3%	64.7%	64.0%	
Mexican-	2,671	2,791	3,367	3,398	3,469	3,498	+2.5%
Americans	9.5%	9.7%	11.4%	11.5%	11.8%	12.0%	
(Caucasians							
of Spanish							
surname)							
Negroes	3,427	3,869	4,134	4,138	4,269	4,390	+2.9%
	12.1%	13.5%	13.9%	14.0%	14.6%	15.1%	
Orientals	2,281	2,251	2,283	2,245	2,164	2,166	−0.7%
(Chinese,	8.1%	7.8%	7.7%	7.4%	7.4%	7.4%	
Japanese,							
and							
Korean)							

Source: Research Report on Pupil Population, Valley City Unified School District 1964–1969.

movement in this southerly direction can be expected. There is also a smaller movement eastward into predominantly Caucasian neighborhoods of Northland and the Greens and a concentrated movement away from Negro and Mexican-American areas.[7] In this context it may be noted that Caucasians are also leaving the city areas while the number of Negroes and Mexican-Americans is increasing (Table 17).

Not only is Valley City's Chinese population dispersed throughout certain areas of the city, but Chinese association centers and churches are not coincident with population clusters. The major Chinese residential areas are not located within or even near the Chinese Association and Community Center, where many major and minor Chinese activities take place (see Figure 5). In fact, Chinese residing in the

[7] Since 1963 there has been a continual loss of Chinese students from the nine elementary schools of high Negro concentration and from eight of the ten schools of high Mexican-American concentration (Research Reports 1963–1968, Valley City Unified School District).

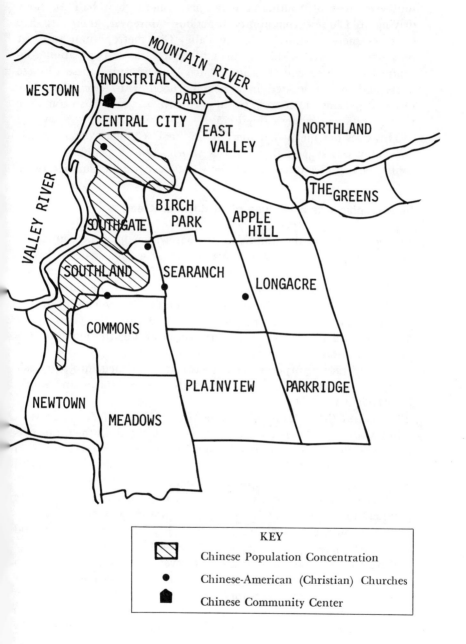

Figure 5. Chinese Population Concentration, Chinese Community Center, and Chinese-American Churches, Valley City, 1968.

southern areas of Southland may spend more than half an hour driving to Chinese community functions. Moreover, there are five Chinese-American churches in the Valley City metropolitan area, yet only one is located within an area of high Chinese population concentration.[8] Three churches are located "just outside" these Chinese areas and one is located in a neighborhood with fewer than fifty Oriental persons. Therefore, Chinese churchgoers must also commute to their religious centers (Figure 5).

This does not mean that there is no "real" Chinese community. It does, however, suggest that the ties which "bind a people together" cannot be considered to depend solely upon geographic considerations.

Demographic Characteristics of Residential Areas

The destruction of the traditional Chinatown enabled the Chinese to disperse and relocate, but not necessarily as a homogeneous racial-ethnic group. The Chinese currently reside in both the central and southern portions of the city. It has been seen that the three census tract areas with a relatively high proportion of Chinese exhibit diverse socio-economic and ethnic profiles (Tables 13 and 14). These major differences are also related to patterns of social organization and rates of acculturation.

For illustrative purposes, these areas can be divided into two basic categories, the Central City and the south area (Southgate and Southland Heights).

The Central City. This area is one of the oldest residential areas in all of Valley City. It is located fairly close to the downtown business and state office section and is bounded by a major thoroughfare on the south. The east and west boundaries are established by proposed and existing freeways. Some of the residences were first built over fifty years ago and show the signs of age; many are considered by city planners to be "very old." Although the houses may appear shabby and run down, the yards are fairly well kept, the streets clean, and neat vegetable gardens common in back-yard plots.

Private homes dominate the area; however, many of them have been turned into apartments with separate front, side, or back entrances for each family. One- and two-story apartment complexes are also scattered throughout this area, an increasingly common phenomenon in the central city. Rents vary considerably but are usually not overly

---

8 Chinese-American churches are churches of Protestant denominations composed almost exclusively of Chinese parishioners. As of this writing, all but one are headed by Chinese ministers.

high. Many of the apartments are small in size and rent from
$80–$120 a month. Converted apartments in private homes can cost
as little as $35 a month. One such dwelling, occupied by a Chinese
family, supports three adults and four children in a two-bedroom
apartment, but such overcrowding is not common.

There is a modest amount of traffic in the streets, but automobiles
owned by people living in this area are usually lower priced and older
than those that come from the direction of the freeway and head toward the center of town.

Although the area is considered "residential," it supports small
family-owned commercial enterprises. The shops include grocery
stores, Oriental food shops, candy stores, barber shops, and laundries,
many of them owned and operated by Chinese and Japanese families.

The ethnic composition of "Japantown," a local term for the
clustering of Japanese within the central city, is as heavily Chinese as
it is Japanese. Moreover, there are Negro and Mexican-American
families living within the area, as well as Caucasians. Although interracial and inter-ethnic social relationships are infrequent and rarely
primary, the neighborhood is rapidly becoming a multi-ethnic community.

The life style of the Chinese living in this area is characteristic of
recently arrived immigrants, working-class people, and small shop
owners. A description of households in this neighborhood will com-
plement a more formal analysis of Chinese settlement patterns by
presenting a more personal and intimate picture of family and home
life.

Mr. G.'s market is located well within the central city in an old
building attached to a large private home. It is papered with Pepsi
Cola and other advertisements and resembles in many ways the old-
fashioned neighborhood store. The aisles between food displays are
very narrow, and the store carries both Chinese and American food-
stuffs. Most supermarkets in Valley City carry a section of Oriental
foods, but in Mr. G.'s store the soy sauce comes in large bottles rather
than the smaller ones, rice vinegar is always available, 100-pound
burlap sacks of rice abound. Chinese cookies are on sale and many of
the cuts of meat and fowl available are those preferred by Chinese,
Japanese, Filipino, and Korean customers.

The Chinese proprietor lives with his family in the attached house.
He is past 50, with graying hair, and wears work clothes. His wife
wears ill-fitting "pants" with a nondescript blouse and apron and has
her hair tied in a bun. His daughter, who comes in to help out while
her husband works at a nearby Chinese restaurant, is arranging the
produce. She is about 30, dressed in cut-off levis, tennis shoes, and a

sweatshirt. Her three-year-old daughter is sitting on a chair in the corner and is busily eating candy. Most of the customers are middle-aged and elderly. They are, for the most part, Chinese housewives who sometimes converse with the owner and his wife in Sze-Yap. Many of the customers are greeted cordially and appear to be regulars. There is a large supermarket located directly across the street which attracts a younger and more mixed clientele.

The Y. family lives on "V" Street in a three-bedroom wooden frame home with a small but well-kept back yard. The living room is tiny and is crowded with low-cost, old, and worn furniture. However, a recently polished wooden dowry chest belonging to the mother stands in one corner of the room. Many pictures of parents, grandparents, and children hang on the walls, and there are both American and Chinese decorative items throughout the home. The television set in the corner has not worked for the past two months. On one wall in the dining room there is a wooden bookcase filled with Chinese-language story books, copies of a San Francisco Chinese-language daily, and Hong Kong movie magazines along with similar English-language publications. Above the case is a paper-thin unframed reproduction of Jesus Christ, held to the wall by thumbtacks. On another wall is a large hutch containing a set of Chinese dishes and kitchenware and some small ivory figurines brought from China. On the bottom shelf is a rolled silk scroll presented as a gift to the father by a Hong Kong artist. A telephone is mounted on the wall and directly under it is a cardboard with Chinese characters and English telephone numbers and a calendar from a local Chinese restaurant. The mother cannot use the English telephone directory and the Chinese names are those of frequently called friends and relatives, local Chinese grocery stores and restaurants, and the home phone of the minister of the Chinese Gospel Mission.

The wooden table in the dining room is covered with a linoleum cloth and three daughters, ages 19, 15, and 13, all sit around the table talking and doing their homework assignments. The kitchen is old and the ceiling has black cooking stains; otherwise, it is immaculate. There are Chinese and American cooking utensils on the wall and metal cauldrons on the stove, and the smells of present and past cooked Chinese foods permeate the room.

The father, in his fifties, and a son, 17, live at home and are employed in a nearby Chinese restaurant as cook and dishwasher respectively. The mother works part-time in a local cannery and the three daughters attend school. The annual family income is about $5,000 and the family does not own a car. The father's older brother and two younger sisters live with their families in San Francisco but are frequent visitors and the house is usually filled with the sounds of children. The Y. family has been in America for eight years, three of which were spent in San Francisco before they moved to the central city.

The South Area. The Southgate and Southland areas can be combined as they are similar in demographic characteristics and quite different from the Central City tracts. The area is bounded by Valley River on the west, a major thoroughfare on the north, and railroad tracks on the east. Its southern boundary is constantly expanding with the growth of the city and may be located around the Valley City Airport at this time.

Most of the homes are of conventional, contemporary or modern design and, generally, less than twenty years old. The streets are wide and lawns are spacious, kept immaculate by the owners, often with the help of Japanese gardeners.

There are few apartment complexes but for those present, rentals start as $150 and some exceed $250 a month. There is usually little traffic in the suburban streets, but the cars parked in driveways are recent models, in the medium-to-expensive price range. Many families own more than one car. Small neighborhood businesses are generally absent, shops being located in shopping centers on the main arteries. The area is predominantly Caucasian and there is a conspicuous absence of Negro and Mexican-American families.

The D. family resides in Southgate. Their home is of a contemporary brick and wood design with three bedrooms and a den on a half-acre plot. The house is ten years old but has recently been remodeled. It is in the $40,000–$50,000 price range. The living room is spacious, with plush shag carpeting and modern furniture purchased from an expensive local store. There are two comfortable leather chairs aside a large sofa. The older miniskirted daughter is watching television while her younger sister is reading a science-fiction novel. There are many framed pictures of the family, particularly of the two daughters, on the fireplace mantel and the two large floor-to-ceiling bookcases. All of the reading material in the house is in English. Both Valley City daily newspapers are delivered and the crossword puzzles are partially completed. The room is also filled with trophies won by the mother and father, both of whom are avid golfers. The color television is in the den, where the family often relaxes before dinner; a black-and-white set is in the older girl's bedroom. The den furniture is less expensive but nevertheless attractive. There are framed art pictures on most of the walls, including a Chinese silk screen scroll. Two Chinese vases appear in the foyer. The kitchen is sizable, with all electric appliances, including a washer-dryer, a dishwasher, and other built-ins. The entire house is centrally air-conditioned. Chinese spices and herbs are found in one of the cabinets, but the food is American rather than Chinese. A five-pound prime roast is defrosting on the counter and rice will certainly be served with the evening meal. The back yard is partially a flower garden with camellias, Chinese pireas, and azaleas. There is room for a swimming pool, which the family plans to build next year. The family owns three cars, a 1968 Cadillac, a new Mustang, and an older Chevrolet; the Mustang was bought on time but cash was paid for the other cars.

The father and his two brothers are partners in their own produce company. The mother is not employed. The two daughters, 19 and 17 years old, attend a local college and high school respectively. The older daughter is engaged to a graduate engineer. The family has lived in Valley City for the past twenty years. Both parents are American-born.

Unfortunately, detailed statistical data about the Chinese populations in the central and south areas of Valley City are unavailable. However, it seems plausible to suggest that the social-economic profile of Chinese residing in the central area is not unlike that of large urban Chinatowns, while the Chinese residents of the south area are practically indistinguishable from their non-Chinese neighbors.

Chinatown populations have, according to Yuan (1966:321–32), a larger percentage of males to females in the most marriageable age groups. They are generally older than the non-Chinatown populace and exhibit a higher degree of illiteracy. The low educational achievements of Chinatown residents are reflected in their occupations: more manual and service jobs than white-collar work, and a higher rate of unemployment. This means a lower family income than is true for non-Chinatown groups, which results in a higher participation of women in the labor force in order to make ends meet. Chinatown populations also exhibit a higher percentage of adults and youngsters who do not speak English adequately.

Conversely, residents of the south area enjoy a more favorable sex ratio, are younger, better educated, and are employed in more prestigious occupations.

Ethnicity and Social Relationships

The central city area still tends to be "home" to the majority of older Chinese immigrants and their families. It also supports more recent immigrant arrivals as well as a scattering of Chinese students and young couples who are just starting their educational and occupational careers. The area is heavily populated with working and lower-middle class Caucasians and also houses Negroes, Mexican-Americans, and Japanese.

Among the older Chinese residents, interracial relationships, when indeed such social relationships can be said to exist, are clearly of a secondary rather than a primary nature. For example:

> Mrs. G., a Chinese widow of 60, spends most of her day sitting on her front porch or tending her small back-yard garden. She has lived next door to the Gonzales family for over two years and, although both she and Mrs. Gonzales speak English and work the same shift at a local cannery, she has spoken to her only twice that she can remember. When asked about her neighbors, she replied, "Now, mind you, I am not a bigoted person. I know many other people but we don't really have anything in common. We have different ways and even like different foods, so I like to spend my time with my Chinese friends who are more like me."

> Mr. B., a recent Negro addition to the neighborhood, says, "I moved out of Birch Park (a Negro ghetto) and this really is a nice place to live, even though it's getting a little old. But these Chinese really get me, man. They are the most closed-mouth and clannish people I have ever known."

Even Chinese-Japanese relationships suffer from limited contacts and unpleasant experiences in the past tend to become factors significantly influencing social interaction.

> Mr. K., a Japanese-American citizen, has lived in the central area all of his life, but he still remembers when his family was relocated during World War II. "I had to sell my home to the Chinese grocer for next-to-nothing. Since then I have had little to do with the Chinese."

> Mr. T., a long-time resident and a family association leader, claims: "The Japanese may say they are my friends but I know that when they invaded my home in China they took our land and put me in a prison camp. I am friendly when I shop in their stores but I have never invited them to my home."

Older Chinese families—foreign-born, Chinese-speaking, and employed by Chinese in restaurants and supermarkets—rarely mix socially with different racial or ethnic groups. Hostile attitudes toward other "peoples," strengthened by both voluntary and involuntary segregation and a desire to preserve their historical and cultural heritage, keep such interaction at a minimum.

Younger and more recent immigrant families, hampered by their lack of facility with the English language, are unable to participate directly in American life. One young man, for example, still walks a mile to work because he is afraid he will get on the wrong bus. These families socialize primarily with other Chinese-language speakers, including older immigrants, and rarely with outsiders.

Generally speaking, residents tend to have more social intercourse with people living in the same area, who are likely to belong to a similar socioeconomic group. However, cross-cutting visiting patterns are common, particularly when Chinese parents and children reside in different areas.

Linguistic and cultural barriers do tend to break down among high school and college-age youth; yet primary social relationships are still largely limited to other Chinese. Schoolroom and playground may be shared with majority and minority groups, but relationships often end there. In both high school and college cafeterias, minorities may be observed to cluster together and eat their lunches at separate tables.

Thus far, the central area has been treated as a "neighborhood" and not necessarily as a "community." A community also implies co-operative communal activities, a shared identity with other residents based upon social commonalities, and considerable interaction at the secondary and, especially, at the primary level. In Gans' words, a community "is more than purely an ecological or statistical construct and some of its qualities can perhaps be captured only by the sociologically inclined poet or artist" (1962:11). While it may be presumptuous to expect primarily interracial parties, teas, and gossip sessions among residents, considerable reciprocity at weddings, funerals, and other important rituals, as well as at less personal activities such as church and school functions, might well be expected. Although there are exceptions, however, this is generally not the case for central area residents.

A "social togetherness" does, however, exist among members of the same ethnic group. The absence of a Chinese ghetto does not mean the destruction of ethnic identity. A ghetto is also in a very real sense a cultural community that expresses a common heritage, a store of common traditions and sentiments. It is not so much a physical fact as a state of mind. Within the central area, these historical and cultural ties are strong indeed, and Chinese are linked with other Chinese neighbors. As one resident describes:

I am so happy we moved here, it is such a friendly place. I just love the people on my block, Mrs. W., Mrs. L., Mrs. H. (all Chinese). I always call them on the telephone and we play mah-jong. We shop together and I have gone to all their children's weddings. I sometimes feel like I am in

China, but there everyone was my friend or family. I just skip the other people here and stay with the Chinese.

Although friendship should be distinguished from kinship, the basic building block of Chinese social organization, these informal and ethnically centered community relationships play an important part in Chinese cohesiveness. They perpetuate Chinese social and cultural identities and reinforce them through shared activity. Because these informal relationships overlap, they tend to become multiplex and carry over into more formal activities. By excluding non-ethnic residents from their gatherings, the Chinese strengthen a feeling of separateness and maintain ethnic and racial boundaries. Thus, different social systems exist side by side with no true mixing. Social interaction between the groups becomes intermittent and, when it does occur, it is permeated with hostile undertones (Lee 1960:57).

Central area residents create a pluralistic sub-system within the larger community and thereby defy melting-pot ideology. They encourage in their children the development of derogatory stereotypes of other groups and discourage assimilation into the dominant culture. Chinese residents in the central area are best characterized as "traditionists" (see Chapter 10) who, as a group, control and dominate an important segment of Chinese community life.

The Chinese who reside in the south area are primarily American-born or immigrants who arrived as young children. There are also some financially successful older immigrant families. Most south area Chinese tend to be middle class in occupation, income, and education.

The area houses few minority peoples other than Chinese and Japanese and thus is overwhelmingly Caucasian, over 88 per cent in most census tracts. Yet it is also, after the central city, the largest area of Chinese population concentration. This concentration reflects a desire to continue and preserve intimate social contacts with other Chinese, but not necessarily to preserve a traditional way of life. Residential clustering, a practice common to many ethnic minorities,[9] is also a Chinese social characteristic, one in which class differences are as significant as ethnic identity.

Edward G., a recent south area resident, states:

We used to live in the city but I had a good opportunity to buy a home in

[9] Glazer and Moynihan (1964:162) report that Jewish residential concentration is not confined to the immigrant generation or the poor. It is characteristic of the middle and upper-middle classes and of the third generation no less than the second.

the Northland area. I decided against it because I and my children would be strangers there. I have never been discriminated against because I am Chinese, yet I feel more comfortable living near other Chinese who are successful like I am.

Residential concentration, however, may be the result of other less obvious factors. Mr. S. remarked:

> My wife and I both make a good living. We went to college and have fine jobs. I chose to move to the south area because I didn't want to live where too many other Chinese lived. If there was a Chinese next door prior to moving in, I probably wouldn't have considered moving there. I see enough Chinese already. Even though I was born Chinese, I have adopted many good middle class habits, and I am an American.

Residential propinquity of Caucasians and Chinese is a demographic fact in both the central city and south area. But Chinese-Caucasian social relationships are far more cordial in the south area. Chinese and Caucasian neighbors do share "coffee talks" and constantly chat with one another as they mow their lawns or wash their cars. They often attend one another's children's graduations, weddings, and parties. Yet they still manifest a tendency toward Chinese exclusivity regarding the more personal relationships.

> We had a Chinese New Year's party at home and invited some of our Caucasian and Japanese neighbors. We all certainly had a fine time. But for the most part we still usually attend predominantly Chinese parties, and our husbands belong to predominantly Chinese clubs. I still cannot tell my Caucasian friends about some personal problems in my life. Only another Chinese could really understand.

> My daughter had been going to parties with a white boy. We walked over to meet his parents and although they were very polite the conversation was strained. I spoke to Mrs. R. later and we both agreed that our children should not see each other so often because inter-racial marriages do not often work.

Regarding interaction with other minority people, the feelings of Caucasian neighbors are as much of a factor as their own. For example, Stanley F., age 12, met a "colored boy" bicycling in his neighborhood. They played together in his family's yard, yet his mother never invited the boy inside. She told Stanley:

> It's all right with me if you play with them but if I invited him into my

home some of our neighbors wouldn't like it. It might be best not to play with him any more.

Many native-born Oriental-Americans are growing up in Caucasian neighborhoods with a way of life that tends to be more American than Chinese (Sung 1967:234). Chinese, Japanese, and Caucasian youngsters often play with each other. When they become older, they date and go to mixed parties and consider individual personalities more important than racial or ethnic heritage. However, there is still little social mixing with Negroes and Mexican-Americans and marriage partners are still most often Chinese (Weiss:1970).

As in the central city, informal friendships among Chinese residing in the south area are strong and form a base for organizational life. Overt prejudice against Caucasians is diminishing but interracial marriage is still discouraged and there is little mixed activity at a more formal organizational level.

The Chinese settlement in the south area, however, illustrates very effectively two important structural features of Chinese life: first, the increasing acculturation of the Chinese into American social and economic patterns; and second, the development of sub-societies based on social class within the Chinese communities.

Residence and Social Class: Inner City and Suburb

Ianni's study of Italo-Americans (1957) suggests that residential mobility is an index of the acculturation of an ethnic group. While the immigrant generations cluster in less desirable neighborhoods, the native-born children of immigrants, the first generation, and particularly the native-born children of native-born parents, the second generation, establish residence in more desirable neighborhoods outside the colony. Acculturation becomes a necessary although not always a sufficient preliminary to acceptance in such neighborhoods. Moreover, the residential dispersion of a minority group can only be understood as part of the group's incorporation into the dominant social system. Residence is clearly a measure of the rate of acculturation (Ianni 1957:72).

Lieberson (1961) has also concluded that differential residential segregation of ethnic groups in American cities is a significant dimension of behavioral assimilation. Furthermore, the magnitude of a group's separation appears to influence other aspects of its assimilation, like citizenship, intermarriage, ability to speak English, education, and occupation. Residential dispersion is a basic prerequisite for ethnic assimilation and an important factor in interpreting and predicting differences is social behavior (Lieberson 1961:57).

Finally, Lee concludes:

> "The degree of assimilation and acculturation attained by a given ethnic group can be measured by the distance between the original quarter and their present residence" (Lee 1960:56).

Thus, as Chinese become more acculturated and/or financially success-ful, it will become increasingly vital for them to move to suburban areas to demonstrate their new status (Lee 1960:325). Families who live in Anglo-neighborhoods generally represent the same social and economic status as their neighbors (Marden and Meyers 1968:91), and their residence (address and home) will be directly related to their occupational-educational gains (Sung 1967:251).

These conclusions are best illustrated by Mr. L. and his family:

Cho-Lung L. (immigrant generation)

I come to this country 1930. I work as Chinese dishwasher. In business of cousin. Fourteen hours a day work. Come home to room. Have one room for wife and two son. I read little (Chinese) paper. I play fan-tan in hall. I don't speak American. I don't understand these people.

Adam L. (first generation)

I went to Valley City High School and studied my lessons hard, and worked after school as a grocery delivery boy. I later opened up my own small shop with the help of my relatives. I moved so I could have a house for my father and my family. On weekends we would go to Chinatown in San Francisco. I belong to my family association but only go for the New Year's banquet. I am proud I could send my sons to college to become engineers. When business became good we moved to Southland in a very comfortable and large house. My sons speak English very good but they have forgotten third dialect (Sam-Yap). They still do me great honor.

Barclay L. (second generation)

Well, Dad's a little too "Chinesey" for me but he's really O.K. I go to college and belong to ——— fraternity. It's all white except for two Japanese guys. All this Chinese jazz is in another world. I used to go to the language school but quit after a year. Dad still pays for me in the association but I have never been there. When I graduate I'll leave this old town and get away from all these old Chinese.

Although the major Chinese population shift is from the central to the south area, there is concurrently a movement of Chinese peoples into distinctly middle- to upper-class Caucasian regions to the east and north, where Oriental families are hard to find.

Two processes are operative in these areas: first of all, a general acculturation through the adoption of American standards and norms; and secondly, a partial structural assimilation through some participation in Caucasian community life at the primary level. Accelerating these trends is the fact that many Chinese do not participate in any form of Chinese community life at all, thus excluding themselves from membership in more formal Chinese organizations. There are exceptions, to be sure, yet day-to-day living and intensive interaction with non-Chinese will tend to reinforce these trends for future generations.

One immigrant family moved from the midwest to Valley City in order for the children to be exposed to Chinese people. Ironically, they chose to reside near their Northland restaurant. Their sons and daughters now live and study in a predominantly non-Chinese world, frequently date Caucasians, and are abandoning Chinese traditions almost as fast as they adopt Caucasian ones.

However, there are also forces that tend to reinforce Chinese solidarity. It would be wrong to assume that Chinese movement into Caucasian areas will automatically mean the loss of their Chinese identity. Etzioni (1959:258) suggests that a group can maintain its cultural and social integration without having a territorial basis. Common bounds are still reinforced through clubs and organizations at all age levels and through religious and traditional institutions as well as family visiting patterns. Moreover, discrimination against the Chinese, although normally not overtly practiced, is nevertheless evident in Chinese exclusion from certain prestigious Valley City associations and country clubs.

In general, Chinese residence patterns reflect both ethnicity, a sense of peoplehood, and social class, a ranked position usually dependent upon occupation and education. As regards Chinese cultural behavior, differences of social class seem as decisive as those of ethnicity. Middle-class Chinese tend to share viewpoints with and to have many of the same social values as middle-class Caucasians, although they share a different ethnic and cultural-historical racial background. Yet, with regard to social participation in primary groups, the Chinese tend to confine themselves to their own social class segment within their ethnic group. Thus the Chinese tend to participate in a social field circumscribed by both ethnic group and social class boundaries.

The Chinese in Valley City are exposed to pressures both from within their own group and from the outside. They are very much aware of their Chinese identity and easily express these feelings. A middle-class Chinese living in the south area states:

> I am still Chinese and don't you forget it. I am concerned with this Chinese community but also with all the Chinese in America and with the Chinese people of the world. I am proud of my ancient traditions and when any Chinese person is insulted it affects me as well.

Yet the fact that this man is also college-educated in America and engaged in professional activities is, perhaps, as important as his ethnic identity:

> I don't live the same life as the poor Chinese immigrant. I feel just as uncomfortable talking to an F.O.B.[10] as I do to an Indian. We may both be Chinese but we have different interests. We like different foods and want different futures for our sons and daughters. I feel most at home with other Chinese who have the same background and share the same problems.

Gordon (1964:51) calls these social class divisions, which are created by the intersection of the vertical stratifications of ethnicity with the horizontal stratifications of social class, the "ethclass." Ethclasses constitute distinctive social groupings with different goals and with different means of attaining these goals. As we shall see, ethclass conflicts often lead to dissension and factionalism within the Chinese community.

Thus, both acculturation and social class play important roles in the structuring of the Chinese community. In the forthcoming chapters, attention will turn to the effects of ethnic-class variables on the structure and function of organizational groups.

[10] The term "F.O.B." means "Fresh off the Boat" and generally refers to newly arrived immigrants. The term also refers to a cultural orientation that is Chinese rather than American. Thus, people who exhibit Chinese mannerisms in both their attitudes and behaviors may be referred to as "F.O.B.'s."

9

Contemporary Population Characteristics

Demographic Profile

THE POPULATION FOR VALLEY CITY, California, as of January, 1970, was 254,413 (U.S. Census 1970). The city is surrounded by an extensive urban sprawl, referred to as the Valley City Metropolitan Area. In 1968 the population count for this area was 634,200. If the contiguous areas of Westown and Northland are also included, the population is almost 800,592 (U.S. Census, 1970. The figures in this chapter will refer to the Valley City Metropolitan Area and are based on the 1970 U.S. Census figures.)

Valley City is predominantly Caucasian, but other racial and ethnic groups are also represented. Mexican-Americans (Caucasians of Spanish surname) account for approximately 7 per cent; Negroes, 4.7 per cent; Japanese, 1.5 per cent; Filipinos, 0.9 per cent; and American Indians 0.4 per cent (see Table 18).

In 1970 there were 10,444 persons of Chinese ancestry residing in the Valley City Metropolitan area. This figure represents 1.3 per cent of the total metropolitan population (U.S. Census 1970). In 1970 Valley City ranked seventh among metropolitan areas in Chinese population, surpassed only by San Francisco-Oakland (88,108), Honolulu (48,288), New York (76,208), Los Angeles-Long Beach (40,798), Chicago (12,454) and Boston (12,025) in that order (U.S. Census, 1970).

Sex Ratio. The Chinese sex distribution in America, predominantly male in 1890 (94.6% males), has steadily approached a more equal

Table 18

Ethnic Minorities in the Valley City Metropolitan Area

Ethnic Group	Number	Per cent (approximate)
Negroes	37,911	4.7
American-Indian	3,559	0.4
Japanese	11,804	1.5
Filipino	3,442	0.4
Chinese	10,444	1.3
Others*	5,220	0.7
MINORITY TOTAL	72,380	9.0
Caucasian (Majority) **	728,212	91
TOTAL POPULATION	800,592	100.0

*This category includes Hawaiians, Koreans, Aleuts, and Eskimos.
**Mexican-Americans are considered Caucasians of Spanish Surname. The 1970 Census does not include a separate listing for Caucasians of Spanish surname.
In 1960 Mexican-Americans accounted for approximately 6% of the total population. It is estimated that there are approximately 70–80,000 Mexican-Americans currently residing in the Valley City Metropolitan Area.

Based upon 1970 U.S. Census statistics, PC (1) – B6.

pattern. By 1960, 57.1 per cent of American Chinese were men and 42.9 per cent women (Kung 1962:33).

Sung's 1960 figures for Valley City's Chinese placed the total Chinese population at 6,457. Males numbered 3,540; females, 2,917. The number of males per 100 females was 121, the lowest for any continental American city with a Chinese population exceeding 2,500. The corresponding figures for the San Francisco and Los Angeles areas were 128, for Chicago, 154 and for New York, 161. In 1970 there were 5,362 males and 5,082 females resident in Valley City.[1]

According to Immigration Service reports of Chinese immigrants admitted from 1948 to 1959, the number of females per 100 males was 177.4, making this a predominantly female immigrant group. Liberalized immigration laws admitting wives and children as non-quota persons, particularly the Refugee Relief Act of 1953, has measurably helped to balance the sex ratio (Kung 1962:33). However, since the 1950's female immigrants have been under 39 years of age; therefore

[1] Department of Industrial Relations, Division of Fair Employment Practices, State of California, Bulletin: *Californians of Japanese, Chinese, and Filipino Ancestry*. This publication is hereafter referred to as CJCFA.

a sex discrepancy still exists for the middle aged and elderly groups. The prognosis is for a continuing equalization of the sex ratio.

Age Distribution. In 1960 the age distribution by sex for the Chinese in California was as follows:

AGE GROUP	MALES	FEMALES	COMBINED
Under 35	58.8%	69.7%	64.3%
35–44	14.6%	13.6%	14.1%
45 and over	26.6%	16.7%	21.6%

Source: CJCFA (1965:10). A more detailed distribution is prepared in Tables 19 and 20.

Specific Chinese age-sex distribution data for Valley City cannot be obtained since this breakdown is unavailable in census data. Such figures would most probably follow the national trend, however, which shows the following characteristics:
1. A shift from a more mature to a more youthful group.
2. A more symmetrical age pyramid, more balanced for males and females in the same age bracket.
3. A small but growing group of elderly persons, in which the men outnumber the women 3 to 1 (Sung 1967:119–21).

Nativity. The number of American-born Chinese has steadily increased since the early days of Chinese settlement in America and they now outnumber the foreign-born group. In 1960, 51 per cent of the

Table 19

Chinese Age Distribution by Sex—California 1960

Age group	Males	Females
Under 5 years	11.2%	13.5%
5–9 years	11.6%	13.3%
10–14 years	9.2%	10.7%
15–19 years	4.5%	4.8%
20–24 years	6.0%	7.3%
25–34 years	16.3%	20.1%
35–44 years	14.6%	13.6%
45–54 years	11.6%	8.9%
55–64 years	8.8%	4.9%
Over 65 years	6.2%	2.9%

Source: CJCFA 1965:19.

Table 20

Chinese Age Distribution by Sex—U.S.A. 1960

Age group	Males	Females	Combined	Change since 1940
Children (14 and under)	30.0%	36.9%	34.4%	+ 6.8%
Young adults (15–29)	18.6%	21.3%	19.9%	−11.3%
Mature adults (30–44)	22.8%	24.4%	23.6%	− 2.3%
Middle age (45–59)	17.4%	12.2%	19.8%	+ 4.1%
Elderly (60 and over)	11.0%	4.2%	7.6%	+ 0.6%

Source: Sung 1967:122.

Chinese were native-born, while 39 per cent were born in China (Sung 1967:269). A 1960 survey of thirteen western states (including California) places the native-born population as slightly higher at 68.5 per cent (CJCFA 1965:49). Kung (1962:39) estimates that by 1970 the native-born Chinese population will be in the neighborhood of 70 per cent and by 1980 as high as 80 per cent.

At the same time, a considerable number of foreign-born Chinese have acquired American citizenship. This increase in the number of naturalized citizens might have important implications in reference to suffrage, should the Chinese ever decide to cast their votes as an ethnic bloc.

Education. In 1960 the educational picture for Californians of Chinese ancestry was one of extremes. A relatively high proportion of both men and women, 29.2 and 23.2 per cent respectively, had completed at least one year of college, but approximately 40 per cent of the populace had not gone beyond the eighth grade (CJCFA 1965:11). About 80 per cent of the males and 60 per cent of the females with no formal schooling are, however, over 45 years of age (Sung 1967:126).

The educational level attained by Chinese persons 14 years and over in California is shown in Table 21. Nationally, the number of median school years completed for Chinese females is 11.7, a full grade higher than Chinese males at 10.7 (Sung 1967:126). In Valley City the situation is reversed: Males have completed an average of 11.5, females only 10.7, years of education (CJCFA 1965:26).

Educational opportunities in the Valley City area, aside from public and private elementary and secondary schools, include two junior colleges, one state college, and a University of California campus at a nearby community. Valley City College, one of the tuition-free two-year junior colleges, attracts many Chinese college-age youth. At the end of the 1968 spring semester, 401 Chinese (14.3% of the total school population) were enrolled. Summer school attendance by Chinese was estimated at 12.6 per cent of the total registration figure (Weiss 1968b:1).[2]

Because of its distance from major Oriental residential areas, the other Junior College has a negligible number of Oriental students. The same dependence between school location and residence is demonstrated by the fact that 88 per cent of Valley City College's Chinese students graduated from two out of five local high schools (Weiss 1968a:4).

Male students tended to major, in order of preference, in engineering, chemical and biological sciences, business administration, and technical studies. Females were enrolled primarily in business administration, technical studies, and social science. More than half of all

Table 21

Educational Attainment for Chinese, 14 Years
and Over, in California 1960

School level completed	Males	Females
No formal schooling	15.8%	18.7%
Grades 1–4	6.9%	5.8%
Grades 5–6	6.6%	5.4%
Grade 7	3.3%	2.0%
Grade 8	8.2%	6.8%
Grades 9–11	13.9%	13.2%
Grade 12	16.1%	24.9%
College 1–3 years	15.9%	14.3%
College 4 or more years	13.3%	8.9%

Source: CJCFA 1965:25.

2 In July, 1968, I was director for the Valley City Chinese Community Research Project. Questionnaires were distributed to students of Chinese ancestry at Valley City College. Eighty questionnaires were returned to my office by 20 per cent of the 400 attending Chinese students. The responses were coded on IBM cards. A frequency and percentage distribution was obtained through the services of the Valley State University Computer Center.

Table 22

Income for Chinese in America, 1959

Income group	Per cent
Under $1,000	3.3%
$1,000–$2,999	12.7%
$3,000–$4,999	21.5%
$5,000–$6,999	20.8%
$7,000–$9,999	20.1%
$10,000–$14,999	14.4%
Over $15,000	7.2%

Source: Sung 1967:322.

students planned to continue their education. Yet more females than males indicated that they would seek immediate employment upon graduation (Weiss 1968a:16–17).

Chinese students at the area's four-year institutions, Valley State University and the University of California, are also heavily enrolled in engineering and science programs.

Family Income. Over 70 per cent of Chinese families in America have incomes over $5,000 per annum. More than 40 per cent make at least $7,000, and more than 20 per cent make over $10,000. The family income for Chinese in America is shown in Table 22.

Median family income for Chinese nationally was reported as $6,207 (Sung 1967.322); for Valley City, the figure was $6,089. The median income for males was $4,192, over $500 per annum more than for San Francisco's Chinese men and slightly higher than that for the Los Angeles-Long Beach area. However, the median yearly income for females in Valley City was $1,897, about $100 less than that for San Francisco Chinese women and less than female income in the Los Angeles-Long Beach area (CJCFA 1965:45). Median annual income for whites in Valley City was $5,437 for males and $1,927 for females (CJCFA 1965:45).

Employment. The occupational distribution for Valley City's Chinese indicates that approximately 60 per cent of employed males were engaged in professional, managerial, proprietory, clerical, or sales classifications. About 70 per cent of the female labor force over 14 years of age, 800 persons by census count, were employed in clerical, operative, and kindred jobs (CJCFA 1965:40). Specifically, Valley City's Chinese are concentrated in three major areas: over 40 per cent in wholesale and retail trades, about 19 per cent in public administration, and about 17 per cent in manufacturing (CJCFA 1965:31).

Although Valley City and San Francisco men are somewhat equal in regard to professional and technical employment, Valley City has over 7 per cent more male managers, officials, and proprietors, about 6 per cent more sales personnel, and about 9 per cent less service workers. For employed women, Valley City has about 8 per cent more operatives, which includes laundry, service, and restaurant personnel. Otherwise the occupation patterns are similar. Using industrial indices, Valley City employs 6 per cent more people in wholesale and retail trades and almost 11 per cent more in public administration than does San Francisco.

Unemployment rates reveal that the Valley City rate for both males and females is 4.2 per cent, approximately 1.2 per cent less than for San Francisco-Oakland and about .5 per cent less than for the Los Angeles-Long Beach area (CJCFA 1965:43). Unemployment rates for Valley City's white males and non-white males are 5.4 per cent and 10.9 per cent respectively (CJCFA 1965:43).

Demography, Social Organization, and Acculturation

The characteristics of the Chinese in Valley City have changed radically since the transitional period, 1910–1940. Since 1930 the population has increased about *700* per cent, from 1,366 to about *10,000*. This population increase may be seen as a function of a higher birth rate, lower mortality, and increasing migration supported by a Chinese economic concentration in small businesses, which demanded, in turn, a large and heterogeneous population base (Lee 1949:427; Sung 1967:119). Expanding state and federal offices in Valley City also attracted a large number of Chinese from San Francisco-Oakland, the Bay Area.

In-migration from other states and from other countries was minimal when compared to figures for the San Francisco-Oakland and Los Angeles-Long Beach areas. From 1955 to 1960 in-migration to Valley City was reported at 216 persons from other states and only 224 from other countries. The in-migration rate from other countries during this five-year period was 3,335 for San Francisco and 1,601 for Los Angeles (CJCFA 1965:21).

There has been a considerable increase in the youthful age brackets as well as a smaller one in the number of elderly persons. At the same time, the sex ratio has become more balanced, and this accounts for an increasing number of married adults. The most dramatic shift has been in terms of nativity, for today American-born Chinese outnumber the foreign-born two to one.

Changes in occupation, income, and education are also significant. Never before have the Chinese of this city, and in America in general, enjoyed more prestigious occupations, higher incomes, and more advanced schooling. Their educational and social mobility is a function of decreasing discriminatory practices and of a general acceptance by Americans in the professions, commerce, and industry.

These youthful, married, American-born, educationally, occupationally, and residentially mobile Chinese have had a significant effect upon: (1) the behavioral and structural assimilation of the Chinese into American society; and (2) the organizational structure of Valley City's Chinese community.

Population and Community Structure. Valley City is sufficiently large to support a "traditional Chinatown." Rose Hum Lee (1949:425) considers a Chinese population of 250 as the lowest limit necessary to support Chinatown life. Yet Valley City could not be expected to support as diverse and complex an organizational system as do the larger Chinese communities in San Francisco with a Chinese population of 53,250, in New York with 36,503, or in Los Angeles with 19,402 (U.S. Census, 1960, Non-white Population by Race:217). Valley City's Chinese community is more likely to be less segmentary and less hierarchical than that of cities with a larger population. However, the present population of about *10,000* will allow for the establishment of new Chinese organizations, different in both structure and function from the more traditional forms.

A smaller Chinese community will also exhibit less racial visibility, particularly if residential restrictions are minimal, residential mobility being both a cause and a consequence of acculturation and structural assimilation. From 1950–1960 Valley City's Chinese were rapidly leaving their traditional Chinese quarters, and during the summer of 1969 the last physical vestiges of Valley City's traditional Chinatown were being dismantled. The failure to establish a new traditional Chinese enclave is directly related to the age-sex-nativity characteristics of the Chinese.

Nativity and Culture. The majority of Chinese in Valley City, both adults and youth, have been raised and educated in America and their reference group is, for the most part, more American than Chinese. Many of them no longer possess a "traditionist orientation" and feel that the aims and methods of the more traditionist associations are old-fashioned and do not cater to their contemporary interests as Americans. More serious is the fact that many of them no longer possess the most important prerequisites for participation in traditionist organizations—Chinese (Cantonese) language ability.[3]

Growing up in the American social system makes one an unlikely candidate for traditional organizational positions; for those who do join, conflict with the already established leaders is all but inevitable. Thus a growing American-reared and American-educated youthful population will lead to a decrease in the social and economic functions of traditionist associations and will restrict their potential for growth through recruitment. Consequently, Valley City's native-born, English-speaking people have established their own organizations at both the adult and youth levels.

Males and Females. A more equal sex ratio means a greater opportunity to marry and raise a family. The percentage of married Chinese in America in 1960 was 59.7, an increase of 6.7 per cent since 1940. The percentage of married females was 69.4, 4.9 per cent over the United States average. Of the women, 76.3 per cent had found mates by age 20, and only 7 per cent were unmarried by the time they reached 25 (Sung 1967:124).

Marriage leads to a more fulfilling family life and means a decreasing dependence upon traditionist male-centered associations for certain social and sexual needs. Recent immigrants entering the community with their wives and families are less dependent upon family associations and are less likely to enter into traditional Chinese organizational life. Moreover, it can be expected that an established family will participate more in the activities of the larger community and thereby increase contacts with non-Chinese in religious, economic, and social institutions, which in turn increase the rate of acculturation into the American system.

A more equal sex ratio also leads to more intra-community dating and social activities and less dependence upon other Chinese communities for mates and social life. Growing intra-community social relationships may weaken ties to other Chinese centers in America, restricting identification with non-community Chinese at both the familial and organizational level.

Occupation and Organization. Employment statistics in Valley City

---

[3] One survey conducted among Valley City College Chinese students indicated that less than 20 per cent of those responding to questionnaires could speak, read, write, and understand Cantonese. Only 40 per cent could speak and understand this Chinese language, although one-third of the respondents were not American-born (Weiss 1968a:6).

and the United States indicate that the major occupations of the Chinese tend to be similar nationwide. Wholesale and retail trades predominate. Aside from both small and large independent merchants, Valley City's Chinese own, manage, and staff four major supermarket chains consisting of eleven, eight, four, and four stores respectively. Supermarkets tend to be owned by particular Chinese families. They are located throughout the city and cater to a predominantly non-Chinese clientele.

There are many Chinese restaurants. (The Chinese Business Directory of California, 1966, lists 66 Chinese restaurants.) The larger eating establishments serve both Chinese and American food, but even those specializing in Chinese food do not cater to Chinese customers exclusively.

Many Chinese professional and technical employees work for non-Chinese organizations, primarily state, federal, and aerospace agencies located in the Valley City Metropolitan Area. Chinese are also well represented in the fields of medicine and dentistry, and, to a lesser extent, in the legal profession.

Assuming that the first five occupational categories listed in the CJCFA are the most prestigious—a safe assumption since they include professional and technical employees, managers, officials, and proprietors—the percentages for Valley City and other cities can be compared. The combined percentages of the five top occupations for males total 58.5 per cent for Valley City's Chinese but only 46.2 per cent for Chinese in San Francisco and 48.1 per cent on the national level. The combined percentages for white, Japanese, and non-white males in Valley City total 46.7, 54.9, and 20.1 respectively (CJCFA 1965:37, 40; Sung 1967:321–22). Thus, the employment categories of the Chinese in Valley City compare very favorably with those of whites and Japanese in Valley City and are slightly more prestigious than those of Chinese in San Francisco and on a national level (see Tables 23 and 24).

Moreover, the current occupational picture for the Chinese, both nationally and on the local scene, is characterized by a growth in professional and technical categories, illustrated by a six-fold increase, from 2.9 per cent in 1940 to 17.6 in 1960. The operatives' category is still predominant but decreasing rapidly (Sung 1967:127).[4]

Many of Valley City's Chinese are occupationally mobile and already enjoy more than a minimum standard of living. As they continue to

[4] A more detailed analysis of Chinese occupational changes is to be found in Beulah Ong Kwoh's doctoral dissertation, 1947. A summary is available in Kwoh (1947:192–100).

Table 23

Occupations of Chinese in Valley City, San Francisco, and Nationally by Sex, 1960

Occupation	Males			Females		
	Valley City	San Francisco	U.S.A.	Valley City	San Francisco	U.S.A.
Professional, technical, and kindred	14.4%	14.5%	18.4%	8.4%	9.4%	16.8%
Farmers and farm managers	1.8%	.7%	.7%	–	.1%	.3%
Managers, officials, and proprietors	19.1%	12.0%	15.4%	4.1%	3.3%	5.4%
Clerical and kindred workers	9.2%	10.6%	7.6%	32.4%	33.5%	30.1%
Sales workers	14.0%	8.4%	6.0%	5.9%	8.5%	8.0%
Craftsmen, foremen, and kindred workers	6.4%	7.9%	6.8%	–	1.0%	.8%
Operatives and kindred workers	13.1%	12.6%	12.6%	37.7%	29.7%	21.3%
Private household workers	.5%	1.8%	.9%	1.5%	1.6%	1.5%
Service workers (except household)	13.6%	22.3%	22.7%	5.4%	5.8%	8.6%
Farm laborers and foremen	1.9%	.6%	.4%	–	.5%	.4%
Laborers (except farm and mine)	2.5%	1.9%	1.7%	1.6%	.1%	.3%
Not reported	3.5%	6.7%	6.6%	3.0%	6.4%	6.3%

Source: CJCFA 1965:37, 40; Sung 1967:321–22.

Table 24

Industrial Distribution for Chinese in
Valley City and San Francisco, 1960

Industry	Valley City	San Francisco
Agriculture, forestry and fisheries	3.4%	1.3%
Mining	–	–
Construction	2.5%	2.3%
Manufacturing	17.4%	17.4%
Transportation, communications, and public utilities	2.8%	4.4%
Wholesale and retail trade	40.7%	34.7%
Finance, insurance, and real estate	1.7%	5.3%
Business and repair service	.7%	1.7%
Personal services	5.2%	8.9%
Entertainment and recreation	.2%	.7%
Professional and related	4.8%	9.3%
Public administration	18.8%	8.1%
Not reported	1.8%	5.9%
Totals	100.0%	100.0%

Source: CJCFA 1965:30–31.

enter into the mainstream of American economic life, traditionist association control over its members and the Chinese community at large is decreasing rapidly. In the years before World War II Chinese were categorically discriminated against in professional occupations and had to depend upon their family associations for the livelihood. Some of the traditionist associations, particularly those that control large business enterprises, still award kin-based job contracts and help recent immigrants and native sons find employment, but their role as a major clearinghouse for jobs has ended.

The successful businessman or professional is no longer content with playing minor roles in Chinese organizational life. For those who enter into "association politics," there is usually much conflict with economically less successful elders who nevertheless may control association activities. These younger men are more likely to find satisfying companionship and pertinent business contacts among their peers in the new organizations which can better serve their needs.

Selective Migration. The relatively high educational level in Valley City, the higher family income, lower unemployment rate, and better occupational distribution for males are most likely a function of selective migration. Valley City is not, and never has been, a primary receiving center for new immigrants, nor is there a multitude of menial laboring jobs available in the community. Therefore, Valley City does not attract the many recent immigrants whose English language ability and educational skills are minimal. Eventual migration to Valley City for both the native-born and immigrants appeals to the more educated people who can take advantage of the state, federal, and aerospace employment opportunities in the city. Moreover, Valley City does not provide the "Chinese atmosphere" of either San Francisco's or New York's Chinatown and the less acculturated are unlikely to find either economic, social, or spiritual security in Valley City.

10

Patterns of Social Organization
in Overseas Chinese Communities

THIS CHAPTER WILL EXPLORE: (1) Crissman's model of the social organization of overseas Chinese communities, (2) possible modifications of and additions to Crissman's model, and (3) the construction of a revised model focusing upon Chinese social organization in America.

According to Crissman (1967), the patterns of Chinese immigration, cultural adaptations, and present status as minority groups in overseas communities can be quite diverse. Yet, beneath the veneer of cultural and historical differences, most major Chinese communities, particularly those of Southeast Asia and North America, are based upon a similar organizational pattern—a structural motif built upon hierarchy and segmentation and derived from patterns indigenous to China.

The Segmentary System

All Chinese living in a given area comprise a Chinese community in that they stand apart from the rest of the population. But Chinese communities are not homogeneous; they may be further divided into a hierarchical series of "sub-communities," [1] each segment being internally autonomous, with its own leaders and recognized member-

---

[1] The use of the term "sub-communities" follows Crissman's (1967) definition. A general term such as "sub-group" is preferable.

ship. Sub-communities are usually formed on the basis of a number of criteria. One of the most important of these criteria is speech groups, which reflect major differences in language (i.e., Cantonese, Hainanese, Hokkien, Teochiu, etc.). Languages, except for Hakka, are associated with discrete localities and can also be expressed in geographic terms.

Geographic distinctiveness is not limited to language groupings but may be based upon counties usually associated with dialect differences, market areas, and even single villages.[2] Speech communities often segment into sub-communities based upon such provenance.

Another distinction upon which sub-groups may form is surname. There are several hundred surnames in use in all of China. Inherited patrilineally, they ideally delineate exogamous units. Surname groupings do not have to depend upon demonstrated genealogical relationships, for it is assumed that all men who share a common surname are related. Surname group identity may be extended to persons of different surnames provided that they share a bond of blood-brotherhood or longstanding historical association. Surname group identities can also be manufactured when expedient.

Each Chinese person has a surname, native place, and speech group. Should all the distinctions be applied, the Chinese community would be crosscut by a multitude of overlapping and interlocking subcommunities. However, not all sub-communities are recognized in any one community. The criteria utilized for segmentation, as well as the points of segmentation, vary and depend upon historical factors such as immigration history, the number of different groups present, and special interests of the community. Segmentation in different communities does not always follow the same pattern nor is it necessarily symmetrical.

Generally speaking, the first major segmentation is along speech groups, which can further segment upon locality and/or surname identity. When surname and locality criteria are both operative independently at the same level, overlapping sub-communities are formed and individuals belong to more than one segment.

A single speech group community usually segments upon distinctions of locality, usually the county (hsien). They may then divide by surname groups which may in turn segment upon smaller locality dimensions. The basic unit is, however, the village, and while a single village may contain different surnames, further segmentation is rare.

2 Every Chinese has a "native place" where his lineage is localized and where his ancestors are buried. He may never have seen his native place but it is his permanent home and can never be changed.

At the highest level, all Chinese overseas communities are ethnic communities consisting of people who share, and are conscious of, a common ethnicity different from that of the host population. Most urban overseas Chinese communities are corporate groups defined by: (1) endurance over time despite changing membership (diachronic continuity), (2) internal organization and leadership, and (3) the right of all members to participate in the group's activities.

The definition, however, of both ethnicity and participation is relative and has no absolute boundaries. Members may, over time, shift their allegiance to that of the host country and some members of the community will always consider themselves more "legitimately Chinese" than others. Residents of the ethnic community may participate in all the activities of the community, in only some of the activities, or in none of the activities.

The territorial parameters of the ethnic community are also definitional and may shift correspondingly over time. For purposes of this essay, however, the Chinese living within a single metropolitan area constitute the relevant unit of analysis.

Segmentation does produce separate sub-communities, but the division is less than final and does not preclude sub-community cooperative endeavors. Segments will combine and dissolve depending upon particular circumstances.

"In some contexts, the whole Chinese community is united and acts together, while in different situations small segments act independently against each other. Opponents in one situation are allies in another" (Crissman 1967:193).

Moreover, organizational hierarchy within the ethnic community parallels the segmentary structure. Therefore, members of the smaller sub-communities are represented by their leaders in larger groups, and they in turn by their leaders in the highest-level organizations. Leadership positions at ascending levels are often filled by the same persons, producing an interlocking system in which most leaders have official positions in numerous organizations at all levels.

Finally, participation in speech group, locality, and surname sub-communities varies with the degree of the individual's acculturation and identification with the host population. Persons with strong Chinese identities are apt to be more involved in these organizations than are persons whose Chinese identity is slight. Participation in these organizations usually grows weaker with each succeeding generation.

Crissman's Model and Structure in Valley City

Crissman's model for overseas Chinese community structure is based upon the following assumptions:

1. That all pertinent organizations are contained within a single hierarchical and segmentary framework.
2. That all organizations owe their allegiance to a common ideology and recognize a single political-legal system.
3. That leaders of all high-level organizations are also officials or representatives of lower-level groups.

Yet, when a Chinese community evidences a lengthy historical continuity and its population increase is primarily due either to a high birth rate or to internal immigrations rather than to overseas immigration, there will come a time when the native-born sons and daughters will reach adult age and wish to establish their own identities. Such a situation can occur when Chinese become acculturated and, as a result, no longer owe their primary allegiance to the traditions of their forefathers or to the organizations that attempt to perpetuate such traditions. Acculturation accentuates the differences among generations and the generational membership criteria of certain groups become so pronounced that they are distinguished by distinctive linguistic terms (e.g., native-born *Peranakans* are separated from the China-born *Totok* fathers in Indonesia. In the United States these terms are *Chuk Sing* and *Chuk Kak*). These distinctions are also appropriate in the Chinese communities of the United States and most particularly in Valley City.

Like most overseas Chinese settlements, Valley City's Chinese community possesses the potential for a hierarchical and segmentary system. Given the demographic characteristics of this population, there are various theoretical possibilities. Although only one major speech group is represented, segmentation could proceed along locality designations, leading to a division into three sub-communities. Each sub-community would then be characterized by a distinctive dialect and represent immigrants from one or more counties respectively. Each sub-community could be further segmented on single-county and even single-village loyalties (see Figure 6).

An alternative possibility is segmentation into both locality groups and surname groups at the same level. Surname groups constitute basic units while locality groups may be further subdivided as outlined in Figure 6. However, there is an area of overlap and some indi-

SPEECH GROUP LEVEL
(Cantonese)

LOCALITY GROUP LEVEL
(each segment is
represented by a
dialect difference)

COUNTY LEVEL

VILLAGE LEVEL

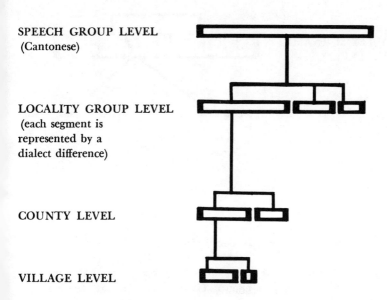

Figure 6.   Hypothetical Model I: Social Structure in Valley City.

viduals have the choice of participating in either the surname or
locality group. This situation is diagrammed in Figure 7.[3]

Chinese communities in Manila (Amoyot 1960), Thailand (Skinner
1957, 1958), and Semerang (Willmott, D. E. 1960), are based upon
speech group, locality, and surname associations. The Chinese in New

[3] Surname communities are always formed on the basis of both a name and some
criterion of locality. They are perhaps functionally as significant but structurally
subordinate to locality communities. They are always contained within some territorial community even if such is taken to be the total Chinese community (Crissman
1967:191).

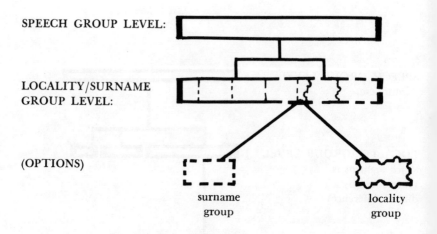

Figure 7.   Hypothetical Model II: Social Structure in Valley City.

York (Heyer 1953) and in San Francisco (Lyman 1961) belong to a single predominant speech group, Cantonese, but are further segmented by dialect, district, and surname. The Chinese community in Valley City, however, is based solely upon surname identities (see Figure 8).

Segmentation into surname groups is probably the result of a historically small population, most of whom were emigrants from a single county (Toishan), coupled with a preponderance of one dialect (Sze-Yap). Representatives from other localities and dialect groups lacked sufficient numbers to form competing groups.

Sub-groups based solely upon surname identities cannot internally constitute a segmentary system nor can they form a hierarchy since they cannot divide further and no two surnames are any closer than any other two. Moreover, sub-communities based upon one surname cannot contain smaller sub-communities based upon others.

Thus the contemporary alignment of Valley City's traditional Chinese community organizations is based upon a single criterion surname identity. This does not make Valley City's Chinese community organization a simple phenomenon. It does suggest, however, that organizational complexity will be based upon other characteristics that will require an analysis along dimensions different from those that Crissman has discussed.

SPEECH GROUP LEVEL:

SURNAME GROUP LEVEL:

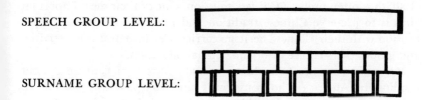

Figure 8.   Model for Social Structure in Valley City.

The Tripartite Model

The utility of Crissman's segmentary schema for analyzing overseas Chinese social structure should not be denied. His model is particularly applicable to both the traditional (1850–1900) and transitional (1900–1940) eras in America. However, his model does not account for the growth of new organizations, a response to changing patterns of Chinese adaptation. It is perhaps more helpful to consider today's situation in terms of a tripartite Chinese community system, each sub-system being autonomous from the others and each exhibiting its own organizational structure, leadership, and ideology. Crissman's segmentary system will be considered as one of the three sub-systems.

This tripartite model is most useful for understanding Chinese communities with longstanding histories whose members exhibit differential rates of acculturation into the mainstream of the social and economic life of the host society. These organizational sub-systems are a reflection of (1) the informal and/or formal ideological commitments of each group, (2) the major goals of the group and the means by which they obtain these stated goals, and (3) the sociological profiles of the group's members.

These three sub-systems can be defined as "traditionist," "modernist," and "activist." In any given Chinese community, individuals with traditionist, modernist, and activist philosophies live side by side. For analytical purposes, it is necessary to examine these orientations separately.

Traditionists include those Chinese who adhere to the values, attitudes, themes, and sentiments reminiscent of traditional Chinese society. Although they live in America, they are oriented more toward a "sojourners" lifestyle (Siu 1952). They are most responsible for perpetuating Chinese stereotypes, and when Chinese and American values clash, they often prefer a Chinese solution. One of their most important aims is to preserve Chinese tradition and history. This strong identification with their Chinese heritage carries over into multiple activities and guides their choice of organizational affiliation.

Modernists, on the other hand, include citizens of Chinese descent residing in America who consciously and conspicuously pursue an American lifestyle and who willingly embrace their American heritage. When faced with important decisions, they frequently opt for an American solution, and their organizational life is strongly influenced by their American social perspectives. Although they are interested in social and financial mobility, they choose to reach these goals by direct participation in the American economic-educational system and rarely by challenging the basic tenets of that system. Their American identity is basically middle-class, white Anglo-Saxon, and Protestant. Modernists rarely embrace radical philosophies of any nature.

Activists are also concerned with their identity and heritage, both as Americans and as Chinese. But, unlike traditionists and modernists, their plans include, as least philosophically, radical changes of their present position as an American minority group. Their programs are geared toward social action and their goals center upon changing both the traditional image of the Chinese and certain aspects of the American social system itself.

Traditionists, modernists, and activists basically are cultural types. They share a common awareness of their Chinese ancestry. Although modernists may prefer American material comforts and intellectual styles, they nevertheless consider themselves to be Chinese and feel most comfortable in the company of their Chinese comrades. Activists express their identity as Asian-Americans rather than narrowly as Chinese and subsume their Chinese exclusiveness under an Asian-American banner.

However, not all Chinese in America wish to be identified with Chinese associations, although they may share traditionist, modernist, or activist sentiments, and many do not become active participants in community life. Some exclude themselves completely from formal organizational affiliations while others realize their social needs by joining predominantly non-Chinese groups. This analysis of the formal organizational structure of the Chinese community will not include those who are not active participants in Chinese associational life.

Membership in the traditionist family associations is ascribed since it is based upon surname and every Chinese is a member automatically.

For purposes of this discussion, active participation will be defined as either involvement in the decision-making process of the group or attendance at most of the group's major functions. Modernist and activist groups are voluntary associations and prospective joiners must actively seek membership. Members of voluntary groups who regularly attend meetings and some major events will be considered to be active participants since decision-making in voluntary groups is often conducted at public meetings.

Today's traditionist[4] associations are basically concerned with the preservation and continuation of their Chinese heritage. Their organizational activities reflect this primary concern. They support the Chinese language school and the weekly showing of Sunday afternoon and evening Chinese language movies, provide for the social and recreational needs of their senior citizens, and sponsor dinners and other festive occasions stressing the history of their Chinese identity. Many of their active leaders are foreign-born and primarily Chinese-speaking, may have little formal education in either English or Chinese, and are chosen by a quasi-democratic process which assures their continuation in controlling positions. Their meetings, conducted in the Cantonese language, are scheduled irregularly and organized in a style in which the subtleties and nuances of decision-making, often obscure to Caucasian understanding, remain traditionally Chinese. Their involvement in extra-Chinese affairs is often limited to community events emphasizing Chinese history and customs. When they must deal directly with the Caucasian superstructure, they are formal and polite and interact primarily as representatives of their organizations, rather than informally on an individual basis.

Modernist organizations are primarily concerned with establishing and maintaining an American-Chinese identity. Their events and programs are ordered around their members' social and recreational needs, which often emphasize their American self-image. Leaders are democratically elected and are often persons who have achieved success in the Caucasian economic structure. Their regularly scheduled meetings are conducted in English, in an informal and casual manner, with serious business occasionally interspersed with jovial remarks. Ceremonial observances, when practiced, are often directed at American symbols. While many of their major functions reflect a Chinese heritage, this identity is transmitted via a modern American idiom.

---

4 Traditionist associations are those oriented toward traditional Chinese values. I prefer "traditionist" rather than "traditional" because these associations are not necessarily traditional in the sense of having existed in pre-contemporary China. It is their orientation rather than their existence that is traditional (Willmott:1967).

Caucasians are usually invited to their major events and members of the groups deal directly with their Caucasian counterparts on an informal social basis.

There is presently a relatively new and still emergent grouping among Chinese youths of high school and college age. Members of this current Chinese generation—the Asian-Americans—are also concerned with their heritage and identity, but as Americans and as Orientals, rather than as Chinese. They receive little support from older community leaders and only a passive acceptance from most modernists, who do not understand their goals or their association with the philosophies of their "Black and Brown brothers." Unlike their elders in both groups, activists are creating a new image in a pan-Asian solidarity. Their emphasis is upon Asians rather than Chinese, and their programs call for social action and consequent change. Through ethnic study programs, lectures, and seminars, as well as other means, they are reassessing their Oriental heritage and, in the process, are re-examining old and new Oriental stereotypes, attitudes, and experiences that their parents and grandparents prefer to ignore.

The terms "traditionist," "modernist," and "activist" have been chosen to represent and reflect an overall cultural orientation. The assignation of all Chinese to these three basic divisions does not take into consideration all the complexities pertinent to social interaction. The categories do not take into account overlapping memberships or individual choices in all situations. However, this discussion is concerned with the functions of organizations rather than the personalities of individuals. When the Chinese join a group and become active participants, they are playing roles as group members. A young activist may still take part in family celebrations and treat his parents with filial respect when the situation does not call upon his attitudes and activities as a member of an activist group; however, when he behaves as an activist, he does differ considerably from members of other groups.

The cultural categories chosen—traditionist, modernist, and activist—may be shown to be highly correlated with, though not determined by, certain commonly used demographic-sociological variables such as generation, age, language, education, and occupation.[5] In the

---

[5] Sex and ethnicity do not have the same predictive power as generation, age, language, and occupation. They are, nevertheless, worth mentioning.

The Chinese association in this community are male centered and male dominated. Women's groups, whether formally or informally recognized, are often adjuncts or auxiliaries of male organizations, and this is particularly true for the most important traditionist and modernist groups. In activist organizations, however, females participate equally as members and leaders.

following section the relationship of these variables to the cultural typology proposed will be examined.

Cultural Categories and Sociological Variables

It is common for an acculturating minority group to base its organizational identities upon generational differences, the Japanese in America affording one of the best documented examples. Each Japanese generation in America is designated by a specific term—Issei, Nisei, Sansei, etc. The terms refer to the progression from immigrant status (Issei) through the first generation of American birth (Nisei)to succeeding generations of American-born persons (Sansei, Gonsei, etc.). There is also a special term (Kibei) to describe those individuals who, although born in America, were reared and educated in Japan but currently reside in the United States. Although these terms are based upon generation, they are often utilized as indices of cultural adaptation within the host society, with Isseis being the least acculturated, Niseis constituting a transitional stage, and Sanseis and groups beyond considered most acculturated. It has also been suggested that there are distinct psychological profiles associated with each generational group (Lyman 1969). Moreover, and most important for the purposes of this study, the social organization of Japanese-American communities is structured along generational lines (Kitano 1969: 7–12).

Analysts of Chinese social life in America, particularly Lee (1960), have used similar and roughly equivalent terms for Chinese. Early immigrants have been called sojourners (Siu 1951) and are referred to as Chinese-Americans, while the term American-Chinese designates the native-born children of these immigrants as well as succeeding generations of American-born persons. There is no specific term for American-born Chinese who were educated in China although this situation is also well documented. An expansion of definitive categories based upon generation previously suggested (Weiss 1969), would add "Americans of Chinese descent" to represent the native-born children of native-born parents (equivalent to Sansei).

The groups discussed in this chapter are part of the Chinese organizational system, yet not all non-Chinese are summarily excluded from membership in all organizations. Traditionist groups are limited to Chinese exclusively. Modernist groups, however, while overwhelmingly Chinese, sometimes admit Japanese and even a few Caucasians. Activist groups, with their pan-Asian ideology, are specifically organized to include all Orientals. According to this investigation, peoples of Negro or Mexican-American ancestry have never been admitted to any Chinese organization.

These terms also have socio-psychological connotations but they are less useful for an analysis of Chinese community social organization than they are in the case of the Japanese because they often group together what must be separated and create false dichotomies. For example newly arrived Chinese immigrants should not be grouped with Chinese who, although born in China, have resided in America for thirty years. Nor should both elder and youthful immigrants be grouped under the rubric of "Chinese-Americans"; they may share a common birthplace and speak a common language, but their differences are often more significant than that which they hold in common. Similarly, the residents of Chinatown should not be classified with the residents of primarily Caucasian suburbs, though they may both be American-born United States citizens. Finally, the occupational variable must also be considered; bus boys in Chinese restaurants do not interact comfortably with school teachers and civil engineers.

Nevertheless, since generation is indicative of cultural orientation, generational categories may be used as gross indicators of more meaningful cultural categories, becoming thereby important referents for Chinese community structure.

1.   Traditionist organizations tend to draw their membership predominantly from the immigrant Chinese-American population.
2.   Modernist organizations are primarily staffed by first-generation, native-born American-Chinese, though they may also include some Chinese-Americans.
3.   The members of activist organizations are drawn from all generational categories, but particularly from second-generation, American-born Chinese.

Age categories[6] are also significant structural referents, as organizational life tends to be based upon peer-group formations. People in similar age groups share much with their own age mates that they do not share with either their parents or grandparents. This "generation gap" is as much a phenomenon for the Chinese as it is for other Americans. Moreover, age groupings are a good index for marking the acculturation process, the more youthful indicating a greater degree of both extrinsic and intrinsic acculturation patterns than the older groups. Finally, there are some general principles regarding organizational identity and age groups:

1.   Traditionist organizations are largely staffed by the elderly and middle-age adults.

---

[6] Age categories selected are as follows: children—14 years and under; young adults—15–29; mature adults—30–44; middle age—45–59; and elderly—60 years and over (Sung 1967:122).

2. Modernist associations are mainly composed of mature and young adults but may include the middle-age group as well.
3. Activist groups are generally limited to young adults. Their members are rarely over thirty years of age.

The ability to speak and understand Cantonese, the Chinese language spoken in organizational meetings, is a prerequisite for participation in the affairs of the traditionist organizations. Members of modernist and activist groups may be fluent in Cantonese, but organizational meetings are always conducted in English. Thus, English language knowledge is essential for participation in these organizations. Language abilities, usually the result of residence and education, are highly correlated with generational and age categories. The ability to be conversant in the English language is one of the best indices of acculturation.

Members of minority groups in America tend to restrict their primary social relationships to people within their own racial-ethnic group and, within that group, to people of similar social status. Organizational membership is, to some degree, also based upon shared interests stemming from a common educational and occupational background, but these characteristics are less useful for predicting formal group affiliations than are language, age, or generation.

The structure of the Chinese community, then, based upon its members' individual orientations and represented by their associational identities, clearly follows divisions created by differential rates of assimilation correlated with shifts in reference groups. In particular, the Chinese community in Valley City is significantly split along these lines into traditionist, modernist, and activist groups. This type of socio-cultural differentiation is supported by a wide range of minority assimilation studies.[7] It is frequently recognized and verbalized by the Chinese members of the community.

Anthropologists are concerned with developing classifications that are culturally meaningful. The proposed typology emphasizes the cultural determinants of group identification and therefore, hopefully, is superior to a classification based solely upon demographic-sociological variables.

[7] E.g., Goldstein and Goldscheider (1968), Kitano (1969), Glazer and Moynihan (1963), Gans (1952), Gordon (1964).

11

Traditionists

THE INTENTION OF THIS chapter is to examine critically the structure
and function of traditionist organizations as well as the role they play
in integrating the various elements of the Chinese community and in
preserving a Chinese identity in America.

Most important is the Chinese Benevolent Association,[1] which, as the
highest-level traditionist association, acts as a governing or consolidating agency for all formal traditionist groups. Ideally, this agency is
composed of representatives from all pertinent Chinese organizations
and thus assumes the right to speak for all Chinese in the community
(Lee 1960:148–49). Theoretically, each local C.B.A. is under the jurisdiction of the national Chinese Consolidated Benevolent Association,
often referred to as the "Six Companies," with headquarters in San
Francisco. Realistically, however, each local C.B.A. is autonomous,
governing its own constituents. Because of proximity, however, those
in California maintain a close relationship with national headquarters.

The C.B.A. is the highest-level organization in the Chinese community and, as such, unites the community's diverse elements, cutting
across and superseding familial, linguistic, and district loyalties.
Whenever the Chinese community wishes to give the appearance of a
unified group or to combine its resources, it acts through the auspices
of the C.B.A.

The organizations represented by the C.B.A. include the eight
family associations, the single tong, the Confucian Church, the Chi-

1 Hereafter abbreviated as "C.B.A."

nese language school, the Chinese community drum and bugle corps, the Kuomintang, the Anti-Communist League, and the Chinese Women's New Life Movement, the only official woman's organization. The family associations, both numerically and politically, constitute the most important faction within the C.B.A. Activist and modernist groups are not members, with the single exception of the modernist Civic Club, which was invited only recently to attend meetings. However, the modernist association member rarely sends representatives to meetings and generally does not participate in C.B.A. affairs unless there is specific interest in a particular program. Thus their active participation in the C.B.A. is variable and, most of the time, minimal. Most important, then, is the fact that the C.B.A., which ostensibly represents the entire Chinese community, excludes the modernist and activist sub-communities in the city from formal participation in its affairs and, by doing so, restricts its representation to the traditionist populace.

The structural characteristics of traditionist organizations and the processes by which they make decisions and implement policies are by and large identical, so similar, in fact, the family associations can be singled out for analysis and used as a blueprint for other traditionist organizations. When appropriate, examples will be drawn from other traditionist organizations, primarily the C.B.A.

Patterns and Processes of Traditionist Organizational Life

There are eight family associations[2] in Valley City; four are single-surname associations, while four are multiple-surname associations linked by long-standing historical or fictional ties.[3] Like the C.B.A.,

---

[2] Family associations are also referred to as "clan associations" (Willmott 1964), "family-name associations" (Heyer 1953), or "clans" (Lyman 1969). The term *Kung saw* means "public assembly," and is the usual designation for a family association. Some family associations may also use the term *tong*. Many of the words in the association names are terms for family virtues. For example, *Gee How Oak Tin* means "most filial relations."

[3] The origin of a multiple-family association, as described in a family association document, is reproduced below.

The S. Y. Association consists of three families—L., F., and K. The history and the origin of these names date back four thousand six hundred sixty-five years.

Four thousand six hundred sixty-five years ago, China had an emperor named Hwang Ti. One member of his cabinet at this time was named L. Goan, who was from the territory of Sai Ling. Because of this friendship, Emperor Hwang Ti became acquainted with L. Goan's cousin, L. Jo. Eventually she became the emperor's queen. She was very talented in her work with silkworms, and she developed the silk industry. This is the beginning of the L. name.

Valley City's family associations are nominal branches of national associations with headquarters in San Francisco. Although branches engage in cooperative ventures, primarily fund-raising, each branch retains internal autonomy, the ability to regulate its own affairs. Family associations may have the same title all over the world but there appear to be no formal links between associations in different countries (Willmot 1964:34).

In contrast to family associations in Singapore (Freedman 1960) or Manila (Amyot 1960), where these organizations link territorially disparate groups, associations in Valley City appear to be a means of breaking down the over-sized single province group. The reason for this difference in organization is the fact that the overwhelming majority of Chinese in Valley City come from a small section of Kwangtung Province and all speak dialects of Cantonese.[4] Those associations that are made up of more than one surname involve surnames that are relatively rare in Valley City and might be unable to support an association of their own.

The size of family associations varies. The largest, consisting of three surnames, claims 3,000 to 4,000 families and has historically dominated Chinatown life in Valley City; the smallest association consists of less than 100 families. One aspect of family associations that is not shared with other traditionist organizations is the criteria for membership.

Membership. Membership in family associations is ostensibly based

---

About this same time, Emperor Hwang Ti sent his prime minister, a member of the L. family, to the F. San territory to settle troubles and disturbances. The emperor's prime minister was the son of Aye Yee Mong. After success in settling the problems of the F. San territory, he decided to remain and make his home there. He changed his name to F., and therefore became the first F.

In the year 1127, Fong Sam Tit of the Tang dynasty had a son who served under Emperor Soong Goe Dong. His name was Fong Yee Ping, of the Soong dynasty. He served as a member of the emperor's cabinet and he held the position of a supreme court justice. Because of his great deeds for his country and the fact that the emperor's wife was the daughter of Fong Yee Ping, he was awarded the name K. by the emperor. From that day forth he became known as K. Yee Ping, and that was the beginning of the K. name.

The above incidents relate the originality of the names L., F., and K. These three families are associated together under the name of S. Y. Association. The words "S.Y." are symbolic of a swirling river which flows from its source and continues on and on till it reaches its deeper and larger channels. The history of the S. Y. Association is, therefore, very similar to the river, whereby it goes back from the K. name to F. and then to L. This is the reason for the united brotherhood among all these three families.

4 The eight counties of heaviest Chinese emigration to America are depicted on the map in Chapter 4.

upon surname. There is a Chinese saying: "Everyone has to belong" (Heyer 1953:60), and any person of a given family name is automatically a member of the appropriate association. One family association constitution reads:

> ". . . All the Clansmen of the ———, ———, and ———, three families who are living in Valley City and its vicinity are members of the Valley City ———, ———, and ——— Association."

Thus it would appear that membership is an ascribed status for every Chinese, immigrant or native-born. But Willmott regards such organizations as voluntary:

> "Although the concept of the Clan, which embraces all those of the same surname, continues to exist among overseas Chinese, the associations based upon clanship by no means include all the resident members of the Clan. These are voluntary associations" (1964:33).

Although the family association in Valley City often claim the support of the entire surname community, they generally regard active membership as a voluntary commitment. One Valley City family association specifies in its constitution that:

> "Any descendant of the ——— families in America who wishes to join and whose application has been approved . . . is eligible for membership."

It is, therefore, inappropriate to discuss membership in family association without distinguishing between degrees of membership. Useful for sociological analysis are the following categories of membership, categories which may or may not be recognized by family associations:

1. *Token membership*: Those Chinese who are included as members by the association because they possess the appropriate surname or have been registered by their parents without their knowledge or approval.
2. *Nominal membership*: Chinese who register as members, usually by giving a small monetary donation at the annual Chinese New Year's banquet, but whose participation is largely limited to attending this major function.
3. *Participatory membership*: Limited to Chinese who generally attend festive and ceremonial functions, regularly contribute to association coffers, and take advantage of association facilities and procedures.

4. *Full membership*: Those Chinese who participate in the decision-making apparatus of the association, either as participating members or as elected or appointed officers.

This chapter is concerned primarily with the activities of full and participatory members.

Membership lists are rarely disclosed[5] even when these lists are made available they are very probably inaccurate. Many associations maintain cumulative lists and others count all males possessing the requisite surname as members. It is a common practice for fathers to register their children as members even though the children deny their membership. Membership in the family association is also open to unmarried women of a given surname, yet there are few women members. Women who are active in association affairs usually participate in the associations of their husbands, where they are often asked to perform the tasks of cooking and serving for banquets and celebrations. In Valley City these women often are the official hostesses at New Year's dinners and other family association events.

As is the custom of Chinese clanship, family associations base membership upon patrilineality, a married woman becoming a member of her husband's group. Also, celebrations and fund-raising programs include many related non-members; they function to build within the Chinese community feelings of friendship, mutual aid, and trust and allow a host of affines and consanguines to congregate and reaffirm familial loyalties.

Informants state:

My name is Mah and we have no family association in Valley City. I have always gone to the dinners of my wife's association and always donate a substantial amount to their needy causes.

I am a widower and leader in my family association, but I always hold a special place in my heart for my deceased wife's kinsmen. I am welcomed at their festivities and have helped one of her relatives when they were beset with financial difficulties.

The ties of affinity are strong indeed and, as suggested by Gallin (1960) for Taiwan, these relationships are usually characterized by good feelings and reciprocity. They cross-cut surname identities and incorporate all "relatives" in a pan-Chinese sodality.

Association Officialdom. All family associations have the same

---

[5] Because many Chinese entered this country illegally, they are reluctant to make public any information that might be used against a relative or friend.

basic type of administration. The major officials always consist of a chairman (president), one or two vice-chairmen, a Chinese secretary, an English secretary, and a treasurer. In addition, there is a senate (an advisory committee). Each association has a number of standing committees as well as ad hoc committees. The larger associations have more official positions, such as assistant secretaries, auditors, public relations men, etc., while the smaller associations operate with fewer elected and appointed officials.

Each year a new slate of officers is chosen. There are few restrictions placed upon continuous officership save that the chairman and major officials are usually limited to two consecutive terms of one year each, while minor officials are restricted to three consecutive terms. Senators can serve for an unlimited number of terms.

Theoretically, all officers are elected by the entire membership. A slate of nominated candidates and a ballot are either sent by mail or delivered in person to all members, who then choose from the list of candidates. Anyone may express an interest in being nominated, but the nominating committee consists of a small group of men. They are either present or past officers or powerful men in the community, and in actuality they control selection of the slate of candidates. Thus, although the election is democratic, the selection of candidates rests exclusively within a small, influential group.

The chairman is the most conspicuous officer of the family association. He is the official representative and therefore the spokesman for the entire association. Although, in theory, any member may hold this position, some practical restrictions exist. First, because the business of the association is conducted almost entirely in the Cantonese language, the chairman must be fluent in Cantonese; he is, therefore, almost always a native-speaker. Secondly, the Chinese generally equate wisdom with age and experience. Thus the chairman is invariably a China-born older man, an immigrant who has resided within the Valley City community for many years, and who consequently has participated in association affairs and has always been a past officer. Thirdly, the chairman is expected to contribute generously to the association and its events, and to other causes within the Valley City Chinese community and in other cities. He is usually a man of property and wealth and tends to have a steady income either from investments or from a well-established business. Should the chairman not be a man of wealth, he is then well educated and, as a scholar, a respected member of the Chinese community. Finally, the chairman is expected to spend a good deal of his time on association affairs. Many chairmen are either retired or senior partners in a business that does not demand too much of their time.

Although language ability, age, wealth, education, and availability are governing criteria for all association posts, much more flexibility exists for other officers. The constitutions of the family associations state explicitly the duties and responsibilities of each officer. The following description is excerpted from the regulations of the Valley City branch of a large association and is entitled "The Duties of Officers."[6]

"The Chairman—in charge of all the affairs of this branch association, having the duty to supervise and to guide each department to promote the associational business. He has to execute all the resolutions internally and represents this branch association externally. He also presides at the meeting.

"The vice chairmen—assisting the chairman in handling all affairs. When the chairman is absent, a vice chairman will act as chairman. The vice chairman who drew more votes than the other in election will first act as chairman. When the chairman and vice chairmen are absent, the senate president will act as chairman. When the senate president is also absent, the vice senate president will act as chairman.

"The Chinese secretary—responsible to draft and to keep all Chinese dispatches, circulars, letters, and the minutes of the meeting, and to keep the seals. The clerks have to assist the secretary in handling the Chinese clerical work.

"The English secretary—responsible to draft and to keep all English dispatches, circulars, letters and the minutes of the meeting. He also has the duty to negotiate with the westerners or Caucasians and is responsible to interpret. The clerks have to assist the secretary in handling the English clerical work.

"The officers of social intercourse—under the chairman's direction, representing the branch association, to perform the activities of social intercourse with our members and with other people.

"The auditors—responsible to audit the accounts of receipts and payments of the branch association. After audit, they have to report to the general meeting and to answer the questions made by our members regarding the accounts.

"The treasurers—in charge of cash receipts and payments for the branch association and performing the duties of bookkeepers. The treasurer has to post a copy of the accounts of cash receipts and payments on the wall inside the association building each month. In every meeting, he has to report the financial situation and to submit the evidences of deposits to be audited. Each of the three treasurers will take his turn on duty for four months. One who drew more votes in election will be on duty first.

[6] This is a literal translation from the Cantonese original. It was obtained from an officer of the association.

"The business manager—in charge of the records of Chinese and English papers, membership registration books, and all the archives, having the duty to assist each department to perform their activities. The employment of the business manager is recommended by the chairman and approved by the general meeting. Only our clansman is qualified to apply for this job.

"The business clerk—responsible for cleaning the building, delivering circulars to call a meeting, keeping all furniture and equipments, in charge of entertainment activities and other miscellaneous works such as the hoisting of flags.

"The president of the senate—acting as chairman when the chairman and vice chairmen are all absent. In case the chairman, vice chairmen, or other officers are not able to fulfill their responsibilities, the senate president has the power to summon the senators to hold a meeting and to propose corrections or impeachments.

"The vice president of the senate—having the power to assist the senate president is handling public affairs. When the senate president is absent, he has the power to execute the duties of the senate president.

"The senators—having power to propose, to second a proposal, to criticize, to show their opinion by a vote, and to question."

Decision-making powers and the chain of command pass from chairman to vice-chairmen to senate president. The senate, consisting of thirty-five senators, has the right to approve new policy as well as to re-examine older statutes. The offices of chairman, vice-chairmen, and senate president are important and influential posts and are usually held by powerful personages. However, official position is not always coincident with the ability to implement policy or to influence votes. Persons who hold the office of "senator" or of "chairman" of one of the standing committees may be the real politicians while those who hold the important-sounding posts may be figureheads. The true dimensions of power are visible only in the actual decision-making process. *Decision-making "Chinese-style."* Protocol and procedure govern the behavior of association affairs, but the formal, and particularly the informal, rules are rooted in Chinese tradition. Two of these procedures are "face-saving" and "propriety."

The term "face" has been defined as the positive social value a person effectively claims for himself by the *line*[7] others assume he has

---

[7] Goffman (1967:5) defines a "line" as a pattern of verbal and non-verbal acts by which a person expresses his view of the situation and, through this, his evaluation of the participants, especially himself.

taken during a particular contact. He may be said to "maintain face" when he presents an image of himself that is internally consistent, that is supported by judgments conveyed by other participants, and that is confirmed by evidence conveyed through impersonal agencies in the situation. A person may be "without face" when he participates in a contact with others and does not exhibit the behavior expected of participants in such situations. He is then likely to feel ashamed or inferior. One may "save face" by sustaining an impression for others that he has not "lost face." One may "give face" by arranging for another to take a better line than he might otherwise be able to take (Goffman 1967:1–9).[8]

Theoretically, saving face is the ability to hold one's own behavior in check to spare another's feelings. It also involves not admitting the true conditions of a situation when it can prove embarrassing to either party. It demands that one must often refrain from doing or saying something for fear of losing face. For example, Chinese parents may refuse to go to court but instead refer their children's cases to a lawyer to appear on their behalf. They are concerned about the comments of their kinsmen and friends should they be forced to appear at the hearing (Lee 1960:348).

Face-saving also involves indirect rather than direct methods of interaction and is subtle rather than overt. It functions to exert strong control on in-group behavior, often prevents outsiders from learning of suspicious activities, reduces active conflict, and justifies the existence of China-oriented norms and behavior (Lee 1960:134, 141). This practice covers a multitude of sins and allows powerful personages to place a burden on the less powerful by charging that the latter caused them to "lose face." Fear of losing face often results in the leaders winning while those who dissent from leading opinions are unwilling to publicly display their own views. It is often used as a device to shield calculated misdeeds (Lee 1960:394, 430, 437).

Propriety refers to the proper order of things, be they objects, actions, or personnel. It is firmly based upon the traditional precepts of filial piety, respect for the elders, and the principles of familism. Propriety demands that Chinese have due respect for those in positions superior to them and enables them to accept their positions and keep their assigned status and rank (Lee 1960:135–36). It often encourages them to be secretive and cautious about their own desires and guides them not to humiliate other people for their own gains (Heyer 1953:150).

---

[8] See Hu Hsien-Chin, "The Chinese concept of face," *American Anthropologist* 46:45–64, 1944, for a more detailed discussion of face-saving.

Although association meetings may appear to exhibit democratic or at least consensual procedures, face-saving and propriety enter into the subtle nuances of traditionist association decision-making. One full member states:

> We were in the committee meeting to discuss our new building. I did not like the way the light switches were placed, but I said nothing. If I were to question the placing of the fixtures, I would be challenging the chairman of the committee and everyone knows he is a very powerful person and all listen to what he says. Were I to criticize his acceptance of the architect's plans, he would lose face and both of us would be ashamed.

Contributions to worthy causes are expected of association officers and there is a direct relationship between the amount contributed and the status of the official. A low-ranking member always waits until a known leader announces his contribution and then pledges his share. It would be extremely rude for him to announce his contribution first, for it might embarrass the leader into making a more generous pledge. This informal code is further reinforced by the fact that contributions are sometimes listed and made public, not only to the members of the family association but to the entire Chinese community.[9] The same system operates for relationships between family associations, and one clever Chinese fund raiser remarked:

> If I can persuade the ———— Association to pledge $100, I know the ———— will want to better that amount, and the ———— Association, which is the largest and richest, will have to at least double that money.

Not only should a leader first make known his position, but a respected man may choose to show his displeasure at a suggestion by not discussing it. One member reported:

> I suggested that we ought to support the development of low-cost housing. I expected Mr. W. to support this proposal. I was surprised when he remained silent. All eyes looked to him for approval. I understood that his silence meant that he was not in agreement with my suggestion and that the matter was promptly dropped.

---

[9] Contributions, for example, for the support of the Chinese language school or the Chinese drum and bugle corps are often posted on a bulletin board in the Confucius Church. Donations to family associations are posted in the family associations' headquarters. The name of each contributor and the amount contributed are conspicuously displayed. Donations at New Year's range from $2 to $500; however, the majority are rarely over $30.

Subtlety in decision-making is truly an art and is best illustrated by the following case:

> It was recommended that Mr. C. and his wife be sent to the Stockton Association dinner. Mr. L., a past president, said he liked the idea but also suggested that Mr. G., an older man, be sent along with him. Mr. C. then announced that he regrettably would not be able to attend and that Mr. G. be the family association representative at the Stockton affair.

The suggestion to send Mr. G. along with Mr. C. and his wife as co-representatives and not send Mr. G. alone enabled the past president to "save face" by not suggesting that Mr. C. was really too young to represent the association. Were he to do so, he would cause Mr. C. to "lose face." Mr. C. realized that he was not the most qualified to attend the dinner and by withdrawing his name was also able to save face.

Furthermore, any person who wishes to challenge a leader should be a leader in his own right.

> Mr. L. wished to invest association capital in a particular real estate scheme. He was opposed by Mr. F., who had previously managed association funds. No one else would speak and a silence crept over the meeting. Finally the two leaders agreed to set aside the suggestion and to discuss it at a later date after they had had time to discuss the matter among themselves.

Yet a leader can also use his influence and his status to take advantage of his position:

> Mr. K., although not an official of the ———— Family Association, was a known leader in the association. At one time he borrowed a substantial amount of money from the association. He has not repaid his loan. Many of the association officials think that he should start to repay it, a little at a time, but Mr. K. claims that he is unable to do so. Some of the younger members suggested taking Mr. K. to court, but the older members were embarrassed about it and disagreed. To this date, nothing has been done about Mr. K.'s repayment of funds.

Actual voting generally proceeds by democratic processes and there is usually little outright verbal contesting of a decision. Face-saving, propriety, and informal caucus by leaders before the actual vote serve to iron out any differences of opinion and complete consensus is the rule rather than the exception.

C.B.A. officialdom is similar to that in family associations in both form and function. Saving-face and propriety play important roles in decision-making, and money and influence buy prestige. The officers and directors are, for the most part, elderly and mature China-born males who have resided in Valley City for at least ten years. The primary language of meetings is Cantonese, meetings are irregularly scheduled, and the important standing and ad hoc committees consist largely of the most powerful individuals within the traditionist structure.

There are twenty-one officers in the C.B.A.: a president, two vice-presidents, three Chinese secretaries, three English secretaries, three treasurers, two auditors, two Chinese and three English public relations officers, two counselors. Eight heads of traditionist organizations serve as directors in addition to thirty-five other duly elected directors.

Profiles of Officials. One of the most important characteristics of traditionist organizations is the social make-up of its leaders. Such a sociological profile is an integral part of a discussion of traditionist organizational structure because (1) it enables us better to understand the cultural orientation of the leaders by examining the degree to which they participate in the mainstream of American life; (2) the basic background data are preparatory to analyzing the development of areas of conflict both within a given group and in its relationships with other organizations; and (3) it is germane for examining the continuous and overlapping dimensions of Chinese community structure.

The detailed empirical data needed in order to reach justifiable conclusions as to the nature of this sociological profile can be drawn from an examination of the largest and most influential family association in Valley City. The other family associations and traditionist groups are similar, both in their organizational administration and in the profile of their leaders.

The family association under discussion lists twenty-three titled officers: a chairman, two vice-chairmen, three Chinese secretaries, three English secretaries, three treasurers, two auditors, two public relations officers, a custodian, four Chinese school counselors, an advisory committee chief, and an assistant advisory committee chief. In addition, there are presently forty-two members of the advisory committee senate. A profile of officials listed is shown in Table 25.

From Table 25 we derive a composite family association official who is China-born, married to a China-born spouse, 55 to 70 years old, residing currently in the Central City section of Valley City, having been a Valley City resident for at least thirty-five years. While he is a native speaker of a Cantonese dialect, his English language ability is fair or

Table 25

Profile of Officials for One Family Association

I. *Given Name*

	Chinese Given Name	English Given Name
Titled officers (23)	13	10
Advisory committee (42)	28	14
Total	41	24

II. *Residence*

	Areas of Chinese Concentration*		
	Central City	Southgate	Southland
Titled officers	16	1	2
Advisory committee	20	5	4
Total	36	6	6

	Other Areas of Residence			
	Low Income Area	Middle Income Area	High Income Area	Outside** Valley City Metropol- itan Area
Titled officers	1	3		
Advisory committee	5	6	1	1
Total	6	9	1	1

*Central City is a predominantly low income area, while Southgate and Southland are middle to high income areas.
**The official residence of one advisory committee member is Colusa, California.

III. *Marital Status*

Married	Single	Divorced	Separated	Widowed
19	1	0	1	2

Table 25 (continued)

IV. *Age*

	Over 60 (15)			
Over 80	79–75	74–70	69–65	64–60
1	3	3	3	5

	Under 60 (8)			
59–55	54–50	49–45	44–40	Under 40
3	1	3	1	0

V. *Birthplace and Spouse's Birthplace*

	China-Born	American-Born
Self	19	4*
Spouse	18	4

VI. *Length of Residence in Valley City* (*years*)

Under 35 (6)						Over 35 (7)	
Under 5	6–15	16–20	21–25	26–30	31–35	36–40	Over 40
1	1	1	1	2	0	7	10

*Of the four American-born officers, three have American-born wives; one is single.

VII. *Formal Education*

	In China		
No Formal Education	Grammar School	High School	College
6	9	8	0

	In America			
No Formal Education	Grammar School	High School	College	Post-Graduate*
16	2	0	4	1

Table 25 (continued)

VIII. *Language Ability (speaking and understanding)*

Cantonese				English			
Native-Speaker	Good	Fair	Poor	Native-Speaker	Good	Fair	Poor
19	2	2	0	4	2	6	11

XI. *Occupation*

Professional	Technical and Skilled Craftsmen	Owners, Managers, Merchants	Semi-skilled and Unskilled
4	2	14	3

*Of the five persons with an American college education, four are American-born.

poor. Although he is or was the owner, manager, or proprietor of a Chinese grocery or supermarket, he has, at best, the equivalent of a Chinese high school education and, more often than not, little or no formal education in America. In addition, he has held official and advisory posts in his family association for the past ten to fifteen years and presently holds a similar post in at least one other traditionist organization.

The data also indicate that most officials have not participated in the mainstream of American life, primarily because they lack the necessary social, educational, occupational, and, most importantly, language prerequisites for such participation. Their life styles are also more reminiscent of the sojourners of the traditional era than of acculturating Chinese-Americans. Many Chinese youth refer to them as anachronisms of another place and time. In short, they spend and have spent the major portion of their lives within the sheltered security of the Chinese world.

Yet, in spite of their apparent lack of extensive formal education, they have, typically, the qualities required of successful owners, managers, proprietors, and merchants. They run their own business enterprises and enjoy a comfortable standard of living, by any criteria. Lest the erroneous conclusion be drawn from the aforementioned data that association affairs are governed by hard-working but somewhat inept and doddering old men, the reader is cautioned to be fully aware of the following summations:

1. In practice, leadership in the association is not exercised by the total body of officials and advisers. The affairs of the association are ordinarily controlled by fewer than fifteen of these men and, for all practical purposes, less than a handful can dominate all decisions. General meetings are only irregularly scheduled and the actions taken by the entire membership are likely to have been predetermined in informal agreements. A few powerful persons who, by virtue of their position on important standing committees, control association revenues and expenditures make most of the decisions.

2. While their academic credentials may not be overly impressive, these individuals are most likely to be quite wealthy and to have wisely invested their monies in the American economy. One leader, for example, owns over 1,000 shares of stock in a major communications network and lives comfortably from his dividends alone. Another is the president and general manager of a chain of supermarkets.

3. Family associations are viable economic corporations as much as they are ethnic social clubs. They own considerable properties and derive the majority of their income from such enterprises. For example, the cost of construction for one association's new building is $300,000, while a housing development planned by the association will cost close to two million dollars. Such investments of capital demand much legal and financial acumen.

4. Some association officers and advisers are professional people such as lawyers and architects. They are American-born and American-educated and are respected members of the larger Valley City community as well. While they do not usually dominate association affairs, they are a valuable resource, readily available as knowledgeable consultants.

Nevertheless, the officers' participation in American life is largely limited to secondary relationships with other Americans. Their primary loyalties, reference groups, and cultural orientation are clearly Chinese. The leaders of other traditionist organizations exhibit similar characteristics. Some C.B.A. leaders, however, are better educated and have a more cosmopolitan outlook.

Overlap and Continuity. Most persons who are important members of the traditionist community hold positions in several traditionist organizations. For example, the vice president of the C.B.A. is also the president of the Kuomintang and the chairman of the board of directors of the Chinese school, in addition to being an officer in his family association. Thus, the leadership of traditionist organizations shows substantial overlap, and decision-making in middle-range organizations like the family associations is performed by the same personnel as in the highest-level organization, the C.B.A.

In addition, overlap exists within individual organizations as well: Table 26 gives the composition of some of the more important standing committees within the association previously discussed. On the basis of the information presented, it can be seen that the titled officials make up the majority and control family association committees and that they are elected to these offices by virtue of being a titled official. Remaining members of standing committees are most likely to be advisers. Non-officers are rarely members of these standing committees. Moreover, the five or so paramount leaders are always elected or ap-

Table 26

Internal Overlap in Decision-making Committees

Name of Committee	Number of Members	Members Who Are Also Titled Officials	Members Who Are Also Advisers
Property Management Committee	19	15	4
Officials	6	6	
Old members elected to serve for another year	5	5	
Newly elected members	5	3	2
Alternates	3	1	2
Affairs Preparation Committee	21	(20)	
Officials	3	3	
Committeemen	18	(17)	
Board of Directors	24	18	5
Chairman	1	1	
Vice-chairman	1	1	
Chinese secretary	1	1	
English secretary	1	1	
Treasurer	1	1	
Members	12	10	2
Alternates	7	3	3

pointed to all important standing committees. The power to persuade and predominate in the financial and ceremonial aspects of association life is primarily in the hands of a few powerful personages.

Another structural feature of association life is the continuity of its officers, as seen in Table 27. The same members are returned to official posts year after year. Furthermore, some officers have served as association officials for over forty years. In some family associations, positions are switched every two years, while others hold "democratic" elections. The end result is similar—little change in association officialdom. The system is so inbred that members frequently state that the decision to elect a man for a post often depends on his having previously served in a similar position.

The principles of overlap and continuity, a feature of intra-organizational structure, are also an important facet of intergroup activities. Officers of family associations are often also officers of other traditionist organizations. For example, the treasurer in the previously discussed family association is also the treasurer for the C.B.A. and the vice-chairman of the board of directors of the Chinese school. His wife is a leader of the Chinese Women's New Life Movement. Another individual is the English secretary for no less than five traditionist organizations. Table 28 makes apparent this overlap among officers of family associations and the leadership of other traditionalist groups.

This interdependent, interrelated, and interwoven system, fostered by continuity and overlap, provides a number of implications. First, through a system of what are commonly called interlocking directorships, the control of all affairs within the Chinese community is invested in less than a score of leaders. Secondly, this system encourages

Table 27

The Continuity in Titled and Advisory Offices

	Number
Titled officers who have held a titled or advisory position for the past two years	22 (96%)
Titled officers who have held a titled or advisory position for the past five years	21 (91%)
Titled officers who have held a titled or advisory position for the past fifteen years	19 (83%)

Table 28

Overlap of Officials in One Family Association

Traditionist Group	Number of Officers	Overlap with Family Association Officers
Chinese Benevolent Association (Titled officers)	21	8
Chinese Benevolent Association (Advisers)	35	15
Chinese Benevolent Association (Property Management Committee)	5	2
Chinese School Board	5	2
Anti-Communist League	4	2

a stable and self-perpetuating organizational scheme in which decisions affecting one segment of the system are likely to have similar results in all segments. Stability and continuity allow for long-range planning with a minimum of conflict. The continuity of the system over long periods of time is also ensured, fostering multiplex relationships among titled leaders and advisers. Such a system reinforces group solidarity and is characterized by a high esprit de corps among the ruling elite. Thirdly, and perhaps most important for small Chinese communities in overseas lands, the structure aids in keeping alive the culture of the "old country" by a plethora of similar ceremonies and festivities. At each event the same emotions are expressed, the same people make the same speeches, and everybody feels that he belongs.

However, the system allows for few innovations and little change in the programming and planning of community activities. It does not bend easily and novel ideas are rarely accepted. Because of the interlocking nature of the various organizations, potential changes in one segment are perceived as a possible threat to all. Those in leadership positions tend to view younger Chinese as a threat to their way of life, and these people are covertly or openly dissuaded from participating in association affairs. At this point in time, younger and more acculturated officials, though few in number, are becoming increasingly dissatisfied with associational policy and are beginning to challenge the privileges of the leaders, thereby challenging the traditionist system itself.

Functions of Traditionist Associations

During the period 1850–1900, traditionist organizations controlled the warp and woof of American Chinatowns. During the transitional period (1910–1940), Valley City's associations continued to dominate Chinese political-economic and social-cultural activities, even as demographic and social changes were modifying the patterns of Chinese life in America. Today many Chinese-Americans who have entered the political-commercial world of the greater society find themselves less dependent upon these traditionist associations. Yet the associations continue to provide goods and services for a dwindling portion of the Chinese population, primarily the elderly and recent immigrants. Both groups have experienced difficulties in entering into the mainstream of American life.

Thus, the once extensive functions of the traditionist associations have been reduced significantly in the political-economic sphere. On the other hand, they have taken on a new importance in their cultural-social aspects.

The major functions of the traditionist organizations today are:
1. To preserve and continue the cultural and historical Chinese identity of their people.
2. To provide for the physical comforts and social needs of their members.
3. To regulate internal disputes and to act as a regulatory agency resolving differences with other associations and with the outside community.

Chinese Historical-Cultural Continuity. If the Chinese in America are to maintain their ethnic exclusivity, it is imperative that they observe traditional and customary practices. These events include a series of cyclical rituals which reinforce mutual ties as well as their allegiance to both their ancestral heritage and to the political system of Nationalist China. In this section three such events will be discussed. Two are of traditional vintage, the Chinese Lunar New Year and the celebration of Confucius' birthday, and the third, observance of Chinese Independence Day, has a more recent origin.

During the two weeks of the Chinese Lunar New Year, each family association in Valley City provides traditional activities climaxed by a dinner celebration for its members. The association halls are rarely large enough to accommodate the crowds, so most family associations must hold their annual dinner at a Chinese restaurant. The largest family association holds its feast in the association hall but, because of the large turnout, also provides dining facilities in the nearby Confucian Church.

On Tuesday, February 6, the ——— Association's blue and red neon signs light the chilly evening air as a chartered scenicruiser pulls away from the association headquarters. Two Valley City policemen are present to direct the arriving San Francisco and Stockton visitors and to regulate traffic in the area. Flowers front the entrance and red papered signs in Chinese proclaim the New Year and wish the association future prosperity.

The lower level room, which usually serves as a gathering place for older men, is alive with the noises from the gaming table as one to fifty dollar bills are exchanged across the board by elderly and mature Chinese men wearing dark suits and white shirts.

The small kitchen is overcrowded and busy as the smells of Chinese cooking permeate the air.

Upstairs the tables for dining have been set and women, some dressed in cheong-sams and some in American-style clothing, act as hostesses serving Chinese pre-dinner snacks along with American hors d'oeuvres. The officials, identified by the red ribbons on their jackets, greet the arrivals. Men also sport red carnations and the women, pink corsages. Small children receive red packets of money (lei sei) from relatives and family.

Across the street in the Confucian Church, the 55 or so tables set up in the gymnasium are crowded and the dinner is already under way. Older men and young boys do the serving and the chatter of family small-talk is heard across the room. When the meal is finished, paper "doggie bags" are supplied for the remaining food. The family groups leave at 6:25 as another crowd enters for the second and final shift.

Back at the association hall, the seven-course dinner is being served. Seagrams whiskey bottles on each table are being emptied into paper cups. Men are making donations, and red slips of paper showing name and amount in Chinese are being posted on a board. During the dinner and afterwards, local and out-of-town guests are introduced with great rounds of applause for the more distinguished visitors. The officers make speeches and the guest of honor, a California Chinese congresswoman, gives a carefully prepared speech in Cantonese and in English praising the success of her Valley City "cousins."

This celebration is best characterized as a rite of intensification. As noted by Taylor (1969:114), such rituals are calendrical or cyclical occurrences held in association with events which occur repeatedly within the society. The ritual is consummatory rather than instrumental because the ceremony is a legitimate end in itself.

Honigmann (1963:171) suggests that one of the major functions of the ritual is to unify and solidify the attendant group. This is accomplished by validating and reinforcing conventional values and behavior. The group gathers to hear appropriate sentiments expressed under stirring circumstances and to renew the strength of those sentiments. The excitement these ceremonies kindle makes the participants intensely aware of themselves as a select group. This heightened sense of membership intensifies the group's solidarity and helps to insure its continuity.

The relationships between age and youth, and men and women, follow Chinese ideas of propriety and deference. The giving of the *lei-sei*, a gift of money usually in a red envelope, to children, the unmarried and young childless couples, the donations, and the services provided by the women reinforce the conventional status arrangement of the community.

Not only are the Chinese marked off from all other peoples, but the members of the association are distinguished from members of other Chinese groups, a social fact emphasized by inviting guests from other Chinese organizations to witness the generosity of their "kinsmen." The constant hallowed references to the association's prestige, evident in the speeches, unfailingly arouse a warm sense of identification. The people are proud and their emotional commitment leaves them unwilling to look too frankly at the group's shortcomings. The banquet ritual also functions to unite all "cousins" within the national association, as witnessed by the attendance of distinguished visitors from the San Francisco, Stockton, and Los Angeles association branches. This feeling of brotherhood was eloquently expressed by the congresswoman's reference to all the members as "my cousins."

Although each association holds a separate feast, the ceremony focuses upon the Chinese New Year and, in doing so, is an "all-Chinese" event. This association will reciprocate and send its representatives to the other associations' dinners, which are held at different times exactly for this reason. It is most significant that during the New Year's celebration members of different generations, who rarely cooperate and usually do not attend the same functions, minimize their differences and joyously feast together as a single family group.

However, most of the more acculturated, primarily native-born, young adults (15 to 29) are conspicuously absent. Many of them consider the ceremony boring, wearisome, and meaningless, for it is a reflection of Chinese loyalties that conflict with their American outlook; they do not wish to be reminded of their Oriental heritage. Nevertheless, a few do attend, bowing to their elders' wishes. Thus the

New Year's banquet, on the one hand a symbol of Chinese identity, also expresses the widening gulf between the rapidly assimilating Chinese and the larger Chinese community.

In the more traditionist households in Valley City special Chinese delicacies are prepared or imported from San Francisco specialty shops. Housewives scrub floors and rearrange furniture for anticipated guests, the boys get haircuts, and there are new dresses for the girls.[10] There is much visiting among friends and neighbors, and some Caucasian guests, particularly in the south area, are included. For the more adventuresome, a trip to San Francisco's New Year's parade, followed by dinner at a Chinese restaurant, is in order.

The New Year's celebration lasts for about two weeks. The association halls are open, dinner is served, and gambling activities continue deep into the night. Those attending, however, are likely to be older men who would normally frequent the association halls throughout the year.

Cohesion is further reinforced by the use of affective symbols. Red-paper envelopes (lei sei), red badges, flowers, firecrackers, and Chinese delicacies are all symbolic of a Chinese tradition, as are verbal and non-verbal behaviors. Each association has an altar with a picture of a usually mythical founding ancestor. Offerings to this ancestor are infrequent and are individual undertakings, but the smell of burning incense has meaning to all Chinese. These symbols are powerful guides to insure proper behavioral responses to specific occasions. They blend the components of the moral and jural order with the sensory excitement of emotion (Turner 1964:30) and reinforce an identification with the present Chinese community while maintaining a continuity with past traditions.

The Chinese New Year's banquet reinforces the feelings of Chinese solidarity, but attitudes and behavior of those present reveal some basic conflicts. The most influential and prestigious members dine in the hall, while the less-involved are shifted to the Confucius Church. Although the food is prepared in one kitchen, certain delicacies are served only in the hall. Most of the speeches are in Cantonese and the non-speaker, often bored with the proceedings, engages in competing conversation. Quarrels, and occasionally pushing and shoving, break out between members over real and imagined slights and, under the influence of alcohol, there are some heated exchanges. Elders are often annoyed and dismayed with some rather unfilial actions of their sons. Conflicts of Chinese life in America do not escape representation even

10 A similar pattern was reported by Dare (1959:35–37) for San Francisco.

at these unifying rites. But harmony transcends these divisions and, in the context of the occasion, these rivalries are underplayed, for the ritual demands that emphasis be placed upon what all members have in common.

These rituals, therefore, reinforce the sense of commitment to certain cultural values, drain off tensions that may threaten social stability, bolster feelings of confidence and security, and provide a strong sense of unity. They also serve to strengthen the members of the group and rekindle the fires of kinship and clanship, thus rebuilding the foundation necessary to maintain their identity in a changing world over which they may have no immediate control. In such changing times this ritual stressing the cultural roots of the Chinese takes on a larger significance than in times past.

Another important event in the ceremonial life of this Chinese community is the celebration of Confucius' birthday.

The celebration of the birthday of Confucius is scheduled to start at 6:00 P.M. in the auditorium of the Confucius Church, yet there are fewer than twenty people present at that time. At 6:15 a black and white movie in Cantonese, with Chinese character subtitles, begins to run. As the movie continues, the leaders of the C.B.A., dressed in dark suits and white shirts, start to arrive. At 7:30 P.M., the drum and bugle corps makes its entrance, assembles on the stage, and presents a medley of songs climaxed by an interpretive rendition of "Wendy."

The corps leaves by 8:00 P.M. and the official activity commences. A large screen with a portrait of Confucius is lowered. In front of the screen, flowers that serve as an offering of respect are displayed on a wooden table. The C.B.A. leaders assemble on stage and lead the audience in the singing of the Chinese national anthem. Each leader is individually introduced and gives a short speech in Cantonese honoring Confucius, at the end of which they kowtow three times to his portrait. The guest speaker is a Chinese professor of history from a nearby university. He lectures in English although he comments that perhaps he should do so in Chinese. His presentation is on the relevance of Confucian ideals to the present situation and he exhorts his audience to continue to follow the universal teachings of this sage. But his style is geared to the college classroom and his lecture meets neither the needs nor the expectations of the audience, who talk throughout his speech and seem to pay little attention to what he says. The second speaker, a C.B.A. leader, also cannot hold the attention although he does speak in Cantonese.

Four and one-half hours later, the ceremony is concluded and the 200 or so people assembled, primarily elderly men and women with a sprinkling of younger Chinese immigrants, depart.

It seems as though many celebrants attend to see the Chinese movie, to visit with friends, and because it is Saturday evening and there is nothing else to do.

The third celebration is held on October 10 and is called the Double-Ten Commemoration. It is the Chinese Independence Day, the equivalent of the American Fourth of July. The ceremony is almost identical to the one performed on Confucius' Birthday. Again a Chinese movie is shown, the drum and bugle corps performs, the Chinese national anthem is sung, reverential bows are directed, this time to a portrait of Dr. Sun Yat-sen, and the speeches in Cantonese are presented by local leaders. In addition, twenty Chinese language school children sing several songs. As usual, the audience appears to be restless, one elderly gentleman falls asleep, and many people leave before the speeches are completed.

Provision of Physical Comforts and Social Support. In addition to encouraging cultural-historical identity by sponsoring ceremonial and commemorative celebrations, traditionist associations are also instrumental in meeting some of the social and psychological needs of their members.

Every Chinese community has its share of the elderly, primarily older men who, although they have resided in the United States for many years, have spent most of their lives in Chinatown, on the fringes of the American community.

"Among the aging males are the sojourners who have been unsuccessful . . . they find seclusion in Chinatowns and manage to exist without steady employment and income, living in the headquarters provided by their . . . associations. They maintain a rooming house existence and culture, devoid of family and normal social contacts. They likewise avoid contacts with the larger society, finding security within a predominantly Chinese social milieu" (Lee 1960:330) .

This rooming house atmosphere is also enjoyed by married men with families who are either retired or infrequently employed. Unable to return to their Chinese homeland, they too are more comfortable and secure in a Chinese rather than an American world. It is primarily within the association halls and in nearby rooming houses owned by the associations that elderly men may pass their remaining days in a congenial atmosphere reminiscent of more traditional times.

The headquarters of one particular association is bordered by a small gas station and a narrow alleyway. The building itself is about fifty years old and is of a design that is typical for the period. From the street it appears to be a two-story building, but a side view reveals that there is also a basement floor. The top two stories consist of offices and a "shrine" complete with an altar, a place for incense burning and the lighting of candles. During the New Year's dinner, the room serves as a central banquet hall. Most of the activity, however, occurs in the basement. It is an open room with perhaps seven large wooden circular tables and some old wooden chairs. There is a gas furnace to the left of the entrance and a black-and-white television set against one wall. At the rear of the room is a Chinese kitchen.

The occupants are mostly elderly men, dressed in shabby, usually rumpled, clothing. Mah-jong or cards are available and at one table four men are decisively placing their "tiles." They keep up a constant conversation in Sze-Yap, which centers upon the intricacies of the game. Occasionally, one of them will loudly proclaim his successful play, and some coins change hands. Other men are seated reading the Chinese-language newspapers delivered daily from San Francisco, while one man, his head resting on the table, appears about to fall asleep. Chinese-language newspapers from New York, San Francisco, and Los Angeles are scattered around the room, as are some local English dailies and magazines and other Chinese reading materials. A mail rack on one wall holds but few envelopes. Coffee and cake are available throughout the day and evening on a smaller table near the kitchen, which is attended to by the association custodian. There are a few notices on the wall in both English and Chinese. One announces a forthcoming Chinese movie whose proceeds will be used to support the Chinese language school; another announces a recent committee, and a third lists the contestants for the Miss Chinatown pageant in San Francisco. The television is constantly on but the occupants of the room rarely watch it.

Though the seasons change and the days grow shorter, the activities remain the same. When it rains, the hall will be a bit more crowded. Sometimes a few elderly women will "visit," but they do so infrequently, and in the evening some younger men will sit at the tables for games of mah-jong, dominoes, or cards. Men will enter and leave to eat in nearby restaurants, visit a gambling establishment, or return to their rooms.

The associations continue to provide a haven for their members, as they have in the past. The facilities are open to all members but serve primarily as a meeting place for elderly men, who gather to discuss their lives and their problems, their successes and their failures, to speak to their friends of their families, both in America and in China or Hong Kong, and to spend time before they return to their wife, family, or their empty room.

The hall also serves as a depository for receiving and sending mail and as a clearinghouse for information about Chinese events in the local community, in San Francisco, across the country, and in Taiwan. Dinners are often served on traditional Chinese holidays like Ching Ming, Moon Festival, and All Souls Day, which are celebrated with festivities in the association hall.

The association usually waives the dues or donations of its older members and often pays those over sixty-five a small stipend which supplements their Social Security or welfare payments. Donations are sometimes solicited from members to help their needy cousins; thus the indigent and infirm are somewhat provided for. The associations guarantee a funeral for the poverty-stricken and for those who do not have relatives in this county. These funerals are generally less expensive and the banquet afterwards less elaborate than those paid for by individual families, yet the service and funerary provisions are adequate and respectful. The dead are usually buried in a local cemetery in Valley City since the practice of sending the bones of the deceased to China has been discontinued because of difficulties with the Chinese authorities.

The association also maintains contact with its branches in other cities and with the government in Taiwan. Visiting dignitaries—for example, Taiwan's Consul General or the chairman of the association's San Francisco branch—are officially welcomed by resident family associations.

In addition to strictly association-sponsored projects, the associations cooperate with each other and help to maintain the Chinese language school and the Sunday showing of Chinese-language movies at the Confucian Church. Most cooperative activity is conducted under the auspices of the C.B.A., to which all family associations belong.

Although the associations attempt to provide a Chinese identity for all their members, their daily activities provide recreation and sociability for but a small section of their membership. Association facilities and events attract the elderly and the immigrant almost to the exclusion of the native-born and more acculturated, and particularly the young. They serve as a bastion for those who cannot or will not participate in the life of the larger community. Their concerns reflect their image as a tradition-oriented and China-centered group. Thus, associations aid in widening the gulf between the generations, a practice which results in estrangement and conflict. But by maintaining a Chinese port in an American sea, they function to make life more pleasant and more meaningful for the elderly whose numbers may be decreasing but whose needs remain.

While the family associations cater primarily to the needs of elderly men, the C.B.A., as the highest-level traditionist organization, attempts to unite the entire traditionist community by providing Chinese-language movies. These are shown each Sunday in the Confucian Church at approximately 2:00 P.M. and 7:30 P.M. Admission ranges from a $0.50 donation to a $2.00 charge, depending upon the quality, prestige, and length of the films; the money is used to support the Chinese language school. The movies, advertised in the San Francisco Chinese papers, are changed weekly and vary considerably in quality, ranging from black-and-white productions from Hong Kong depicting modern comedy, romance, and adventure, to full-color spectaculars of traditional Chinese history and mythology. Most of the movies are in Cantonese (Sam-Yap) while a few are in Mandarin. All have Chinese character subtitles and a few include English subtitles as well. Attendance varies from fewer than 100 persons to over 700, but the audience is always composed primarily of elderly Chinese-speaking men and women, with a scattering of younger adults, teen-agers, and children. Some sit silently, engrossed in following the movie plot, while others chat throughout the performance. Young children grow restless, often leaving and re-entering the auditorium, and not a few fall asleep in their chairs.

Chinese senior citizens look forward to this weekly event. The movies offer them a temporary respite from the American world outside, a chance to relax with age-mates and to see once again the familiar scenes of their youth. Most important, it gives them an opportunity to remember their cultural legacy by spending a few hours in a world that is particularly Chinese.

Movie day is also enjoyed immensely by the younger immigrant population who are not familiar with the English language and with American scenarios. It affords them a pleasant afternoon or evening before they must return to their low-paying, long-houred jobs. They often bring their young children and carry their babies, thus sparing the expense of a baby-sitter. For them, the movie is a family outing.

Conspicuously absent are the middle-aged and mature adult modernists and the native-born young adults and adolescents, who find the language strange and the plots incomprehensible. They may drive Grandma or Great Uncle to and from the show but prefer to spend their afternoons and evenings elsewhere.

In conclusion, the relative success and persistence of the functions and activities sponsored by the traditionist organizations, ranging from the New Year's celebration to the Chinese-language movies, indicate a viable, if not dynamic, concern with the cultural-political heritage of Chinese-Americans. But even more relevant to this discussion are the social-psychological functions of such celebrations. Mrs. L., China-born and widowed, expresses these sentiments:

> I go to all the Chinese things. I never listen (to) or understand the big shots (C.B.A. officials), but I like to talk to my friends and I love to see the movies. They make me think about my childhood.

Similar concerns are expressed by younger adults, who are in a minority at such events. For example, Mr. C., a dishwasher who came to America five years ago, states:

> I am a lonely man because in America I cannot understand what they do. I like to be with Chinese people and see a Chinese movie or just to hear people talk Sze-Yap. I need to feel Chinese.

Dr. B., a C.B.A. leader educated in America, comments:

> Being Chinese means respecting the ways of our ancestors and honoring our great leaders. I know the people don't really listen to the speeches, but we are, after all, Chinese. If we didn't perform our duties, we would lose our identity and become just Americans.

These events provide an opportunity to socialize, exchange news, gossip, reinforce friendships, and enjoy an evening's entertainment, an activity particularly valued by the elderly, who have few such outlets. These activities take place in a familiar atmosphere and serve as a refuge for those Chinese who feel they are surrounded by an often hostile and confusing American world. In this manner, they serve as reminders of Chinese traditionalism and reinforce Chinese identity.

But while these activities unify the traditionist community, they have little impact on modernists or activists. Their primary appeal is to the less acculturated. Chinese adults who do not speak or understand Cantonese are always conspicuously absent. Few teen-agers attend these events, and even those who speak Chinese prefer other activities. Thus, these activities represent and perpetuate divisions within the community, divisions based primarily upon acculturation and, to a lesser degree, upon age.

The Regulation of Disputes. The third function of traditionist organizations is the settlement of disputes. During both the traditional and transitional periods of Chinese settlement in America, the traditionist organizations were invariably involved in a plethora of immigration cases, in the political and economic control of legal and illegal business practices, and in representing its Chinese members' interests to an often hostile Caucasian world.

"Chinese come under regulation of the American government through their immigration status, their ownership of business, their occupation or ownership of buildings and their possession of income. Among themselves the Chinese know there are disputes, that there is the danger of economic competition, and that there are many ways in which people can be exploited. In such situations, the protective agencies of American society would be considered unapproachable and inappropriate, and American officials would flounder in the complex relationships of Chinatown" (Heyer 1953:80).

In the Valley City Chinese community of the 1960's, traditionist associations concern themselves primarily with the internal regulation of social and economic activities. Associational involvement with the external world has been reduced to legal and financial concerns pertaining to the ownership of property, the redevelopment of such properties, and to other business matters normal to the functioning of corporate groups. Associations function as a regulatory agency concerned with the collection of monetary debts and with the reconciliation of parties to real or imagined insults. Complaints about the mistreatment of a wife or relative and requests for estate settlement involving both domestic and foreign recipients are less common. All of their "cases" for the past five years have involved only older China-born adults. The younger and more acculturated Chinese prefer to utilize the American legal system and do not bring their difficulties before the family association arbitrators. As noted before, they prefer the justice of American jurisprudence which, they feel, deals in facts and whose courts have legal powers to enforce their decisions.

It has also become increasingly uncommon for the family associations to involve themselves in the marital and financial affairs of their members, who are encouraged to solve their problems individually. It is only when anger, frustration, and emotions run high and when individuals and families cannot agree upon a solution that the family association is called upon.

When the family association is asked to render a decision, its suggestion is not legally binding but it carries with it the force of moral and ethical sanction. Since the association does not wish to antagonize its members, it attempts to reach decisions which allow both parties to save face. However, officials and important persons within the association use their influence to seek an advantageous solution for their friends and family. Thus disputes provide them with a vehicle to demonstrate their political-social power.

Any dispute involving members of different associations falls outside the jurisdiction of any particular family association and can only be resolved at a higher level, that of the C.B.A. The C.B.A. is responsible for the settlement of disputes among its constituent organization and most usually is concerned with disputes between members of different family associations.

The kinds of disputes and the manner in which the conflicts are resolved have changed little over the last twenty years and have been adequately discussed previously. Most of today's disputes are settled at lower levels, and the president of the C.B.A. reported that there have been less than a handful of cases during the past five years. He states:

Perhaps during olden times it was common for us to settle conflicts in the Chinese community. Today minor arguments will be settled privately and major arguments about property and money-lending will go to the American courts. It is only the old ones who really come to us. Since I have been president I have known of only two cases.

The first concerned a man who believed he was threatened and insulted by a member of the tong. I spoke to both men myself and found out that all they did was exchange angry words. The man's fear of the tong was unfounded. He just wanted to embarrass him. They later apologized and that was that.

The other was about an officer who borrowed a substantial amount of money but was very slow about repaying it. A younger man suggested that we should insist upon repayment but nothing was done about it.

In conclusion, the liberalization of immigration laws, the reluctance of the American authorities to prosecute violations retroactively, and the involvement of the Chinese themselves in the American legal system, have functioned to decrease the more obvious conflicts between Chinese and American groups. In addition, increased Chinese reluctance to seek aid from traditionist associations, combined with the accelerating acculturation of the Chinese, has significantly reduced the dispute settlement abilities of these associations as well as the need for such services.

Other Traditionist Organizations

The traditionist organizations discussed thus far are concerned primarily with the needs of mature adults. However, to ensure a base sufficient for the continuity of a Chinese way of life, it is important to socialize and educate the young in the tenets of their cultural heritage. One of the organizations designed to deal with this problem is the Chinese language school.

The Chinese Language School. Established in 1908 under the auspices of the C.B.A., the Chinese language school shifted its location in 1909, and in 1931 funds were raised to erect a new building. In 1961 the Confucian Church was erected at a cost of approximately $600,000, and since that time this building has housed the Chinese language school. The church itself is a three-storied building, with an administration office used by the principal and three Chinese teachers and seven classrooms which can accommodate some 300 pupils. Students also use the facilities of a gymnasium and a larger upstairs auditorium capable of seating 1,000 persons. The auditorium is available for all major community events.

On Saturday mornings, Chinese language school begins at 9:00 A.M. On a typical day, sixty (29 boys and 31 girls) of the ninety-odd students enrolled are in attendance. Four classes are in progress with 26, 15, 11, and 8 students in each class. They are taught by the male principal and three female Chinese teachers. Students range in age from six to twelve years, with a clustering around the ages of eight to ten.

All of the classes offer only elementary-level instruction. Imported from Taiwan, the students' textbooks and workbooks are modern, with instructions and descriptions of the lesson in both Chinese and English, a significant departure from the "Chinese-only" format of past periods. At the front of the text all vocabulary words are presented, with the Chinese character followed by the pronunciation in Cantonese and Mandarin, giving both Yale and Wade-Giles romanization for the Mandarin. Mandarin, however, is not taught. At one time adult classes in Mandarin were proposed, but the program was dropped.

Classes are held each Saturday from 9:00 A.M. until noon, and from 6:00 until 8:00 P.M. on Tuesday and Thursday evenings throughout the academic year. Classroom instruction on Saturday is from 9:00 until 11:00, with a 10- to 15-minute break each hour. During the break some students play with a basketball in the gymnasium, while others play or run and talk in the hallways or outside the building. The last hour, 11:00 until 12:00, is often spent in the auditorium, where the children sing Chinese songs to piano accompaniment or practice speeches or other presentations. Song sheets have only Chinese characters.

The lessons are a combination of rote repetition and memorization, combined with more modern teaching techniques. In one class students repeated the lesson after the instructor but were also given the opportunity to read, write, and translate individually. Students generally translated from Chinese to English rather than from English to Chinese. Tone quality is stressed in their pronunciation, as is proper stroking in the "ball-point pen" calligraphy. The formality of the learning process is mitigated by personal remarks and some joking by both students and instructor. Chinese traditions and regard for respect and filial piety are included in the lesson and in the teachers' seemingly impromptu storytelling. When the class valedictorian practices his graduation speech, proper protocol—bowing first to the chairman and then to the audience—is as important as is his Chinese pronunciation.

The language of instruction is English, yet the instructors are all China-born and speak English with recognizable accents. The students are almost all native-born and inter-student communication is always in English.

A description of a Chinese school graduation will acquaint the reader with the flavor of such events. The Chinese language school graduation ceremonies are an exercise in patience and endurance. As is characteristic of many Chinese traditionist functions, the event is thought to be overly long and poorly organized by many of those attending, and audience participation is largely limited to sitting and listening.

On a balmy evening in June, 1969, the Confucius Church's auditorium is filled with over 100 children and, by the end of the evening, more than 800 individuals will be present. Many of them are the parents and relatives of graduates and students, but there are a large number of elderly males and females who frequent traditionist functions as well. At 6:45 P.M., a movie screen is lowered and a silent movie depicting life in Chinese cities starts. The movie is old and the film continually breaks and is re-set by a teenage projectionist. The room has air conditioning equipment but either it is broken or no one knows how to operate it. The auditorium becomes heated as the temperature rapidly climbs to over 100 degrees; the people perspire, conversing with their neighbors as they fan themselves with the evening's program. The second movie shown is a color travelogue in Taiwan. It is also a silent film. At 7:30 P.M., chairs are set up on the stage and a screen-sized reproduction of Confucius is lowered. Throughout the ceremony, children and adults are constantly entering and leaving the building.

By 7:45 the Chinese dignitaries start to arrive. They include the chairman and vice-chairman of the C.B.A., the chairman and vice-chairman of the school board, and the present and honorary-past principal of the Chinese school. The dignitaries and the twelve students (seven girls and five boys) graduating from the sixth grade march on stage to the accompaniment of piano music. The audience stands and they sing the Chinese national anthem. The dignitaries and students bow to the Chinese flag and to the portrait of Confucius three times.

The speeches, all in Cantonese, begin. They recognize the accomplishments of the students, praise the parents for encouraging their youngsters' study of Chinese, recognize the young age of the graduates, encourage them to continue their schooling, mention the teachers and officials by name, and commend the fine work they have done. Each student is presented with a diploma and some receive scholarship and citizenship awards. The class valedictorian praises his teachers and parents; all the students sing a farewell song and, finally, ice cream and cookies are distributed. It is almost 11:00 P.M. when the ceremony ends.

This rite of passage for the students also functions as a rite of intensification for those present. The Chinese heritage, the values of Chinese language education, and the teachers and officials of the community have been officially recognized.

The Chinese language school has been more responsive to the changing conditions of Chinese community than have other traditionist organizations, a response stimulated more by necessity than by choice. The most significant change is a change in primary purpose, a shift to instruction in Cantonese at the elementary level rather than advanced training in both Chinese language and literature. This new direction in curricular emphasis is a direct response to the changing social profile of the student body. Today's Chinese student is between six and twelve years old, native-born and English-speaking, having often had no formal training in the Cantonese language.

Secondly, there is a corresponding modification in the method of instruction. The memorization of lessons, a standard method in times past, has given way to lesson explanation coupled with individual instruction for each student. At the same time, an increasing amount of time is spent in less formal activities—e.g., playing during recess, singing, etc. The language instruction is English, rather than Chinese. Lessons stress tone-quality in pronunciation and proper stroking in calligraphy.

The emphasis is upon teaching, upon providing a stimulating atmosphere for learning. Chinese classics, poetry, and folklore are included in the instruction but only as literature in translation. Yet the students listen eagerly to traditional tales and stories of village life in

China. All in all, the Chinese language school is more like its American counterpart, although many of the students claim it is less innovative and generally less exciting.

Originally, the language school served the function of educating its students in Chinese language and literature. It was important to know the language well because a student's future employment would be dependent to a large degree upon his ability to converse in and read Chinese. Today, Chinese education is rarely necessary for securing a job and Chinese are acceptable to Americans with or without a Chinese education. Moreover, the Chinese language school must now compete with recreational alternatives, and there are many Chinese youths who would rather participate in "Little League" on Saturday mornings.

Although the Chinese population of this city has dramatically increased since World War II, student enrollment has not kept pace with Chinese numbers. Not only has the number of students decreased, but so has the amount of time each student spends attending school. A 1968 survey of eighty Chinese college students revealed that only twenty-nine (36.25%) had ever attended language school. Of those attending, twenty-one (72.4%) had completed less than four years of schooling. Immigrant children, already native-speakers, do not usually attend. First generation native-born average about two years of instruction, while the second generation native-born, if they attend, do so for less than one year (Weiss 1968b).

A majority of the students cease coming by the time they enter junior high school. They often claim they need more time for their American studies and cannot be burdened by Chinese lessons. Parents generally expect their children to attend but are increasingly reluctant to force them to do so, particularly when Chinese school hours conflict with their work or leisure-time activities. Furthermore, the Chinese language school is located far from Chinese population clusters, and the majority of their students depend upon automobile transportation to and from school.

There is a question in the minds of many Chinese, as to the utility of Chinese language instruction today. The dialect of Cantonese taught at the school is Sam-Yap rather than Sze-Yap, the dialect most often spoken at home. These dialects correspond to district divisions in Kwangtung Province. They are two quite different dialects that are barely intelligible. Sam-Yap speakers, geographically and linguistically closer to Canton city, claim that their dialect is purer and relate language to "good manners" and a "more genteel" way of life. Sze-Yap speakers boast that they are the more aggressive in business ventures (Sung 1967:19). Heyer (1953:46) claims that these dialects are closely enough related so that native speakers of one can usually recognize sound shifts of the other. However, Valley City's young Chinese, particularly language school students, insist that "school dialect" does not help them to understand conversation at home. Instructors and students recognize this inconsistency, and, while some parents complain, Sam-Yap is recognized by both school and home as the "proper language" of Valley City's Chinese people.

Support for the language school depends entirely upon the C.B.A. There are expenses in maintenance, lights, equipment, school supplies, etc., as well as teachers' salaries of about $480 per teacher per month. Individual family associations contribute about $2,000 annually, while private contributions and fund-raising events, usually movies, net about $1,000 to $2,000. One family association awards a $100 to $150 scholarship to the highest ranking student. The family associations also pay the tuition of $2.50 per month per student.

Enrollment in the Chinese language school will most probably continue to fall. As Chinese children become more fully acculturated and structurally assimilated within the larger society, the Chinese language school cannot but decrease in importance both to the community and to the individual. A decrease in Chinese language training tends to discourage active participation in family associations or attendance at traditionist functions and can easily lead to the widening of the gap between young and old.

Nevertheless, for the time being the Chinese language school will survive in this community. Although language training is minimal for the majority of students, traditionist as well as modernist parents continue to send their children. Because the school acts as a center for meeting and mixing with other Chinese, the school serves as an agency for maintaining Chinese exclusiveness in a predominantly non-Chinese world. The parents expect that childhood friendships made at school will mature as the children grow up and will result in lasting friendship or marriage, keeping alive a Chinese identity which is continually threatened by multiplex participation in the larger society.

Chinese youth who are unwilling to attend language classes have yet another opportunity to retain their membership in a Chinese organization, one that is geared more to their American ideologies and does not threaten their mixed Chinese-American heritage—the Chinese drum and bugle corps.

The Chinese Drum and Bugle Corps. Bands, drum corps, and drum and bugle corps have always been part of the Chinese experience in America. During the transitional period Valley City boasted three such groups, one sponsored by the C.B.A. and two sponsored by two churches. Many adults who grew up in Chinese-American communities were members of such groups as children and teenagers, and when conversation would shift to the "good old days," they would talk about "their corps" and how they used to play at parades and on holidays and accompany funeral processions through the Chinese sections.

The history of the present drum and bugle corps in the Valley City Chinese community starts on a rainy Saturday morning in 1963 when eleven youths showed up at the Confucian Church for the first organizational meeting. Interest spread and membership grew. During that year, the corps' twenty or so members performed at seventeen local events and, as the Drum and Bugle Corps, made their first out-of-town debut in the Chinese New Year's parade in San Francisco. In 1964 an all-girl color guard was added and the corps launched a massive fund-raising campaign for new uniforms and equipment. The campaign was well publicized in both Valley City dailies and in the Chinese-language San Francisco papers. Donations were sought from Chinese business enterprises and individuals could become patrons for $150 and grand patrons for $500. One well-known Chinese leader volunteered an extra donation of 10 per cent of the total money received. The campaign, climaxed by a benefit ball in the Confucian Church auditorium in December, 1964, raised over $5,000.

The present corps consists of about sixty members between the ages of eleven and eighteen, who perform on thirty-two bugles, eight drums, and one cymbal. In addition, there is a thirteen-member all-girl color guard.

The young adult organizers of the corps and, in particular, its director realized that youthful interest and determination were necessary for the corps' success. However, just as important as money for equipment and uniforms was a place to practice. The organizers turned to the C.B.A., which had both.

At first, Valley City's C.B.A. leaders were skeptical. The corps was run by young men and "children." How could they make it a success without the direct guidance and participation of their elders? Yet the C.B.A. was afraid of losing face if this venture should succeed without its support. This ambivalent attitude led to conflicting practices; some leaders who publicly contributed to the campaign and urged their family associations to do so privately expressed the opinion that the corps would never succeed. After it showed some measure of success, however, they boasted that it was because of their financial support. If it had failed, they would have claimed that they knew it all along. The future success of the corps, however, rests upon its ability to mobilize its own resources. Although officially sponsored by the C.B.A., it is self-supporting and C.B.A. money is not budgeted for corps programs. Yet, as a C.B.A.-sponsored organization, the corps can use the facilities of the Confucian Church rent-free.

When the Chinese language school operated during the week, the drum and bugle corps would use the Confucian Church gymnasium on Saturdays. Language school children who also came to this community center, primarily to use the basket-ball courts, watched the corps practicing and more than a few indicated a desire to join. The C.B.A. directors were not unaware of the corps' popularity but attributed part of its success to Saturday morning sessions. In order to attract young people to the language school and perhaps diminish some of the corps' attractiveness, language school classes were changed to Saturday and the corps had to find other facilities for practice. Clearly, the corps could not be allowed to compete with the language school.

As the corps gained community-wide prestige, some of the C.B.A. leaders became disturbed because the corps did not specifically mention in its title the Chinese language school, a usual practice for such organizations. Some leaders decided that the language school should be officially connected to the corps, so that the corps' prestige would rub off on the language school. They suggested that the name be changed so that people would automatically connect it with the school, although realistically both organizations are quite separate. Moreover, when the corps is mentioned in the Chinese-language newspapers in San Francisco, it is referred to as the Chinese *School* Drum and Bugle Corps. Fortunately, the director was a practical man and did not object to the name shift as long as the corps could use the hall for evening practice. The corps is now known locally as the Chinese Community Drum and Bugle Corps. The young members, however, prefer the name, "The Mandarins," which appears on their pink-and-blue jackets and on identification badges.

In the course of time, the corps has become a drawing card for traditionist community events. One C.B.A. leader states:

> We know the drum and bugle corps is very popular. We wish all our events to be a success. So we want the corps to appear at all of our major events and lend support to the Chinese community. We can use them to attract people.

The corps director, however, disagrees:

> I see the role of the corps in a different light than most of the elders. We do not belong at events like Confucius' birthday because we are not part

of that celebration. Such events are not necessary for the corps' image and frankly I resent the elders' using the kids for their own advantage.

Fortunately, actual conflict is usually prevented. When the director considers it inappropriate for the corps to appear, he usually makes the excuse of a previous engagement. Thus he avoids an outright refusal.

The corps is a focal activity for many of Valley City's young Chinese, particularly because it is the only group specifically organized for the eleven-to-eighteen year age group. Many of its members also play an instrument in the junior and senior high schools. They consider the drum and bugle corps a challenge, an opportunity to compete and win prizes, and a chance for out-of-town travel and adventure. Boys who stay with the corps for a year are often "hooked" and remain until they graduate from high school. The corps appeals to their masculine pride as it involves uniforms, marching, and a military spirit of co-operation. Girls, on the other hand, usually drop out in the sophomore and junior years. At that age girls are becoming young women and their parents may discourage them from further participation, claiming that "parading around" and "showing off your knees" are not proper ladylike activities. The young girls have also begun to shift their interests to other feminine activities, particularly social ones that interfere with the rigorous, often thrice-weekly practice sessions.

In general, parents are enthusiastic about the corps. They claim "it keeps the kids off the streets" and "teaches them teamwork." They often use the threat of not letting their children attend practice if their school grades are not up to par. As a result, the academic standing of the corps' members is above average.

But perhaps most important is the function the corps performs as a meeting place for Chinese adolescents. Parents hope that their children will socialize with other Chinese, particularly at a time when their interests are likely to shift to more active inter-sex activities. Friendships made at corps sessions carry over into late snacks and parties, functioning, as does the language school, as a basis for later adult association. Thus, the corps is able to unite a geographically dispersed Chinese population and affords new families with teen-age children an entrance into Chinese community social life.

The corps consists almost exclusively of American-born Chinese or Chinese who have been raised primarily in this country. The director, noticing the absence of the China-born, states:

Well, the foreign-born kids like the corps and they want to try. They are discouraged when they don't get immediate success and they just don't seem to want to work for it.

Foreign-born Chinese also feel uncomfortable among their American-born peers, feel left out of the socializing, and generally do not have the after-school free time to participate in the corps' activities. The latter statement rather than the former comment perhaps better explains their poor participation. Thus, the corps does not integrate the foreign-born with the American-born, but, rather, accentuates the distinctions and perpetuates these differences.

Although the corps is a youth program, the members wish to become as professional as they can. Thus they do not welcome newcomers with open arms, feeling that previously untrained people will ruin their chances for winning competitions.

Some members want to let competent Caucasians and Japanese into the corps. One member even suggested calling a Japanese boy "Chan" in order to admit him. Opposition to these ideas comes from both parents and elders. Parents see the corps as an opportunity for their children to meet other Chinese. If the corps were to go "interracial," even if only to the extent of including Japanese, many would not let their children attend. The C.B.A. is also against a mixed membership because the drum and bugle corps would no longer represent the Chinese community; it has made it clear that it would refuse the corps the use of the Confucian Hall. The director has been approached by other such non-Chinese corps in Valley City but has turned down offers to merge.

The corps has other problems as well. It is not overly successful in competitions and often must compete against older and more professional groups. The corps' members feel that this competition is good because it "builds character and leadership" and "teaches them to be good sportsmen." However, some adult community members would prefer that the corps withdraw from competitive activities and restrict its playing to Chinese events. They are concerned that losing often does not build a strong character and may make the corps' members feel inferior to Caucasians.

The corps is a youth group and, while its program easily attracts members, its appeal is to their American interests rather than to their Chinese heritage. Corps events are equally divided between American and Chinese events, but even when they play at Chinese events they function as performers rather than as participants. Their repertoire includes traditional marching songs as well as modern swing numbers, all of an American origin, and does not even include the Chinese national anthem.

In this respect, the corps may be regarded as a modernist youth group, Chinese in membership but American in character. Thus it is not surprising that the major confrontations between the corps and the traditionist community concern the corps' racial-ethnic identity. The traditionists wish to retain the corps' Chinese exclusivity and to use it as an instrument for gaining recognition and popularity for the Chinese community. Yet they cannot allow the corps to become more important than the language school. Chinese youth, and their directors, view this organization as another means to enter into the mainstream of American activity, one which combines their Chinese ethnicity with their American heritage. Sponsorship by the C.B.A. allows them easy access to monies and practice facilities. Yet, if the relationship is sometimes an uneasy one between the corps and the designs of the traditionist-oriented C.B.A., it is bolstered by the advantages both organizations can enjoy. For, in the final analysis, both groups benefit from this symbiotic relationship.

Traditionist Youth Organizations. Aside from the Chinese language school and the drum and bugle corps, there are other organizations which cater to the needs of foreign-born high school and college age youths. These groups are not officially affiliated with adult groups, although they are allowed to use the facilities of the Confucian Hall. They serve as a refuge for recently arrived young immigrants who find it difficult to mix with either Caucasians or American-born Oriental peers but prefer to communicate and socialize with their fellow immigrants. There are three such groups in Valley City.

The first two groups, the Drama Club and the Valley City High School Chinese Club, will be discussed as a single organization, because their membership is almost identical. Originally organized by a Chinese minister as a club for Cantonese-speaking Chinese youth, they are now directed by a member of the Chinese Women's New Life Movement. Like most youthful organizations, they plan trips to San Francisco, Disneyland, the Sierras, and other California recreational centers. They also hold parties and attend movies but go to few school and community dances. During the past two years, they have presented a Chinese play in Cantonese and more than a few song and dance presentations of traditional Chinese vintage, all in conjunction with C.B.A.-sponsored events.

Diana T. is a member of the club. She is seventeen, a high school senior, and a rather tall and plain-looking young lady who plans for an eventual career as a medical technician. She formerly attended school in Hong Kong and speaks English with a noticeable accent. She spends much of her free time at home and lives in the central city. She reports:

> I don't mix easily with the American-born kids. They are Americans and want to always act like Americans. I, too, am more like an American every day I live here. But the native-born kids call us squares and they don't even want to know anything about China. They don't even care to be Chinese and I know one Chinese girl who only dates Caucasians.[11] I still want to be a Chinese.

Interest in the drama and high school clubs is decreasing. There are approximately thirty members today but upon graduation from high school most of them will cease to participate actively. For those who continue in junior college, their interests will shift to more adult activities. Some traditionist leaders are proud of the club but say it is poorly organized. Yet they claim not to have the time to "work with these kids."

As these young immigrants continue to attend school and become more fully involved with American life, they will most likely join youthful modernist or even activist groups. Those, however, who join the Chinese working world after their graduation from high school are likely candidates for adult traditionist organizations.

There is also a Chinese club for college students composed exclusively of Chinese foreign students from Hong Kong and Taiwan. Their membership lists fifty of the sixty-eight Chinese foreign students enrolled at Valley State University. They are of a traditionist orientation because they emphasize their Chinese heritage. The club imports movies from Hong Kong, participates in international programs, members don the clothing of their ancestors and speak to organizations of their historical Sinitic heritage. Most members speak Mandarin as well as English.

The club's most important social function, however, is to provide friendly companionship for its members, who, for the most part, have experienced frustration and loneliness. They find it difficult to relate to American-born Chinese, who understand neither their heritage nor their problems and who pursue a life-style alien to their tastes. Their

---

11 For a detailed account of Chinese-Caucasian dating, see Weiss, Melford S., "Selective acculturation and the dating process: the patterning of Chinese-Caucasian interracial dating," Journal of Marriage and the Family, Vol. XXXII, No. 2, May 1970 pp. 273–78.

foreign-born countrymen are, more often than not, immigrants from mainland China, lack formal education, and speak Cantonese rather than Mandarin. Chinese foreign students rarely visit the old China-town area or attend Chinese community functions, preferring instead the security of the University dormitory.[12]

The C.B.A. also recognizes and represents other traditionist organiza-tions—the ———— Tong, the Kuomintang, the Chinese Anti-Com-munist League, and the Chinese Women's New Life Movement. These organizations are of secondary importance to Valley City's tradi-tionist structure because they rarely attract new members, sponsor few events, and their activities usually coincide with other traditionist associations' functions. Moreover, their members are almost always active in their family associations and the C.B.A., with whom their leadership heavily overlaps. For example, every officer of the Kuomin-tang and the Anti-Communist League is also a family association and C.B.A. officer.

Finally, these organizations had all reached their apex during for-mer periods of Chinese settlement in America. The tongs enjoyed a great popularity and influence in the "traditional era," while the others were initiated and rose to prominence during the "time of transition." They function primarily to provide additional Chinese or-ganizational security to an ever-decreasing number of elderly Chinese and to remind them of their past accomplishments.

The Tong. Chinese tongs in America are a product of Chinatown living. Their history is replete with gambling, prostitution, opium traffic, smuggling, blackmail, and similar activities. The infamous tong wars have perhaps been overly publicized and certainly over-dramatized in the American press. They have been discussed in the chapters documenting the traditional and transitional eras of Chinese experience in America.

Since the 1920's overt tong activities in America have substantially decreased; many tongs have changed their name and now operate as merchants' associations or as fraternal lodges (Sung 1968:138). Thus, if the tongs have not completely given up their former enterprises, they have at least gone underground and have substituted blackmail, ex-tortion, intimidation, and slander for overt violence (Lee 1960:165).

---

12 Chinese student groups follow a pattern reported by Chen (1945) for youth and student clubs in New York City. There is a significant split between the China- and American-born, and between both groups and the Chinese foreign students. Inter-club activities are rare, each group preferring to develop separate programs. More-over, members of student youth groups are rarely active participants in either traditionist or modernist organizations.

Today's tong membership in Valley City consists primarily of Chinese-speaking, China-born males over fifty. Many successful businessmen who joined the tong during the days when membership was essential to the operation of any business continue their association with this organization.

Valley City's only tong, an autonomous branch of a large West Coast tong association popularly known as "Freemasons," serves today primarily as a Chinese social club. It holds celebrations at Chinese New Year's and at other holidays, cooperates in the major activities of the C.B.A., and contributes to Chinese fund-raising campaigns. Its internal structure and functioning are similar to those discussed for the family associations, and its involvement with the illicit ventures of the past is largely illusory, although informants have confided that the tong is still active in gambling operations in the metropolitan area.

The Kuomintang. Toward the end of the nineteenth century, patriotic young Chinese, intent on overthrowing the Manchu Dynasty and establishing a republic, organized political associations to bring about a revolution in China (Lee 1960:165). Dr. Sun Yat-sen, often referred to as the Chinese George Washington, became the first president of the Republic of China in 1912 and organized the Kuomintang, the ruling party of Republican China. Since that time, the Kuomintang has maintained branches in America (Kung 1962:217).

These American Kuomintang chapters held periodic meetings to stimulate interest in the home government, held political discussions, showed Chinese movies, entertained party visitors from China, helped to publish the kinds of materials used in the American Chinese language schools, and contributed generously to the war effort (Lee 1960:176). Yet, after the Nationalist Government re-established itself in Taiwan, the local leaders of Kuomintang branches found themselves unable to maintain interest in this organization or to attract new members. As the government of the People's Republic of China rose to prominence on the mainland, Kuomintang activities in America gradually decreased. It became difficult to muster enthusiasm for the Nationalist Government which had promised so much but now was unable even to allow sojourners a return to China (Lee 1960:177).

The Kuomintang Party in Taiwan still sends officials to America who visit Chinese communities and speak of political and economic development in Taiwan. Local branches welcome these visitors with feasts and banquets. Valley City's Chinese community still recalls the time when Dr. Sun and Madame Chiang were their official guests. Aside from sponsoring picnics and movies and participating in the affairs of San Francisco's Kuomintang chapter, Valley City's Kuomintang activities are minimal. Kuomintang headquarters is located in a small room on the first floor of an old and decaying building. The building, however, is rarely used for meetings.

Interest in the politics of Nationalist China has waned considerably and no new political parties have been formed. Most traditionists pay lip service to the government in Taiwan. Unlike some other overseas Chinese settlements (see Williams 1960), their orientation is not toward Communist China. The Chinese community's reaction towards "Communist China" will be discussed in a later chapter.

The Chinese Anti-Communist League. The Anti-Communist League, an offshoot of the Kuomintang, is another traditionist organization whose members are elderly, China-born males. During World War II it was quite active in raising money for supplies and war materials for the Chinese, but it has been inactive since the Communist Revolution. Its members meet, although infrequently, and participate in C.B.A. activities. Not unexpectedly, membership overlaps substantially with the Kuomintang.

The Chinese Women's New Life Movement. In 1939 Madame Chiang Kai-shek sent a representative to the United States to organize American women of Chinese descent to raise funds and to collect clothing and food for Chinese war refugees. The Chinese community of Valley City was the first to respond by organizing the Chinese New Life Movement.

Today the organization continues to hold installation dinners, although the same women hold officerships each year. The organization serves primarily as a female auxiliary to the male-oriented traditionist community. These elderly and mature China-born women act as hostesses at C.B.A. movies, as ticket collectors and ushers at the weekly Chinese movies, and as coordinators at Chinese fashion shows and dramatic presentations. In addition, they also engage in charitable work, primarily among the elderly and recent immigrants.[13]

Extension of the Traditionist Network

The relationship of Valley City's Chinese to the greater Valley City community, to other Chinese communities in America, and to Chinese overseas is also a concern of the traditionist element. The organization most responsible for channeling these contacts is the C.B.A., the

---

13 The Women's New Life Movement claims 750 members, most of whom are housewives (*Valley City News*, January 19, 1971). It is probable that less than two dozen regularly participate in traditional affairs.

highest-level traditionist organization. Other traditionist organizations, particularly the family associations, also maintain relationships outside the Valley City community. The nature and function of these relationships are similar to those of the C.B.A.

At important civic events such as the dedication of new Chinese buildings and ground-breaking ceremonies, the C.B.A. makes sure that local politicians, representatives of the state, photographers, and newsmen gather to recognize the occasion. Important politicians who cannot attend are often listed as honorary guests.[14]

The C.B.A. also represents the Chinese community by participating in local affairs as a Chinese ethnic group. For example, on United Nations Day the C.B.A. was in charge of preparing the Chinese culinary contribtuion and, while the actual food preparation was left to the skills of the Chinese Women's New Life Movement, most important officials were sure to make an appearance. The C.B.A. has also helped to boost attendance at the California Exposition, held annually in August by presenting a Chinese fashion show with music provided by the drum and bugle corps. The C.B.A. also contributes regularly to the City Crusade and to the city's Flower Festival.

The proposed rebuilding of Chinatown directly involves the Chinese community and the Valley City Redevelopment Agency. During one open meeting, a heated argument ensued over a Caucasian restauranteur's refusal to sell his property or remodel it to blend with the Chinese architectural motif. A spokesman for the C.B.A., after patiently waiting to be recognized, stood up and remarked:

> This is intolerable. Either he conform or sell his property or everyone will pull out. That's it, we will all leave and there will be nothing. It would be improper to have that building in our Chinatown.

The agency was impressed and the matter was resolved in favor of the Chinese demand. Though it is questionable that the gentleman had the authority to speak for the entire Chinese community in this matter, the Chinese were able to accomplish their goal by acting as a cohesive unit and by presenting a united front to outsiders.

While many modernists and practically all activists do not recognize the authority of the C.B.A. to speak for them and to represent them in

---

[14] Lee (1960:5) remarked that local political leaders would often attend important C.B.A.-sponsored traditionist holidays, as the Double Ten Celebration and Confucius' Birthday. This may be the case for the larger Chinese communities of New York and San Francisco, but Caucasians rarely attend these functions in Valley City and those that infrequently appear are not politicians.

community affairs, these non-traditionists realize that the community at large considers the C.B.A. as a legitimate spokesman, and this organization is often allowed to represent a united Chinese community.

Participation of C.B.A. representatives in city-wide affairs is characterized by formality; the easy camaraderie and informal friendliness that are typical of interactions between Caucasians are usually lacking. Thus, relationships between C.B.A. and larger community personnel are of a secondary, rather than of a primary nature.

Relationships with other Chinese organizations in other cities are maintained through an extensive network which stretches from New York to Honolulu and from Boston to New Orleans. Ties are maintained through personal communications of families and friends but also through official channels, those of the established branches and chapters of the C.B.A. This network provides the avenues along which peoples, news, and monies travel.

The construction of a new headquarters or old-age home, the renovation and remodeling of an older building, regional events, or the addition of new business enterprises, all may require large amounts of capital. Often a single Chinese community cannot alone afford the entire cost. It is at these times that the bonds of ethnic brotherhood stretch across the country; nation-wide fund-raising, drawing upon ties of family, clan, region, language, and race, enables communities to expand their Chinese facilities and their prestige locally and across the nation.

The traditionist community in Valley City maintains amicable intercity relations by a constant exchange of local officials. Visiting usually takes place during traditional celebrations, particularly the Chinese New Year, and hardly an important event passes that does not attract dignitaries from San Francisco. Valley City's Chinese reciprocate by attending affairs in the city by the Bay. Exemplifying these ties on a personal level, one visitor from the Boston C.B.A. remarked:

No matter where I travel in this country I can always find a home and friends. There are always "cousins" to greet me and welcome me with a Chinese meal and give me lodgings. I, of course, am obligated and will take great pleasure in returning the hospitality. Our association supported the building of the new headquarters and when we need similar help we can always depend on our friends.

Cooperative association ventures, coupled with a constant interchange of personnel and monies, act to unite all Chinese in America in a pan-traditionist sodality. Each endeavor strengthens their Chinese identity, their commitment to Chinese programs and to the associations that perpetuate them.

Official ties to Chinese outside the United States and Canada are reinforced by the C.B.A.'s receptions for visiting dignitaries, actors and actresses, and cultural exchange groups from Taiwan and Hong Kong. Local Chinese leaders who visit abroad are often accorded similar treatment. On a less official level, relatives and friends crossing the Pacific, corresponding via mail, and sponsoring immigrant families in the community, reaffirm Chinese obligations. Yet, generally speaking, although expressions of friendship and cooperation with the Nationalist Taiwan Government bureaucracy are polite, they seem to lack the personal warmth and "good fellowship" characteristic of intercity visitations within the United States.

Relationships with mainland China are minimal. There is no exchange of personnel and little overt sympathy for the Communist cause.[15]

Summary

One of the most important functions of Valley City's traditionist organizations is to perpetuate and continue an allegiance to Chinese identity. The family associations may perform this function for their members, but their activities also stress individual surname loyalties and tend to divide the community. Other groups, such as the Kuomintang, the Chinese school, and the tong, cross-cut particularistic loyalties, but the Chinese Benevolent Association is the one organization that includes all Chinese traditionists, minimizing differences while stressing what is shared by all.

The traditionist community's China-orientation is evident in the activities they sponsor. They present each year a celebration of Confucius' Birthday and the Chinese Independence Day; support the Chinese language school, the Chinese drum and bugle corps, and the Sun Yat-sen Memorial Hall; and sponsor the showing of imported Chinese-language movies. They officially welcome dignitaries from

---

[15] Most traditionist and modernist informants acknowledge the nominal legitimacy of the present government in Taiwan. They rarely speak about "Red China" or a "two Chinas policy." Familiar with American anti-Communist sentiment and perhaps fearful of investigation or harassment by American agencies such as the C.I.A. or the F.B.I., they are reluctant to speak about such matters. A few activists will openly admit that they support Peiking. Chinese foreign students, on the other hand, are willing to discuss Chinese international affairs but are hesitant to commit themselves publicly to a definite position. Communist China's entry into the United Nations will be discussed in Chapter 14.

Nationalist China and from other cities in America, while sending their officials to events in other Chinese communities. They represent the Chinese at civic affairs, receptions, and parades of the larger local community.

In reference to the social organization of New York City's China-town, Heyer (1953:177) concludes:

"Their social organization has been portrayed as useful, familiar, demand-ing, an all-inclusive social matrix which has drawn the Chinese away from reliance on American society and has made possible the cultural insularity of the group."

It is apparent that Valley City's traditionist community, as well, is a self-sufficient organization complex, operating for the most part within an exclusively Chinese world.

Heyer (1953:181) and Crissman (1967:191–93) stress the segmenta-tion and autonomy of each association; to some degree this is also a valid statement for Valley City. However, just as important is the interdependence of organizational life, the overlapping and continuous officerships of key association leaders, and their joint participation in community-wide events. The traditionist world is clearly multiplex.

Yet traditionist organizations cannot and do not integrate the diverse elements of Valley City's Chinese populace. They cater largely to the elderly, the China-born, and the Chinese-speakers. Less than 5 per cent of the traditionist association leaders are members of modernist organizations. None are involved in activist affairs. The traditionist community makes few attempts to include other community segments in their activities, and overtures to other organizations involve not only unequal participation but unequal sharing of revenues and prestige. Although the C.B.A. claims to represent the entire Chinese community, its activities tend to perpetuate and emphasize the dif-ferences among the city's Chinese.

Most traditionists are only partially acculturated—that is, they have adopted only those American traits which do not threaten their Chinese identity. Adoption of intrinsic characteristics, such as a com-mitment to their host society's way of life, morality, sociability, and manner of expression, is minimal, and those traits that are adopted do not interfere with the Chinese value system. Structural assimilation is virtually unknown and the traditionist's relationship with non-Chinese Americans remains secondary.

There are, of course, those within the traditionist system who are not satisfied with maintenance of the status quo. These are, primarily, younger men who have achieved some status both within and without the Chinese community. However, their numbers are small and, because they do not hold the most important positions in associational life, they cannot make policy. In addition, conflicts within the traditionist system are minimized and rarely publicized, in order that the C.B.A. and its member organizations may present a united front to outsiders and further perpetuate the mythology of a homogeneous Chinese community.

12

Modernist Associations

MODERNISTS, AS A GROUP, reflect a cultural orientation that is contemporary, cosmopolitan, and middle-class. They are committed to, and involved in, the major activities of the Caucasian world and adhere to a life-style that is as American as it is Chinese. Were it not for prejudice and discriminatory practices on the part of the larger society, modernist groups most probably would be less numerous and would play a less significant role within the Chinese community system.

Modernists are often the sons and daughters of immigrant parents, who have been reared and educated in America; regardless of their nativity, they have been socialized primarily in the methods and manners of their Caucasian peers and they espouse an ideology that has its roots in the Protestant ethic and the spirit of capitalism. Yet they are Chinese and, as far as they themselves are concerned, are the recipients of an ancient cultural tradition which long precedes Chinese settlement in America. Sociologically more important, however, is the fact that they are full-blooded members of a visible racial-ethnic group. Thus, their organizational life reflects both their Chinese and their American minority identities.

Unlike traditionist associations, whose goals are the preservation and continuation of "traditionality" and whose organization is a product of Chinese social structure, modernist groups enter into community life by adopting the form and format of already existing American organizations. There are basically three types of modernist associations: those concerned with community service and social-political life, those related to a Christian religious identity, and those who emphasize the pursuit of recreational activities. One of the characteristics of modernist associations is the fact that the age range of the membership is more flexible than either that of the traditionist associations, which cater primarily to the elderly, or that of the activists, whose membership is made up almost exclusively of youth. Moreover, modernist groups within similar age categories have a significant number of overlapping memberships, particularly among middle-aged adults, enabling them to integrate the Chinese community more successfully than either of the other groups.

Yet modernist groups are not included in the highest level pan-community Chinese organization, the Chinese Benevolent Association. Although they may co-sponsor some community events, modernist groups, for the most part, function as distinct and separate bodies and are not generally responsive to the policies and control mechanisms of the traditionist community. There is no pan-modernist association and coordinated cooperative ventures among modernists are rare. Like the traditionist organizations, modernist activities attract a distinctive audience and, most important, provide an organizational identity for the acculturated American of Chinese descent.

To reiterate, the critical distinction that separates modernists from all others is the level of acculturation. Not only have modernists adopted the extrinsic traits of their American homeland, but they have adopted the core values, the very foundation of American intrinsic behavior. They enjoy the same experiences and look forward to the same accomplishments as their Caucasian peers. However, they do not and cannot disclaim their Chinese heritage, a Chinese identity based upon the traditions of the past and the social reality of today. Their ethnicity, then, is social and historical, and although some modernists may be unschooled in both the language and customs of their ancestral land, they are nevertheless Chinese. Being the recipients of both a Chinese and American heritage, modernists hold both Chinese and American values, and, depending upon the situation, they activate one set or the other. The holding of sometimes conflicting values is a common phenomenon among people with bi-cultural backgrounds.

The Civic Club[1]

Perhaps the most influential and best known of the modernist organizations is the Civic Club, a community service organization and the local

---

[1] The Civic Club is a pseudonym for the most prominent modernist organization in this community.

Chinese chapter in the International Association of Civic Clubs. The club was first organized in the early 1950's, when members of a Caucasian Civic Club chapter approached a group of influential Chinese businessmen and encouraged them to found a Chinese Civic Club. Organizational help was forthcoming from the San Francisco Chinatown Civic Club, and in 1954 the Valley City Civic Club was officially chartered at a 500-person banquet in one of Valley City's leading hotels.

The International Civic Club charter states that it is non-sectarian. That same ideology is formally stated in the Civic Club's brochure:

"We are a service club. Our purpose is to recognize community needs and develop means of fulfilling these needs. We are non-sectarian, non-political, and we were founded on the Golden Rule."

Yet, it is a fact that Civic Club chapters are organized upon racial and ethnic, if not religious, distinctions. The Civic Club is open to people of all races, yet fifty-two of the currently fifty-six members are of Chinese ancestry. Of the remaining four, three are Japanese and one is a Caucasian. There have never been any Mexican-American or Black members. Within the Valley City District there are "brother" Civic Clubs whose membership is overwhelmingly Black, Mexican-American, Japanese, or Caucasian. The Civic Club's members readily admit that "non-Chinese might not feel comfortable in the club," "that only Chinese seem to be really interested," and that "people of other races can join their own clubs." The four non-Chinese members, however, are not discriminated against, appear to feel comfortable among their Chinese peers, and willingly participate in most of the club's activities. Furthermore, four Chinese members of the club are married to Caucasian or Japanese wives. Thus, the Civic Club is primarily a Chinese organization and, although its activities are not restricted to the Chinese community, it alone among the many local chapters of the Civic Club sponsors Chinese community events.

The Civic Club brochure states:

"We are a group of community minded men; we are your friends. We come from all walks of life. Some of us are businessmen, though many are not. We represent a good cross-section of the community."

The social-demographic characteristics of the members, however, disclose some interesting distinctions (see Table 29). Members tend to be first-generation, native-born, business or professional people between the ages of forty and fifty-nine who live in a middle-class residential area. They are college men who, for the most part, speak English fluently and whose annual family income is over $10,000. The wives of the members exhibit similar social profiles although they are generally less educated than their husbands. Over one-third of the women are not employed.

The Civic Club appeals to men who are engaged in business and professional occupations, typically dentists, attorneys, auditors, engineers, restaurant and supermarket owners, realtors, and salesmen. Their occupations tend to bring them in touch with one another and the spirit of the club is based on their common experiences. The Civic Club is thus an organization united by a middle-class ethos and largely restricted to Chinese members. It serves as a prime example of ethnic-class grouping.

Table 29

Social-demographic Characteristics of Civic Club Members

Characteristic	Number
Nativity	
Immigrant generation	10
First-generation American-born	40
Second-generation American-born	6
Residence	
Central city	5
South area	45
Predominantly Caucasian suburb	6
Age	
Over 60	3
50–59	14
40–49	26
30–39	10
Under 30	3
Marital Status	
Widowed or divorced	3
Married	52
Single	1
Occupation	
Professionals and proprietors	47
Managerial, technical, and sales personnel	7
Other	2

Education

Post-graduate studies	10
College graduate	25
Two years college	11
High school graduate	8
Grade school graduate	2

Family Income (estimate)

Over $15,000	20
Over $10,000	30
Under $10,000	6

English-speaking Proficiency[2]

Native speaker	40
Good	12
Fair	3
Poor	1

Chinese-speaking Proficiency[3]

Native speaker	10
Good	12
Fair	19
Poor	15

Membership in the Civic Club is voluntary. Theoretically, any male person may indicate a desire to join, but since new initiates must be sponsored by members, they are most often introduced to the club by friends and business acquaintances. While membership crosscuts traditional Chinese divisions of surname, language, and territorial identities, it does so only for a segment of the community, attracting, for the most part, business and professional people and catering to persons with an American middle-class background and ideology.

Officers include a president, three vice-presidents, a secretary, a treasurer, and other minor positions, some of which are traditional for all Civic Club chapters. There is a fourteen-member board of direc-

[2] The judgments were made by this observer based upon the following criteria:
Native Speaker: Indistinguishable from American English speaker.
Good: Speaks with slight but noticeable accent; proper use of idiomatic expressions.
Fair: Speaks with heavy accent; little use of idiomatic expressions; resolvable communication difficulties with American English speakers.
Poor: Speaks with very heavy accent; improper use of grammatical constructions; communications problems resolvable only with difficulty.
[3] Judgments were made by group members (native Cantonese speakers) using the same criteria as discussed in footnote 2.

tors in addition to ad hoc and standing committees. Election to office is by secret ballot and is conducted according to Robert's rules of parliamentary procedure. Officers are elected to one-year terms.

Because it is a voluntary organization, it is expected that all members play active roles and the levels of membership involvement previously discussed for traditionist associations are not applicable here. All personnel are full participating members.

Unlike the traditionist associations, where the same individuals have held office for up to twenty years, Civic Clubbers are officers for an average of about five years. It is customary to start in minor posts and then to advance to the more important official and committee positions. While the first vice-president automatically becomes the next year's president, election to other positions does not require having held office previously. Past presidents and directors are officially recognized and continue to influence club policy.

During their first year new members are generally participants only. In their second year they are usually elected or appointed to standing and ad hoc committees, and by their third year they have at least been nominated for a particular office. New members are eagerly sought and are encouraged to join in club activities. They must be sponsored by active members, a process which guarantees the new members' conformity in regard to background, orientation, goals, and values. Because of the club's emphasis on active participation, over 90 per cent of the membership has served on committees and about 40 per cent have been past officers.

This policy of admitting new members who can rapidly advance to positions of responsibility produces a continuous change in leadership. By allowing for new blood and new ideas, the club remains internally dynamic as an organization. Thus is particularly appeals to Chinese men at a time when they are advancing their own careers and becoming leaders in business and community life. In this respect it is unlike traditionist organizations, which demand years of service before admission to official position and recognition.

Like all Civic Club chapters, this Civic Club's activities reflect the major interests of its international organization—sponsoring youth speaker contests and Boy Scout troops, and fund-raising for the blind and the American Cancer Society. It also takes an active interest in Chinese affairs. In the past it has collected donations for needy Chinese families, participated in almost all of the Chinese community's fund-raising drives, and has donated both monies and materials to the Chinese community center. While it continues with these activities, it has increasingly represented itself as the sponsor of certain annual Chi nese events—"China Night," "The Chinese Cultural Revue," and, in conjunction with the C.B.A., "The Moon Festival-Beauty Pageant."

During the second week in February, shortly after the Chinese Lunar New Year, the Civic Club invites the "entire Valley City community" and the members of brother Civic Clubs throughout the area to attend China Night. It begins with a no-host cocktail hour and a banquet at a Chinese restaurant, after which guests proceed across the street to the Confucian Church for the evening's entertainment. Individual dinner reservations are made in advance at $6.00 per person and entire tables can be reserved by a Civic Club.

Both the restaurant and the Confucian Church auditorium are crowded. Over 700 are attending the festivities, over half of them Caucasians, many being Civic Club members. There are few if any Negroes or Mexican-Americans present. A Lion Dance and a Gung-Fu exhibition start the program. Miss Chinatown, Valley City is then escorted to the stage and presented with a bouquet of roses. The highlight of the evening's entertainment is a musical interpretation of the Chinese in American history by past Miss Chinatowns and former beauty queen contestants. A favorite Cantonese song represents the early Chinese immigrants. To demonstrate "merging and change," a well endowed beauty contestant sings Mondo Kane both in English and in Sze-Yap. The rest of the program reflects the modern Chinese. Selections from Flower Drum Song are followed by a rendition of "The Cruel War" to guitar accompaniment and by a modern dance number performed by the current Miss Chinatown dressed in black tights. For a finale, three Chinese beauties, in "mini cheong-sams" and known locally as "The Fortune Cookies," sing and sway to a jazz interpretation of "I Think I'm Goin' Out of My Head."

At the end, all performers appear on stage to a continuous wave of applause and call out "Gung Hay Fat Choy" (Happy New Year with Prosperity) to the audience. Door prizes are presented to the holders of winning tickets, the crowd leaves, and Chinese and Caucasian groups go their own way.

In conjunction with the Moon Festival-Beauty Pageant, yet before the crowning of the new Miss Chinatown, the Civic Club and the Chinese community present a cultural revue. The event is held in the Confucian Church.[4]

Beginning at 5:00 P.M., there is an exhibition in the gymnasium, where original Chinese paintings and silk scrolls from a San Francisco collection

---

4 The Chinese community center is often referred to as the "Confucian Church," its official title. The "church" however, functions more like a hall and is rarely associated with religious offerings or rituals.

are displayed, along with a "natural gold" collection, a historical art display, and the architects' rendering of the proposed new Chinatown complex. The last three exhibits are by courtesy of three local banks.

At this event, Chinese only slightly outnumber Caucasians. Older men wear well-tailored suits but the more youthful sport more stylish clothing. Most of the persons attending are adults rather than teen-agers or children, yet the presentation of the beauty queen contestants attracts members of the younger set. Chinese moon-cakes and tea are served, along with fried chicken and coffee, at booths manned by wives of Civic Club members. A few older people converse in Chinese but the majority of the middle-aged adults and almost all the teen-agers and children speak English. There are few elderly people present.

The celebration in the auditorium commences at 7:00 P.M. with a welcoming address in English by Dr. L., the chairman of the Moon Festival Committee and a very active Civic Clubber. A short speech, which lasts no longer than seven minutes, is delivered in Sam-Yap by the chairman of the C.B.A. His talk seems to command little attention because the audience talks throughout his short address. Entertainment consists of selections from Flower Drum Song, a Chinese dance and fashion show, two Chinese songs sung by the Drama Club, a Lion Dance, and finally a Gung-fu demonstration highlighted by a solo performance by a seventy-year-old Chinese master from a nearby community. At 10:00 P.M. the event ends, although by that time most of the Chinese audience have already left.

The Civic Club maintains its ties with the International Association of Civic Clubs by sending members to national and district meetings, by arranging exchange meetings and dinners with other area Civic Clubs, and by participating in the service and charitable activities of the parent organization. However, in contrast with the stated purpose of the club to participate in both the Chinese and the American communities, the club appears to be primarily concerned with projects related to the Chinese community.

The reasons for joining the Civic Club vary, but they almost always reflect the individual's Chinese and American identities. One past president states:

As my business ventures grew and as I became successful, I knew I was making it. But I never felt really secure with my Caucasian colleagues. I remember one day when my office mates went to play golf at a country club which discriminates against Orientals. I joined the Civic Club soon after that incident because it gave me the opportunity to be with Chinese friends and to belong to a group that was really American.

This concern with a dual identity is also noticeable in a newcomer's statement:

> I had recently arrived in Valley City when one of the officers invited me to a Civic Club meeting. At first I was hesitant because I do not want to restrict myself to only Chinese. But I soon learned that I shared a lot with other members. We are all Chinese but Americans as well. By becoming involved with this group, I am not excluding myself from the non-Chinese world.

This very real concern with maintaining ties to both the Chinese and American communities is almost a preoccupation with today's Chinese adults, as much a concern as it was for their counterparts during transitional times. In former times, however, there were few organizations specifically designed to accommodate the syncretic blending of aspirations.

At the risk of being repetitive, it is necessary to emphasize once again the problems inherent in maintaining a Chinese-American identity. Civic Clubbers are adults, successful in their careers, who have, through their education, occupation, and residence, validated their status as middle-class Americans. For the most part, they are covertly discriminated against in Valley City's older and established civic organizations and, even when they are accepted as members, feel ill at ease as the "token Oriental."

As Chinese they are concerned with their local Chinese community and with the Chinese image, particularly the image they project to the outside world. Participating in the traditionist associations does not appeal to them, as they often cannot easily become members of the inner circle of decision-makers and because the traditionist associations are too preoccupied with perpetuating a Chinese identity that has its roots in China, rather than reflecting the contemporary situation.

It is not easy to fit as equals into the Chinese and American cultural worlds at the same time, and some Civic Clubbers may delude themselves into thinking that they really belong. One former Civic Club member stated:

> By catering to Chinese members the club has prevented my integration into the country of my birth. If I really wanted to belong, I should have joined a Caucasian Civic Club.

Nevertheless, the Civic Club not only provides a significant segment of the Chinese population with an opportunity to express both their Chinese and American heritage but allows them, through their organization, to gain a reputation in the Caucasian world as well. It enables Chinese to keep a foot in both camps—to join contemporary society by establishing secondary relationships with the dominant Caucasian yet to retain close primary relationships with their Chinese comrades.

The dual allegiance to a Chinese and American identity, a recurring theme for modernist groups, is dramatized to some degree at Civic Club functions but is perhaps most evident at their regular meetings. A description of a typical meeting follows.

On the second Thursday in January, 1969, the Civic Club gathers for one of its semi-monthly meetings. The meeting takes place in the banquet room of a Chinese restaurant in the Central City area, where the Civic Club has met since its inception. This Cantonese restaurant is a favorite place for family association celebrations but during the week it is also frequented by non-Chinese blue-collar workers.

The members park their late-model cars, climb a flight of wooden stairs, and enter the banquet room, in which four tables are set for dinner. An International Civic Club rostrum is flanked on either side by an American and a Civic Club flag. Two Speaker's Committee members greet the entrants, collect dues and dinner money, and are busy handing out questionnaires designed to gather information on the reaction to the guest speakers. As the members arrive, they greet each other enthusiastically, jokingly engage in animated conversation, handshaking, and back-slapping. Most of the men are dressed in dark business suits with white shirts, but a few sport more casual dress without ties. Many wear their Civic Club vests under their jackets. The conversation is almost always in English and ranges from television, sports, and past experiences to club or community concerns. Some members are concerned about faltering attendance at meetings and make calls to absent members. There is apparently substantial social pressure placed upon individuals to attend and members may be fined for missing too many meetings.

At about 7:30 the meeting officially begins. The president takes his place at the rostrum and individual members lead the group in singing "America," and in reciting the Pledge of Allegiance to the Flag and a short Christian prayer of thanks. The president makes some in-group remarks and introduces as his guest a Caucasian Civic Clubber from a chapter in a nearby city. A member is applauded for having been elected to the vice-presidency of a local bank and another member is singled out for nomination as Civic Clubber of the Year for the district. His nomination draws many jovial remarks. After a family-style, five-course Chinese dinner for the thirty-two members and their guests, two newcomers are introduced, a pathologist and a local businessman. Miss Chinatown, Valley City is a guest; she arrives late, escorted by the club's only bachelor, a fact that provokes much laughter and some friendly ridicule.

The speaker for the evening is a recently elected congressman from the southern portion of the state. He speaks about his Chinese ancestry and the contributions the Chinese have made to America, a topic that draws comments of approval and some applause from the audience. His speech is spiced with sexual and comical references and provokes much laughter. Some members ask him about campus dissidents; his reply castigates their often violent activities. He is also distressed that taxpayers have to support welfare recipients and he firmly supports the Governor's "creative society." His speech is enthusiastically applauded.

Miss Chinatown is then presented with a recognition plaque, receives a kiss from the president, and is photographed with the guest speaker and other members. (The Civic Club yearly sponsors the Miss Chinatown beauty pageant.) Announcements follow. Members are reminded that they will receive tickets to an event sponsored by the C.B.A., that there will be a no-host cocktail party preceding the annual "China Night" affair, and that a county-wide meeting of the Civic Clubs will be held next month.

The vice-president leads the members in "God Bless America" and at 9:45, except for an eight-member planning committee who remain, the meeting adjourns.

The most striking impression made by this meeting is the fact that, aside from the Oriental faces in the audience and the setting in a Chinese restaurant, it is indistinguishable from a meeting of any American service organization. The symbolic referents—flag, rostrum, vests, patriotic signs, and pledges—are as American as baseball and apple pie. Although one youthful observer once remarked that it seems strange that Chinese adults should be singing of America as the "land where my fathers died," the attitude toward such symbolic statements is respectful and sincere. Secondly, the format of the meetings, the protocol, announcements, introductions, laughter, informality, jokes, and language—in short, both intrinsic and extrinsic signs of acculturation—are evident. Except for a few specific mentions of local Chinese events, there are no indications that the Civic Club is a predominantly Chinese group. The speaker's presentation and the questions following are of contemporary relevance and usually express the viewpoints of typical conservative, middle-class Americans. Most speakers are successful American businessmen and professionals. When the club invited a

Black educator one evening, his comments about discrimination and Black militancy were not appreciated. Most members expressed the view that the way to succeed was through hard work and not confrontations.

In contrast to traditionist organizations, the format of these meetings suggests the strong desire of the Capitol Civic Club to become involved in the processes of middle-class American life rather than to emphasize their Chinese identity in their organization's aims. One officer, speaking for the organization, states:

> Look, you see we are Chinese. Of course we are concerned about our Chinese people and about the problems in Chinatowns. We joined the club because we wanted to work with our Chinese cousins. But we are also Americans. Many of us fought for the United States armed forces and are still in the reserves. We don't want to shut ourselves off from America.

Yet there are also indications that the group is well aware and proud of its Chinese status. The restaurant where the club meets is known for Cantonese cookery. The clubbers relish their Chinese dinner and attack each course with a pleasure and a style that reflect a long-standing familiarity with Chinese dining. As Lee (1960:247) remarks: "Food habits are ingrained from childhood and persist to a remarkable degree."

The meeting is conducted in English, the language preferred for informal conversation as well. But occasionally Chinese expressions are used and, although rarely, there will be some general chatter in Cantonese. For Chinese living outside a Chinatown ghetto bilingualism is not a necessary asset and most Civic Clubbers certainly do not need a knowledge of Chinese language to conduct their business life. Still, about 80 per cent of the membership understands some Cantonese and over 60 per cent can speak it as well.

Feelings of racial and ethnic pride also attest to a Chinese-Oriental identity. Members boast about their children's accomplishments not only because it is a sign of success but because they are Chinese. When the conversation turns to Chinese culture, Chinese society, and, most particularly, to examples of how Chinese have succeeded in American life and have advanced to important positions, faces beam with pride, eyes shine, and identification is strong. Colloquial and ethnic jokes are exchanged; everyone is amused, for example, when congee (thin rice porridge) is referred to as "soul food," but one gets the impression that these references and phraseology are acceptable only when spoken by other Chinese. Moreover, conversation about other racial groups, particularly Negroes and Mexican-Americans but Caucasians as well, can be tacitly and openly derogatory and indicates strong hostile undertones.

Finally, and sociologically most important, one central fact remains. The majority of the members of the Civic Club are Chinese. While it is sometimes possible for Chinese to join equivalent white organizations, the fact that they choose to organize themselves as a separate Civic Club chapter is strong evidence that they prefer the company of their own people to mixed or predominantly non-Chinese groups.

Recreational Groups

Americans have been popularly characterized as a fun-loving people, and America, as a country where recreation is a major industry at the professional as well as at the amateur level. Thus it is not surprising that Chinese born and reared in American society should also put a premium on the pursuit of pleasurable activities.

Among Valley City's Chinese there are three organizations whose major purpose is this pursuit—the Chinese Golf Club, the Chinese Bowling Club, and the Chinese Sports Club. These groups are remarkably similar in both form and function to other recreational groups within the city, save in one important respect: Again the membership is overwhelmingly, if not exclusively, Chinese.

The Chinese Golf Club is perhaps the largest and most prestigious of these organizations, golf being a favorite pastime of business and professional people who recognize that informal contacts made on the green may lead to advantages in political and economic dealings. Although public courses are open to everyone, the membership of most of the country clubs in the area, all of which have a private golf course, seems to be exclusively Caucasian. Such clubs may disclaim any prejudice, but no Oriental families appear on their membership lists. Chinese have been invited as guests and have enjoyed both clubhouses and dining facilities, yet they have not been formally admitted as members. The formation of a Chinese Golf Club might well stem from such discriminatory practices. One Chinese golfer reports:

> Well, they will never admit it but the country clubs won't let us in. That applies to Negroes and Japanese as well. I know this is true. But I like to play golf as well as anyone so I joined the Chinese Golf Club. Sure I could make good use of the social contacts at the ———— Country Club for my business, and at one time I really wanted to join, but. . . .

Yet, should the country clubs open membership to the Chinese, it is highly probable that the Chinese Golf Club would continue to exist, because many Chinese prefer to foster intimate and primary relationships within their own ethnic group.

> I can always play at the public links, although I have to get there early and wait my turn. But I enjoy the game a lot better when I play with my Chinese friends. They are the people I grew up with and, although I do not think I am a prejudiced person, other Chinese are the only people who can really understand me.

First organized in the 1950's, ostensibly for the purpose of playing golf, the club's activities now extend beyond the course. It sponsors picnics, dinners, and other informal activities which the families of the members may attend; in an atmosphere of shared experiences, mellow memories, and Chinese foods, ties of friendship are formed and become bonds that transcend the purely recreational aspects of the game of golf. Unlike all of the organizations previously discussed, men and women have equal privileges and responsibilities as members.

Each Memorial Day the Chinese Golf Club sponsors a tournament which attracts Chinese competition from all over the west coast. Individuals representing similar Chinese clubs in Los Angeles, Stockton, San Francisco, Vancouver, and Honolulu gather and compete for prizes during the day, then dine at a catered banquet in the evening. The food is largely American fare, the band plays fox trots, waltzes, and modern American numbers, but the diners and dancers are Chinese.

Friendship, informality, and extracurricular pursuits also characterize the Chinese Bowling Club, whose members regularly compete among themselves and with other bowling league groups. Similarly, the Sports Club promotes picnics, hiking, and outdoor events. These groups also hold banquets, parties, and informal get-togethers.

All three organizations exhibit similar characteristics and overlapping memberships. Not infrequently, a sportsminded person may be a member of all three organizations; typically, the individual will belong to the Civic Club as well. The modernist character of these organizations is predicated upon the shared middle-class sociological profile of their members, as it was in the case of the Civic Club.

Multiplex relationships strengthen and reaffirm feelings of ethnic identity. In theory, they could provide the basis for a united modernist organizational complex comparable to the C.B.A. Yet these groups prefer to remain organizationally distinct.

I joined the Golf Club because I wanted to play golf. If I was a bowler, I would also join the Bowler's Club and if I was interested in community service I would be a Civic Clubber.

I am a member of both the Civic Club and the Sports Club, but they are two different groups. I joined one club for one reason and the other for reasons quite different. I don't really feel that the two groups have anything in common.

It follows from the existence of separate groups that activities that strengthen political and social effectiveness, competition, and co-operation will be minimal. The modernist community, lacking the means and methods for concerted political or social action, cannot compete with the traditionist sub-community at the same level. There is no supra-modernist organization comparable to the C.B.A. In spite of overlapping memberships, each modernist group is an autonomous club, having no official relationships with one another.

Modernists are proud that their groups are not competitive and are not involved in the petty squabbles and power-grabbing schemes they attribute to the family associations. They claim all this in-fighting gives the Chinese people a poor reputation. Because they do not want to become involved in what they consider disruptive activities, the recreational groups will not sponsor joint events with traditionist associations; although the golf club may hold a tournament during the week of the China Cultural Revue, it claims that the synchronic relationship is purely coincidental.

The Community Service Club

The Community Service Club is relatively new in Valley City. First proposed in December, 1966, and a steering committee organized in January, 1967, the club officially held its first introductory meeting in March of 1967. This club is a young adult group; though it does not restrict membership to any age group, most members are between twenty and thirty-five. In 1967 there were sixty-nine members—ten couples, thirty-one single males, and eighteen single females. By 1968 membership declined to forty-four, a loss of twenty-five; yet twelve members were new recruits, so that the total loss for the club was thirty-seven, over half the original body.

First-generation, American-born Chinese predominate; however, a few members are second-generation and some are even immigrants. Almost all are engaged in white-collar jobs, many in professional and managerial positions. English is the only language spoken at meetings.

The primary objectives of the club, as stated in its constitution, are to:

a.　develop and encourage civic consciousness.
b.　carry out programs for community betterment.
c.　cultivate leadership interest and adeptness.
d.　provide for cultural enrichment and exchange.
e.　represent the Chinese community of Valley City, as appropriate.

But the unstated aims are perhaps more significant. The club serves as a meeting place for young adults who are interested in extending their social contacts to other Chinese, seeking, more often than not, prospective dates and marital possibilities.

> I joined the club because I was lonely. I don't mix well with people and I tend to be shy. Just going to meetings gives me something to look forward to. Perhaps I can even meet a future beau.

> I like the Community Service Club because I can make new Chinese friends who are interested in the things I enjoy. I would like to meet other people too, but I feel more at ease with my own kind.

> I want to meet people and make friends with my own race. I don't care much for the old people. These are my kind.

The Community Service Club is unique in that it is the only Chinese organization designed to cater to the specific needs of this age group, and it is the only group whose de facto membership is limited to young adults. Only three male members are active in their family associations, while less than ten are also members of other modernist groups. For the majority of its members, the Community Service Club is the only affiliation with a Valley City Chinese organization.

The commitment to community service, ostensibly the reason for the club's founding, appears to be of secondary interest to its members. A club-sponsored survey indicated that 80 per cent of those returning the questionnaires favored more social activities as compared to only 20 per cent wishing to provide more service to the community. Thus, most of the club's activities are picnics, dances, outings—intra-club social and cultural functions as opposed to involvement in the community.

One of the outstanding characteristics of the Community Service Club is its members' desire to pursue the same pastimes that their Caucasian counterparts enjoy in an effort better to fit into an American rather than a Chinese world. The club provides an opportunity for Chinese to explore and expand their American identity. A China-born and China-educated member, one of the few also active in modernist affairs, states:

I have no trouble being Chinese. I speak both Mandarin and Cantonese and have gone to college in Hong Kong. But I like my adopted country and want to learn the ways of its people. This organization introduces me to Chinese people by face but Americans by heart.

An American-born member concurs:

I am a graduate student at the university. I belong to many groups but never to a Chinese one before. The Chinese clubs at school have too many foreigners and F.O.B.'s. Not like our club, which is really an American one.

As a service organization, the club runs into competitive situations with the Civic Club, whose national connections and members' professional reputations and resources make it the most influential among modernist groups. When the Civic Club invited the Community Service Club to participate in one of its events, the Community Service Club's membership voted to decline the offer, claiming that participation would not really enhance their reputation. They felt they would merely be used as "free laborers" for the event.

The club also experienced intra-organizational strife; members often could not agree on which community-centered activities should be undertaken. At one meeting they argued vociferously whether or not to extend their activities to include Chinese students at the state college and university. They finally decided to sponsor a welcome tea in September for all Chinese students but, perhaps because no one knew of existing Chinese organizations or even how many Chinese students were in school, the event never materialized. When the drum and bugle corps was raising funds for new uniforms, the club decided to contribute $25.00, but only after lengthy discussion on both the amount to contribute and whether there should be a contribution at all. Of the thirty-three members present at that meeting, only fifteen bothered to vote. Moreover, the club decided not to duplicate traditionist association activities and not to participate officially in traditionist events, although they would occasionally use the Confucian Church facilities for meetings.

Although parties and outings were popular, attendance at monthly meetings steadily declined and some members stopped coming altogether. Factions developed within the club as its original intent to serve the community was challenged by those who preferred a more social orientation. Its demise can be attributed to a general lack of interest in the service aspect. By 1969, only two years after it was founded, the club was clearly floundering. Yet the friendships formed did not dissolve nor did the desire to maintain Chinese social contacts. The result was the formation of a new organization, the Chinese Ski Club, whose purpose was clearly the enjoyment of skiing, camaraderie and good fellowship. It is apparent that the initial high interest in the club was based upon its appeal as a meeting ground for young adults who preferred to establish social contacts and intimate relationships with other Chinese, a need that was not at that time met by any other organization.

Other modernist Chinese groups in the area include both an American Legion post and a Veterans of Foreign Wars post, a Chinese Democratic Club and a Chinese Republican Club, and a Chinese Retail Food Merchants Association. These organizations are similar in form and function to the Civic Club and the recreational groups. They have their counterparts in similar non-Chinese clubs throughout the country and appeal largely to the middle-class portion of the Chinese community who are not active members of traditionist associations.

Organization and Identity

As Chinese acculturation progresses, the desire and need to participate in the many and diverse aspects of American economic and social life will increase. But as long as discriminatory practices against the Chinese people continue and as long as Chinese prefer to share camaraderie and fellowship with other Chinese, modernist groups will persist and flourish, for such organizations perform two functions which particularly suit the Chinese minority. First, they enable them to participate in the activities of their American experience. Secondly, by forming exclusive ethnic groups, they lessen the risk of rebuff from the dominant society and continue to emphasize ethnic solidarity at the primary level.

Each group's desire to maintain its autonomy within the Chinese community rather than join with other modernist groups may well stem partly from the concern of its members to maintain a dual identity. On one hand, members do not wish to advertise their Chinese distinctiveness. Thus, they may insist that their organization is a sports club or a political club and that the fact that they are all Chinese is of secondary importance. On the other hand, they are proud of their Chinese heritage and eager to demonstrate that as American-born *Chinese* they can be part of the American social system.

From the above descriptions it is quite evident that those events sponsored by modernist organizations sharply contrast with those presented by traditionist associations. The following comparison of traditionist and modernist functions explicates significant differences:

TRADITIONIST

Event orientation is directed toward a Chinese past by the celebration of both traditional and Nationalist Chinese holidays. Except in the showing of Chinese movies, events are formal and proper but programs tend to be lengthy. They are geared to remind a Chinese audience of their ancestral heritage. They are ineffectively publicized in both the Chinese and American press.

These functions attract an almost exclusively Chinese audience, particularly middle-aged and elderly adults, and usually include the traditionist leaders. Mature and young adults who attend are most likely China-born and frequently newly arrived immigrants. Teen-agers, adults, and elderly people are usually dressed in conservative but out-of-style clothing. Very young children and infants are often present at these functions, particularly the Chinese movies. All persons attendant are conversant in Cantonese, the primary language spoken at these activities. Attendance at traditionist events, excluding movies, is small, generally less than 200. There are few if any decorative props and admission charges or donations are minimal. The Chinese national anthem usually precedes the event.

MODERNIST

Events focus upon a Chinese identity but are presented in a modern American idiom. The programs are usually well organized and appeal to non-Chinese as well. The atmosphere is friendly and casual and the events are well publicized in the American news media. The audience is composed of both Chinese and Caucasians, generally middle-class professionals and businessmen, and include the modernist leaders. Middle-aged, mature, and young adults are in the majority, few elders or teen-agers are present, and young children and infants are rarely seen. Those that attend are usually well dressed. English is the primary language spoken by all. Attendance often exceeds 500 persons, and props, lighting, musical accompaniment, and decorations are common. Admission charges tend to be relatively substantial.

An analysis of these differences is important because it provides criteria which are useful as indicators of assimilation. The following characteristics are applicable not only to the modernist Chinese community in Valley City but may also serve as indices of the acculturation process for any minority group anywhere:

1. The dominant language replaces the minority language, not only as the language of the presentation but also as the primary language of the audience.
2. The majority of the audience and leadership exhibit sociological characteristics that correspond to those of the dominant society.
3. The content and format of the program are geared to appeal to, and reinforce, an orientation that is characteristic of the dominant society rather than the minority group.

The Chinese-Christian Church

Chinese-Christian churches may be viewed as another institutional aspect of Chinese life in America and, as such, are both a reflection and a consequence of the effects of Chinese acculturation in America. These churches are clearly modernist institutions. Their purpose, to engage their congregation in a Christian life and to provide for their spiritual and social needs, results in an involvement with western philosophical tradition and the American way of life and at the same time de-emphasizes China-centered traditionalism. In both attitude and behavior the church parallels other modernist institutions; although there are differences in personnel, ideology, and activities among these churches and although some may utilize the Chinese language, all espouse a western-Christian-American outlook and are almost exclusively Chinese in membership.

There are presently five Chinese-Christian churches in Valley City.[5] There is little, if any, cooperation between churches, each regarding itself as an independent unit tied more to a national denominational hierarchy than to the Chinese community. They are not a part of the traditionist sub-community and are not represented in the C.B.A., but they are not considered a challenge to the traditionist power structure. Although some traditionist leaders retain their suspicions about Christianity, some prominent members of the family associations are also nominal churchgoers, and most leaders appear to be unconcerned with church activities.

---

[5] These churches are all of Protestant denominations: Methodist, Reformed Church of America, Baptist, Southern Baptist, and Gospel Mission.

Members of modernist organizations are also respected church members and often serve on church committees. Although there is considerable membership overlap, however, churches do not co-sponsor events with Chinese modernist groups, nor do they support modernist activities.

Although the churches have made no effort to be formally represented within Chinese community structure, they do crosscut age, sex, and generation categories to unite, if only temporarily and religiously, these diverse community groupings. The churches, therefore, have the potential for integrating a heterogeneous Chinese population. But, by providing separate activities and, in some cases, separate services for Chinese and English speakers as well as for different age groups, the Chinese churches reflect and perpetuate distinction within the community, adding a religious dimension to ethnic-class divisions. These divisions become apparent from the following description of two Sunday morning church services:

1. The G. Church was established twenty-four years ago, but the small and dilapidated building cannot provide facilities for the entire congregation, so that on warm Sunday mornings classes are held in the adjacent park where small groups of students sit and listen to Sunday school teachers.

   Three separate services are held simultaneously. In the basement kindergarten through sixth grade children lock hands and sing hymns, led by a white teacher and accompanied by a thirteen-member all-girl choir which also makes appearances at the other two services. The children are dressed neatly but many are in hand-me-downs and inexpensive clothing. Behind closed doors on the second floor elderly and mature China-born men and women listen to a youthful Chinese speaker who reads and explains a Biblical passage in Sze-Yap while they copy a lesson written in Chinese characters on the blackboard. The third floor holds the largest congregation, primarily high school and college age youth. Although bilingual hymnals are available, the Chinese reverend conducts services in English, and many of the youth have their own Bibles in which significant passages have been underlined. The services and sermon are of a fundamentalist nature, stressing life in the next world, the mystical experience of conversion, and accepting Jesus as a personal savior.

   Many parishioners prepare home study Bible lessons, printed in both Chinese and English. They attend prayer meetings on Wednesday evenings and most young adherents attend the many religious-social activities, which include retreats, Bible classes, church rallies, suppers, clean-up parties, and outings. Services can best be characterized as emotional and sincere, and it is not uncommon for somebody to suddenly stand up and "proclaim his love for Christ." Informal conversation also revolves around religious motifs. Although the more youthful speak English, they are also conversant in Cantonese. Many of the adults are immigrants who work in Chinese establishments or in canneries at laboring and semi-skilled jobs. They are, as a rule, poorly educated in both English and Chinese, and some of the women speak but few English words.

Services usually are concluded with communion, and the collection plates are filled with numerous but small contributions.

2. Sunday school classes in the C. Church are held in a single-story building adjacent to the main chapel of modern design. They are small in number and often poorly attended. Few teen-agers, high school, or college age students attend Sunday school and the classes are primarily for the younger grades. The service, in English, lasts only one hour and is presented in a dignified and aloof manner by a youthful China-born minister. Parishioners may be characterized as middle-class and middle-aged, employed in professional, managerial and technical occupations. They are well dressed, particularly the women, and all contribute generously to the collection. Attendance is irregular, save for major church days like Easter Sunday, and when the members attend church services their attitude tends to be perfunctory and unemotional.

Each Chinese-Christian church appeals to a different segment of Chinese-American society, primarily on the basis of social class. The church becomes but one more facet of their American experience. The more affluent and acculturated view religion as do many of their American peers—as a social institution with little emphasis upon religious doctrine. The less acculturated and often less educated prefer the company of their social peers and, as characteristic of working-class peoples, enjoy a fundamental, emotional, and more dogmatic approach to religious practice.

One fact of particular interest is the large numbers of youth who attend the more fundamentalist churches. Their religious zeal appears to be real, and conversion to this brand of Christianity seems sincere. Their emotional, as opposed to an intellectual, approach to religion enables them more easily to identify with their church community, particularly because it demands little acculturative sophistication. For many youngsters who, because of their education and background, are unable to participate fully in American community living, the church becomes the only entry into the dominant society, providing them with social and spiritual comforts they cannot achieve elsewhere.

None of these churches overtly challenges Chinese polytheistic, syncretic, or nativistic beliefs or practices. The more fundamentalist groups look with suspicion upon heathens as well as members of other churches, but they do not openly express these sentiments; it is entirely possible that a zealous convert may appeal to "Chinese gods" in the privacy of his own home. The Chinese Church demonstrates a remarkable denominational flexibility and thus can appeal to both modernists and traditionists.

> I am from China. I believe in my ancestors and in their ways of life. But I am Christian too and both ways are good.

The more liberal churches also focus their sermons upon after-life and Christian spirit. They rarely discuss contemporary concerns dealing with youth, sex, drugs, or minority problems, except in passing. As a matter of fact, sermons rarely include references to China or to problems relevant to the Chinese community in America. Without a look at the Oriental faces in the pews, it would be impossible to conclude that this was an exclusively Chinese congregation.

In summary, the growth of the Chinese-Christian church can be viewed as an indication of the increasing acculturation of the Chinese populace. Participating in church affairs is an involvement in American society. Secondly, the diversity of these churches is evidence of the heterogeneity of the Chinese community itself, and individual churches seem to intensify age, generational, and cultural differences. Thirdly, the fact that there are churches which cater to exclusively Chinese congregations indicates the failure of Chinese structural assimilation in religious activity. Finally, these churches are less a part of community social organization than are traditionist and other modernist groups, because they are not involved in major Chinese community programs and events.

Modernist Youth Groups

Most Chinese youth organizations appear to be restricted to high school and college campuses and they include both the native- and foreign-born students. The majority of Chinese college students, however, are not members of Chinese clubs. Chinese students usually spend their time in purely academic pursuits and not a few find social outlets in other college-related groups and activities. It can be estimated that no more than 5 per cent of the Chinese student population are members of Chinese clubs.

There are two such groups within the Valley City area, one at the junior college and one at the state University. They can be considered modernist groups because their major activities and goals are centered around social and recreational pleasures and experiences and are similar to those of other college fraternal or social organizations.

Because of their collegiate focus, these clubs are largely restricted to students. Ages range from seventeen to twenty-five and membership is extended equally to females and males. The clubs confine their activities to planning picnics, parties, and dances. Occasionally they may hold a "Chinese food sale" and may contribute their time and talent to a school-sponsored "cultural review," but their contribution rarely exceeds the lending of authentic Chinese "artifacts" and costumes or, on occasion, a demonstration of Chinese music and dance. Both clubs have but few foreign-born members and almost all of their members who are not native-born have resided in America for many years. The primary, and usually the only, language spoken at meetings and events is English.

Although the structure and functioning of these modernist youth groups could be more fully discussed, the Chinese youth groups on college campuses are rapidly changing their format and are becoming involved increasingly in ethnic studies programs, activities, and events which will drastically change their social motives and cultural outlook. This phenomenon, which has its immediate origins in the late 1960's and promises to grow in the 1970's, has already radicalized student youth groups and has transformed modernist youth organizations into activist groups, the subject material of the next chapter.

13

Activists

IN ORDER TO UNDERSTAND the Chinese activist movement, it is necessary to pay attention to similar movements among other minority peoples and to the widespread phenomenon known popularly as "youth culture." Of paramount importance is the emergence of an attitude toward ethnicity and race which now emphasizes overt pride in color and culture, so that catch-all slogans equivalent to "Black power" and "Black is beautiful" can easily be applied to other minorities as well.

Just as significant is a host of youth attitudes and behavior toward the established political-social regime. These attitudes can be characterized as disenchantment, disappointment, and often disgust with the policies of the American bureaucracy concerning domestic and foreign issues, in particular the Southeast Asian War, pollution, poverty, morality, and racism.

It is these forces that are directly and indirectly responsible for: (1) A reassessment by racial minorities of their image vis-à-vis the dominant Caucasian society and vis-à-vis each other, and (2) the development of organizations, mainly on college campuses, dedicated to changing that image—i.e., the activists.

In Valley City, as elsewhere, priority was assigned to changing the stereotyped image of Orientals, and to that end a change in name was deemed essential. The impetus came from a local Oriental group whose sentiments were expressed in the following way:

"What is the difference, if any, between the terms Oriental and Asian American?

"We realize that almost 95% of the Orientals on campus have used or are still using the term Oriental to describe themselves as a racial group. To most American people, this term has stereotype images—e.g. the sexy Susie Wong, the wily Charlie Chan, and the evil Fu Manchu. To many of us in the Oriental community, we have our own interpretations which differ markedly from that which the majority of the Americans believe. To us an Oriental signifies the quiet, studious, hard-working, generally intelligent individual but who has group apathy. He doesn't care about making waves even though he may be right. He blames the 'establishment' or American society in a subtle way—he resigns himself and accepts his fate—no questions asked. In contrast, what is an Asian American? An Asian-American is an Oriental born or raised exclusively in America—but with one difference. He gives a damn about his life, his work, his beliefs, and is willing to do almost anything to help Orientals become Asian-Americans. In recent years, the term Asian-Americans has been connected with the Third World Liberation Front. Black Student Union, Asian-American Political Association, and other militant organizations that justifies violence —things that are against most Orientals' concept of morality. We also believe in non-violence and to date we have followed this principle. We hope you can be proud some day of the term Asian-American" (Bulletin of the Oriental Student Association, 1969).

This new terminology, Asian-American, is a significant departure from traditionist and modernist Chinese terms because it recognizes the ascendancy of Asian solidarity over Chinese exclusivity. It denies the long-standing historical-cultural divisions that have characterized Asians in America by appealing to what they share—a history of racial discrimination. This is not meant to be a denial of, for example, a Chinese or a Japanese heritage, but it implores Chinese to join with Japanese, Filipino, Koreans, and other "Orientals" in a new solidarity based upon their racial commonality.

In both theory and practice, this Asian unity must be considered a success among activists. There are definite signs of structural assimilation at the primary group level. Asian-American college youth not only cooperate in academic programs but also in social activities including parties, dances, friendship, and dating. The muting of Asian cultural and ethnic divisions by these youth distresses their parents, who, more often than not, have supported these divisions for most of their life. Though some admonish their children for their disregard of ethnic exclusivity, they find it difficult to control their social life. Furthermore, peer group pressure often appears stronger than familial demands. As one Asian-American of Chinese descent claims:

My parents mean well and I try to respect them, but they do not understand what it's all about. We have buried the old hatreds between Chinese and Japanese, and my friends and I must go beyond our parents' "hang-ups." My mother is upset because I am engaged to a Japanese girl but she knows she can do nothing about it.

If traditionist and modernist parents feel threatened by Chinese-Japanese "togetherness," they are even more disturbed about their children's attitude toward other non-whites, particularly Negroes. The philosophy of the movement preaches universal brotherhood and, in particular, a brotherhood of all the oppressed peoples of the world. This spirit demands that Asian-American activists establish a positive relationship with America's dominant minority, the Blacks, and to a lesser extent with Mexican-Americans (Chicanos) and Indians (native-Americans). Cooperation is necessary for practical reasons as well, particularly for the funding and organization of ethnic study programs at Valley State University, a major activist concern. Not all Asian activists, however, are satisfied with this "marriage of convenience." Some are disillusioned by violent public demonstrations and many do not approve of the militant stance taken by their "Black Brothers." Activist leaders, on the other hand, recognize the necessity of co-operation and joint involvement.

Look, maybe I don't really want to be caught up in the Black revolution but people listen to Blacks. Without them and the Chicanos, our demands would go unheeded. If it wasn't for them, there would be no ethic studies program. Besides, they have taught us how to get the establishment to listen to us.

Yet Asian-Black-Chicano togetherness is by and large limited to secondary relationships at the organizational level. Some real friendships do develop, but mixed parties and interracial dating leading to structural assimilation at the primary level are rare. Nevertheless, the activists are the only sub-group within the Chinese community who have established working relationships with other non-whites, a practice often shocking to both traditionists and modernists and one which has accentuated the differences and widened the gulf between the activists and the ethnic groups from which they have emerged.

Activists at Valley State University are few in number, and fewer than fifty of the 300-odd Americans of Asian descent are members of the activist group. Asian foreign students generally shun activist identification and have formed their own organization (see Chapter 11).

Structurally, the activist group is composed of various committees concerned with communications, service, social action, etc., each headed by an elected chairman. It is in the Executive Steering Committee, however, that all final decisions are made. Members of this committee are chosen because of their participation in activist activities, "informally selected according to their interest and involvement," as is stated in their constitution. It is this small group which plans and initiates all activist functions. In 1969 there were ten members of the Executive Steering Committee, of whom two designed and administered a questionnaire to all committee members. The following is a synopsis of the results:

The average age of the leaders is 23.2 years; nine are single and one is married. Five are graduate students, two are seniors, and two are classified as juniors. Almost all are enrolled in social science programs, primarily education and social work, and those who are still undergraduates plan to attend graduate school. Linguistically, seven of the ten claim to understand an Asian language although only three can speak that language well. Their families average annual income is $7,500 and at least half of the fathers are employed in low-status occupations such as restaurant workers, clerks, and laborers. Mothers, when employed, are apt to hold seasonal part-time jobs. Regarding nativity, one leader has native-born grandparents, six have native-born parents, one is native-born of foreign-born parents, and two are foreign-born but have lived in America for over ten years.

Thus far, the profile of activist leaders does not substantially differ from that of non-activist Orientals, but there are some additional characteristics which differentiate this group significantly from all others.

All of the leaders have participated in campus demonstrations and feel that their education is largely irrelevant. They are convinced that racism is ingrained in American society and eight claim to have personally experienced discrimination in the past two years. Those who hold multiple memberships belong to other politically oriented Asian organizations. Practically all of them have dated members of other minority groups, including Blacks, and, while they prefer marriage with a member of their ethnic bloc, marriage is not rated as high among their personal goals as political and social reform. Seven of the ten claim to have tried some kind of drug, usually marijuana. As far as their personal philosophy is concerned, all leaders claim a liberal orientation. Three consider themselves radicals.

One important activist concern is the Asian component of the Ethnic Study Center at Valley State University, established in 1969 to coordinate Black, Mexican-American, American Indian, and Asian-American studies. Activist leaders are substantially involved in the development of Asian-American courses and play an important role in the design, content, and implementation of these courses. As a group, they must approve a course before it can be considered appropriate for Asian-American studies, and they will often question an instructor's suitability.[1] An Asian faculty member officially directs the program, but the students more often than not decide upon policy.

In addition to, and in conjunction with, the Ethnic Studies Program, the activists have established an English tutorial service for immigrants and foreign students, provide volunteer interpreter service for persons who have difficulty with the English language, recruit disadvantaged Oriental students for an educational opportunities program, plan cultural programs, provide speakers, run workshops, and organize Oriental art and culinary displays.

However, only the leaders and a few followers are consistently active in such endeavors. Moreover, activist activities rarely include other than college-age youth. For example, in April, 1970, a University-wide cultural program titled "Asian Perspective 70" featured a nationally known Chinese-American authoress. Her lectures were held on campus only during the day; most of the resident Chinese community were unable to attend. One leader, when questioned about her schedule, exclaimed, "Gee, we never considered an evening lecture. I guess we didn't think of the Chinese in town."

Generally speaking, the college campus seems to be more sympathetic and receptive to activist programs than does the Chinese community. Many California universities, colleges, junior colleges, and a few high schools support Asian-American activist groups. Although their official titles, slogans, and degrees of militancy vary, their programs are similar. Leaders meet at conferences and other activities, and coordinated programs and protests are becoming increasingly common, but at this time most groups are preoccupied with developing their indigenous format.

Conflict Without Compromise

It is not only their organizational alliance with activist Black and Chicano groups which has estranged the Chinese activists from the

---

[1] The Ethnic Studies Center offers but few courses. Most courses are offered by individual academic departments. Activists are concerned about instructors who, they feel, are either prejudiced, poorly prepared in subject areas, or not in sympathy with activist aims. If they feel a course—titled, for example The Asian Experience in America—offered by such a person is not compatible with their ideas and ideals, they will not consider that course part of the ethnic studies curriculum. The course, however, may still be offered in an academic department.

established traditionist and modernist organizations of the Chinese community. Strained relationships and poor communications also stem from conflicting ideologies, partially a product of the difference in age makeup, activists being under thirty, but more substantially due to cultural divergence.

Reared in America, activists are heavily influenced by the American youth culture, one of whose major tenets is a rejection of the values of their forefathers. Among Chinese activists this criticism takes two major forms. First, activists claim that former generations have been "whitewashed" to the extent that their experiences of prejudice and discrimination have been deleted from history. In their opinion, the reluctance of their parents to face racism as it exists today stems from their past refusal to openly discuss and publicize such actions. They often accuse their parents of being "Chinese Uncle Toms" who seem to be satisfied with an almost white rather than a yellow identity. Secondly, they feel that both traditionist and modernist organizations spend too much time and money furthering their own ends at the expense of the Chinese community as a whole and that these groups have done little to improve social conditions for the Chinese, particularly the immigrant poor. The result: estrangement from, and mistrust of, Chinese community leadership, leading to relationships characterized by hostility and suspicion.

At the organizational level there have been few cooperative activities, jointly sponsored events, or official channels of communication between adult traditionist and activist groups. Nor are any of the above seriously contemplated, though both groups believe each could benefit from cooperative endeavors. When activists solicited the support of a traditionist group they failed, and some traditionists expressed the following opinions:

They make friends with anyone. Don't they know there are some races you just can't trust?

These people are not all bad. I believe we need young blood to help us grow. After all, they are educated and can help us, but they do not understand respect.

On the other hand, when the Chinese Benevolent Association planned a community fund-raising campaign, activists stayed home and claimed:

What, help them raise money? For whom? A clique of old men who have everything anyway, too much. Do you know what they will do with their money? Build another hall and exploit the poor some more or gamble it away.

> How can we be expected to work with them? They will want to tell us what to do and how to do it. All they want is free labor.

> I asked my father what this money is for. He tells me it is for China. I never heard of anything so ridiculous.

At this point it is difficult to assess the nature of the activist-traditionist dialogue. Verbal abuse is common for both groups, as are sloganeering and emotionality. Relationships between the groups, when indeed relationships can be said to exist, are characterized by generational mistrust and a cultural disparity over propriety and priorities that do not easily lead to cooperative endeavors.

In their attempt to marshall financial and verbal support for an Asian-American ethnic studies program, activist leaders addressed the Civic Club. What follows is one young leader's impression:

> We were politely received and, because everyone understood English, they listened. I could sense, though, a feeling of tension in the air. It was as if they really did not want to hear some of the things we said. Like when we talked about the struggle of all minority peoples, they wanted to separate the Chinese from everyone else. When I mentioned that we Chinese had, in the past, profited from exploiting Chinese immigrants, they didn't want to believe it, although they knew it had been true. I don't know if they really understand what ethnic studies are all about. Some of them think that we should study Chinese culture and learn the language but that we should keep out of politics.

> When I introduced one of my friends, they were nervous because he had a beard and long hair, but they did listen. That is more than I can say for some of the families [traditionist family associations]. Many of them wished us good luck with our program, but they didn't offer us any financial help or any real encouragement. I can't really blame them. They all have good jobs and they don't want to get involved in anything controversial. I was angered, however, when one man asked, "Does the University know what you are doing?" How naive.

Civic Club response to the talk ranged from moderate support to outright disapproval. One officer mentioned what seemed to be a unanimous concern:

> What we question is the need for such programs. The Chinese have always done well in school and business and in professional careers. We have thusly gained the respect of the white race. What good does it do to talk about discrimination? We all know what it was like. Why bring it up again?

It appears, then, that the activist organization, its programs and its goals, have little appeal to either the traditionist or the modernist elements within the Chinese community. The reasons are many and varied and are heavily influenced by age, generation, and cultural outlook. They are also concurrently influenced by the acculturation process, activists being most acculturated. Activist involvement in social-political movements is a strong indication of their involvement not only into the greater American society but into the sub-system specific for youth. It is particularly in this arena that activists differ from modernists in their view of security, racism, and society.

Chinese modernists, as a group, are neither secure in their status as Americans nor in their relationship to other Americans. They are overly concerned that they will be subject to the prejudice of this society if they do not blend into the American setting. They tend to think themselves as Chinese who are living just like successful Caucasians. They are often hostile to persons of Negro and Mexican-American ancestry and feel that the other minorities should work hard, should follow the Chinese example. They are also willing to work for change but within the established bureaucratic-governmental system. They rarely encourage dissent.

Activists are equally insecure about their status as Chinese in America. They are greatly concerned with the Japanese experience in World War II and are fearful of a similar experience should a confrontation with China occur. Yet, unlike modernists, they do not wish to blend into the American society. They are Chinese, Asians, a Third World "colored minority." They see discrimination against any minority as a disaster for all and preach "togetherness" with Blacks and Browns. They join other campus militants in demonstrations and put less, rather than more, faith in our present social system.

Activist Philosophy and the Search for Legitimacy

Asian activist philosophy is similar to the philosophies of other radical and revolutionary movements, and is not ordinarily a part of the academic traditionality of most of our collegiate institutions. While there may be less agreement concerning specific goals and means, most activist programs appear committed to, at least, a general policy. These aims are:

1. Self-determination for all Asians.
2. That the Asian-American is best suited to assess and to deal with the needs of Asian-Americans. Programs are to be designed,

run, and taught by Asian students and academic institutions must respond to these programs.

3. Programs must have a strong community-oriented focus in which actual community work is stressed.
4. The plight of Asian-Americans and of all minority peoples is a direct result of racism which must be exposed and eliminated.

These statements affect both the nature of academic instruction and community involvement.

The courses offered under the umbrella of Asian-American studies can be divided into two distinct categories. Those which place primary emphasis upon Asian history, philosophy, language, culture etc. . . and those which stress an Asian-American identity and experience. Courses in the former category are apt to be taught by academicians who are Asian studies scholars. They hold advanced degrees and may be non-Asian. While part of the Asian-American curriculum, these courses also attract a majority of students whose majors are in other areas.

Courses dealing with the Asian-American experience however, are often taught by Professors of Asian ancestry or by Asian graduate students. When non-Asians are involved in the teaching of these courses they must be approved by an Asian student committee. These classes attract a predominately Asian student body. Both types of courses usually include readings (library assignments), evaluations (written/oral), and papers or projects. Yet the spirit and substance of the classes are quite different. Identity and experience classes include more group discussions, discussions in which subjectivity is as popular as objective evaluations. The student leaders (instructors) are more facilitators and topic organizers than they are lecturers, and the issues chosen for presentation often include highly emotional subjects dealing with discrimination, alienation and racism. Course assignments also stress participation in, or attendance at relevant community/college events.

Activist activities in the colleges and universities are steadily increasing and are having a significant impact upon the academic community. As their programs continue to expand so does their desire to become legitimate and representative organizations entitled to the same recognition and privileges granted to other organized groups. Once satisfied to merely establish courses on the campus, activists have now achieved recognized minors and majors in Asian-American studies. Moreover, they demand that their curriculum be granted the same "status" as the more traditional social science disciplines. They are actively encouraging the seeking out and hiring of Asian personnel and increasing the allocation of funds for their programs. At Valley City College an Asian-American student group led the successful fight for the appointment of an Asian counselor. Academic departments at Valley State University have increased their efforts to hire ethnic minorities at the staff and instructional levels, and the administration has allocated special funds for the hiring of minority personnel. But perhaps the biggest obstacle to achieving academic recognition is activist insistance that Asian-Americans, by virtue of their ethnic experience are better qualified to instruct and administrate these programs than any non-Asians. Finally, there is a strong desire among some activists to report upon and to analyze their own affairs and to discourage the research of non-Asians in these subject areas.

Activist programs within the community are also expanding. In the past year they have established an Asian Center located in a wood and brick house in the central city. The Center's staff is primarily recruited from Valley State University and City College students yet also includes non-student staff and advisors, many of whom are volunteers. Among the Center's more publicized programs are the services provided to the local Asian-American community. These programs include efforts to establish low-cost housing; educational, employment and social services to the elderly and the immigrant indigent; the provision of translators for non-English speaking persons; and a tutorial program for Asian public school children.

While it is not our intention to evaluate the Center's programs, some pertinant observations seem in order. First, the establishment of the Center along with the organization, coordination and planning of its activities has resulted in a strong "esprit de corps" for its more active members. Many secondary relationships among these activists have developed into primary ones. The Center has also become a spiritual as well as a physical symbol of Asian-American unity so that even Asian volunteers and clientelle who minimally contribute and participate in the Center's activities identify with the Center. Secondly, the Center has now become a community institution and must compete and cooperate with other organizations for prestige, monies, and recognition as a legitimate spokesman for the Asian community. Cooperation has not always been easy, for the powerful and moving experiences that contribute to the Center's solidarity have also tended to minimize diverse strategies. While this has strengthened camaraderie within the Center it has also made it less tolerant of alternatives. When faced with a conflict situation involving other agencies the membership can become quite hostile. A case in point is the controversy over the Valley City Fund. The Fund is an agency that solicits and collects monies from the entire local community and then distributes these monies to various social agencies. The Asian Center requested money from the

Fund but the Fund refused and questioned the Center's ability to adequately administer their program. Subsequent meetings were held between Center and Fund leaders but communications deteriorated and the Center's request was ultimately denied. As a result the Center openly campaigned in the local community against the Fund and accused them of racism and discrimination in their policies and pro- grams. Cooperation with other Asian groups has been more rewarding. At least one Chinese modernist organization and one Chinese-American church have openly supported and encouraged the Center's activities.

It is difficult to predict the future of Asian activists on the campus and within the community. These groups have but a brief social history and their growth and development will be dependent upon changes in the university and in the larger society. An educated guess is that Activist groups for Asian-Americans will continue, that they will grow in numbers, and that their "alumni" will challenge both traditionists and modernists in the years to come.

14

Understanding the Chinese Community

THE SOCIAL ORGANIZATION OF the Chinese in America is a product of historical precedent and the internal dynamics of community life, but its direction has been significantly influenced by Chinese interaction with the Caucasian majority. The resulting attitudes and their behavioral expressions are largely a function of continuing Chinese adaptation to life in America and can perhaps best be understood as part of the assimilation process.

The Assimilation Process as a Methodological Construct

Behavioral and structural assimilation is an index for detailing the degree of integration of a minority people into the mainstream of their host society and emphasizing the minority's adaptation to the dominant group. Moreover, assimilation often assumes the nature of a desired goal where the minority's retention of cultural and historical exclusiveness becomes an obstacle to those goals. Finally, because there appears to be a visible trend toward increasing assimilation with each succeeding minority generation, it is often assumed, though falsely, that this process is inevitable. Indeed, such assumptions are largely responsible for America's melting-pot ideology; even the fact that most minorities have never been completely assimilated has failed to discourage the myth.

Objections to the ideological dimensions of this process do not invalidate its use as a sociological measuring rod. Assimilation variables have been seen to be useful and valuable instruments in the attempt to analyze the degree of integration of the Chinese into the mainstream of American society and the effect that differential assimilation has on community social organization. But there are further difficulties in utilizing the assimilation process as a social yardstick, for the rate of acculturation is not the same for all aspects of Chinese socio-cultural life. Some areas of human activity, such as occupation, housing, and clothing, give ground easily, while others, such as language, diet, and customs, are clung to more tenaciously. Generally speaking, Chinese adoption of American material traits proceeds more rapidly than the adoption of American ideology. Moreover, it is not always possible to recognize if a typically American strategy has replaced a typically Chinese one, particularly when the outcome appears to be similar in both cases. For example, Chinese utilization of the American educational system as a means to achieve social status does not conflict with a traditional Chinese educational philosophy in which both scholars and scholarship are highly valued. Thus, a Chinese student who gets high grades is praised by both Chinese and Americans. However, depending on the observer's point of view, he may have succeeded as an American by being typically Chinese or as a Chinese by being typically American.

Another difficulty involves the mechanics of acculturation itself, because acculturation does not mean the one-to-one substitution of American for Chinese traits. A Chinese son who becomes proficient with knife and fork does not give up using chopsticks. When a Chinese mother joins a Christian church, she may not necessarily give up burning incense for her ancestors. Nor does membership in a Christian church necessarily reflect a commitment to Christ or to Christianity. A bride wearing white lace is wed to her spouse in a Methodist church, the ceremony presided over by a Caucasian minister. After leaving the church in a rented Cadillac, she changes into a Chinese red wedding gown, wears all of her jade and gold jewelry, and ceremonially serves tea to her husband's parents. Neither the bride, the groom, nor their parents consider these ceremonies to be contradictory; in fact, they believe that both are necessary. Valley City's Chinese are, for the most part, the recipients of two cultural traditions. They can, and do, shift identities depending upon the situation and the appropriate reference group. For example, an American-born Chinese dining with his American-born Chinese friends seemed disturbed at the behavior of a group of Chinese immigrants seated at a nearby table. He remarked, "Look how disgustingly Chinese they are! They don't know how to eat. Did you notice how loud they are and how they always talk with their hands?" But when his party was later joined by some Caucasian friends, and when one of them made a similar remark, this same individual became indignant and replied, "Why are you so prejudiced? It's not their fault that they are immigrants. I am Chinese too, and when you speak about them you are including me as well. You know, your table manners may even offend them."

It appears, then, that an analysis of the assimilation process should take into account situational variables and reference group identification. This modification does not, however, invalidate assimilation categories as a means of predicting behavior or as an aid in understanding the social organization of Chinese community life.

The Present Status of Chinese Acculturation

It is the intent in this next section to describe the degree to which acculturation and structural assimilation of the Chinese into the mainstream of American life have taken place. Although until now attention has been focused upon a particular Chinese community, the same assimilation processes, far from being restricted to Valley City, have been well documented for other Chinese communities all over America. At this point a wider perspective will be taken in order to show that similar forces observed to be at work in other communities may result in a similar organizational structure.

The scholarly literature on Chinese living in America strongly suggests that both native- and foreign-born Chinese have been successful in assimilating American culture and behavior. Homer Loh's Philadelphia study (1945:160–73) points out that Chinese enjoy American movies, television, magazines and newspapers, engage in stamp collecting and photography as hobbies, wear American clothing, and adopt American first names for their offspring. Cheng (1948:203–323) further reports that Chinese attend American baseball games, eat American food, attend Christian churches, and celebrate both religious and secular American holidays.

The acceptance of American customs and social ritual has contributed to modifications of personality structure. Abel and Hsu (1949: 286) have found that the emotional control of the Chinese, known for their inscrutability, has altered in favor of the expressiveness and spontaneity descriptive of the American scene, and that American-born Chinese behave more like American-born Caucasians than China-born Chinese. Furthermore, Fong (1965:271) reports that the social and cultural orientations and sentiments of the Chinese shift gradually from the ethnic sub-culture to the larger American society. As the American society continues to become a positive reference group, its norms and values begin to guide as well as modify the behavior and perspectives of the Chinese. Betty Lee Sung tells the familiar story of a woman born in New York City's Chinatown but now living in the suburbs. "She finds it difficult to express herself in Chinese. She smokes, drives a car, throws cocktail parties, wears slacks and shorts most of the time, dances the Lindy, and considers herself 90% if not 100% Americanized" (1967:270). Finally, C. C. Wu (1928) concludes that native-born Chinese are americanized to such a degree that Chinese from China are just as strange in their eyes as Africans are in the eyes of American Negroes.

Valley City's Chinese find the material advantages in American-style living to be very congenial. Not only do they don American-style apparel and observe American social custom, but they are actively engaged in the social stratification system of the American community and compete for prestigious positions at the local level. Chinese, overly successful in internalizing American attitudes, have even adopted Caucasian negative stereotypes of their own minority and some Chinese informants refer to "those Chinese" as "greedy," "sly," "clannish," and "cheap."

Acculturation seems to be related to a person's social profile, the more acculturated being younger, American-born, and fluent in English. They often reside in predominantly Caucasian suburbs, are well educated, and are employed in prestigious occupations.

While we have observed wide-scale acculturation for Chinese in America, there is less evidence for structural assimilation—the large-scale entrance of the Chinese into cliques, clubs, and institutions of American society at the primary-group level. Loh (1947:159) writes that Chinese rarely go to American dancing parties and that their relationship to their American friends is usually limited to business relations. Participation by the Chinese in community life is very slight. C. W. H. Chen (1952:323) adds that although the younger generation has adopted American patterns of dancing, sex, and mating, Chinese youth of high school and college age are generally excluded from white people's fraternities and social clubs. In response, the youth withdraw to associate with their own kind. Yuan (1963:263) claims that the Chinese are accepted in school but not in politics. They are partially accepted in work and housing but not in public affairs and social activities. Grallfs' study (1949:20–22) of a mixed Seattle polytechnic high school reveals that when Chinese students were asked for racial and ethnic preferences for leaders, friends, fellow workers, and dates, the Chinese preferred other Chinese in all four categories. Moreover,

Chinese prefer to participate in private clubs rather than in mixed organizations. Chen (1945:45) further substantiates Chinese exclusiveness and, in her New York study of Chinese student clubs, finds that although many clubs stress American recreational and social activities, non-Chinese members are very rare. Organizational discrimination is also in evidence between American-born and China-born students. Rose Hum Lee (1960:409) concludes that Chinese are treated as Chinese in some situations and as Americans in others, hence they acquire a dual set of responses and are never free from the possibility of differential treatment. Finally, Kung summarizes: "The Chinese in the United States have not been completely assimilated. Complete integration cannot be achieved until the problem of racial bias can be solved and that solution may take several decades and even longer" (1962:178).

Valley City's Chinese face many of the same assimilation problems previously discussed. They have been accepted in the professions of medicine and dentistry and, to a lesser extent, law. Many are successful businessmen, professionals, and technicians. They own large supermarket chains and are heavily involved in wholesale and retail trade and, to a lesser degree, in public administration and manufacturing. Ecologically, the Chinese have spread into formerly "lilywhite" neighborhoods. They find little discrimination in theaters, recreation, restaurant, and public facilities. But the Chinese, like all Asians, are still denied membership in prestigious golf and country clubs as well as some older established organizations and social fraternities. Though no longer overtly practiced, discrimination still exists in many business firms. Moreover, Chinese friendship and social groupings tend to be exclusively Chinese, and even Chinese college students usually attend predominantly Chinese parties and dances, join Chinese clubs, and prefer other Chinese as friends, dates, and future marriage partners.

Without structural assimilation, marital assimilation, large-scale intermarriage with other Americans, and identificational assimilation, the development of a sense of "peoplehood" based exclusively upon American society remains extremely unlikely.

In the course of this study, it has been demonstrated that acculturation is a function of age, nativity, language, geography, education, and occupation. Thus, the Chinese population residing in an American community falls into a multitude of distinct sociological categories. They do not all speak a common language, honor the same institutions, or worship similar deities. They neither act as a corporate group nor do they all pursue common goals, and according to their age and sex they participate disproportionately in both Chinese and American activities. Chinese communities include residents who are second- and third-generation Americans and whose cultural heritage is more American than it is Chinese. Consequently, they exhibit a cultural outlook that is quite different from that of recently arrived immigrants and China-born persons. Chinatowns are no longer the geographically defined population center for the Chinese. Moreover, Chinatowns are rapidly decreasing both in numbers and population as the Chinese continue to migrate to more desirable city and suburban areas. Those who remain in these Chinese enclaves tend to come from specific sociocultural categories and are not a cross-section of the Chinese populace. Finally, Chinese are now employed in a variety of occupations which range from the restaurant busboy to the bank president, from unskilled blue-collar laborers to white-collar professionals.

In spite of the consistent and conscious movement toward acculturation, therefore, not all Chinese are acculturated to the same degree. Acculturation pressures act differentially on various categories, resulting in a population that is heterogeneous with regard to this process.

Nor is there a consistency regarding structural assimilation. Many Chinese residents restrict their primary relationships to members of their own ethnic group, but an increasing number have, because of expanding occupational opportunities, established secondary relationships with Caucasians. A growing minority of Chinese youth under thirty, however, have structurally assimilated at both the secondary and primary level with other Asian-Americans.

In conclusion, two particularly significant findings bear reiteration. First, that acculturation is a process affecting the Chinese in America. This study has clearly demonstrated that both the foreign- and native-born Chinese have adopted many extrinsic, and to a lesser extent, intrinsic traits of the American culture, although they have not simultaneously given up and rejected all the tenets of their Chinese heritage.

A second conclusion is, however, that Chinese primary relationships remain, for the most part, with other Chinese. Although structural assimilation may be a stimulating methodological construct, it has not significantly affected Chinese inter-personal relationships. Structural assimilation, for the majority of Chinese-Americans, remains a myth.

The Chinese-American Community and the People's Republic of China

The nature of the Chinese community vis-à-vis the greater society is dependent, in part, upon political relations between the United States and the People's Republic of China. Two important events deserve attention: the Communist takeover of the mainland in the late 1940's, and the present state of United States-China relations.

When the Chinese were no longer able to make periodic trips or to plan an eventual return to their ancestral village in China, their ties to America were strengthened and the acculturative process was accelerated. Yet, as long as the Chinese could be associated with an unfriendly Communist regime, few Chinese-Americans could feel secure in the United States.

Even today, many Chinese share the fear of incarceration in relocation camps, similar to the Japanese experience during World War II, should United States-China relations become exceedingly hostile. On the other hand, amicable relations might lead to trade and travel between these two major powers, strengthen Chinese-American ties to China, and, in time, once again affect the assimilation process and the organizational structure of the Chinese-American community.

Although Communist-Nationalist divisions pertaining to China may be responsible for intra-community conflicts in Chinese overseas settlements, they are not a divisive factor in Valley City's Chinese community.

In 1971 Communist China was admitted to the United Nations while Nationalist China (Taiwan) was expelled. Most traditionists remained loyal to the Nationalist government of Chiang Kai-shek and appeared to be more upset with the expulsion of Taiwan than with the admittance of Red China. Many modernists believe that the admission of Communist China would be a positive step in the direction of world peace but do not understand why Taiwan had to go in order for the mainland to be admitted. Activists were generally delighted with the recognition of Red China and because they regarded the Taiwan government as a "puppet dictatorship" were pleased with the United Nations changes.

The majority of the Chinese, however, were reluctant to express their feelings and preferred to remain silent.

The Chinese: A Distinct Minority

This study of the Chinese Community in Valley City has dealt with the Chinese as an American ethnic and racial minority. As such, processes common to many racial and ethnic minorities have been viewed, with a particular emphasis upon the development of organizational and family life in terms of conflict and compromise. Yet, while there are structural similarities shared by all minorities, the Chinese community follows a specific historical-cultural motif that is distinctively Chinese.

Unlike any other American minority, the Chinese have developed in their family-name associations an organizational network based upon actual and imputed kinship ties. They have structured their organizational system in such a way that senior male representatives hold key positions simultaneously at all levels within the organizational network. In addition, decision-making procedures rely heavily upon the Chinese principles of face-saving and propriety.

In the religious sphere, Chinese beliefs remain syncretic, eclectic, and accommodate diverse philosophies—in particular, western Christianity. Moreover, the basic Confucian ideal of harmony of man and nature still characterizes Chinese inter- and intra-personal relationships. Family life remains based upon respect for age, filial piety, group cohesiveness, and socioeconomic solidarity. Within the community, Chinese language schools still teach youngsters the fundamentals of reading and speaking the Cantonese language, Chinese national and religious holidays are often celebrated with pomp and ceremony, and culinary and recreational styles continue to be reminiscent of a Chinese heritage.

This is particularly true for the traditionist sub-community. While modernist and activist social life has been heavily influenced by an American style, major events nevertheless focus upon Chinese celebrations and, although these activities appeal to non-Chinese as well, their primary function is a reaffirmation of a Chinese or an Asian identity.

There is yet another distinctive note to Chinese-American society, a distinction based upon racial characteristics. The Chinese are physically distinguishable from both the Caucasian majority and from other minorities. Their racial visibility serves to set them apart from other Americans and their separateness encourages stereotyping, prejudice, and differential treatment.

Thus, in spite of the fact that Chinese settlements in America have been exposed to assimilation pressures for over a century, Chinese community life today cannot be understood except as an expression of a heritage based firmly upon the tenets of Chinese cultural tradition.

Division and Unity

In the introduction to this study, reference was made to the Valley City Chinese community as a holistic and integrated entity. This statement requires further exploration.

A major theme of this research has been the differentiation of the Chinese community. The degree of assimilation has been utilized as a means of distinguishing between its three major segments—traditionists, modernists, and activists. This characterization of a differentiated community is a valuable socio-anthropological construct, firmly grounded in the empirical data collected during fieldwork and fitting both the scholarly and native perceptions of social life.

Differentiation, however, does not necessarily mean that the Chinese community is not an integrated entity. Nor would it be proper to assume that intra-community conflicts always lead to social disorganization. Conflict between diverse segments can also act as a unifying factor for the Chinese community.[1] As Coser (1956:137) states:

"Conflict creates links between contenders. It creates and modifies common norms necessary for the readjustment of the relationship, makes possible a reassessment of relative power, and thus serves as a balancing mechanism which helps to maintain and consolidate groups."

Moreover, social conflict always denotes social interaction. Conflict acts to define group boundaries, thus contributing to the reaffirmation and the identity of the group so that the group may maintain its boundaries against the surrounding social world[2] (Coser 1956:38).

Yet there are also forces which act to integrate the Chinese, forces which crosscut diverse organizational identities, emphasize what is common to all groups, and maintain a holistic and united community: First, all Chinese in this community and in America share a historical legacy. They are the recipients of a continuous cultural tradition which separates them from all other Americans, including those of non-Chinese Asian ancestry. Traditionists attempt to perpetuate and maintain the ceremonial and commemorative aspects of their heritage, and their organizational system remains based upon Chinese structural antecedents. They are Chinese first, and Americans second. Modernists have a dual cultural identity—American and Chinese. Many of their attitudes, as well as their organizational format, are more American than Chinese. Yet in their overall orientation they evidence a strong identification with their Chinese identity, reinforcing the influences that tend to maintain a voluntarily segregated community. Activists, too, are proud of being Chinese. Though they may represent them-

[1] For a contemporary analysis of traditionist-modernist conflict, see David I. Grafstein's "A study in intergroup conflict; some consequences of the emergence of an organization in Boston's Chinatown," *Cornell Journal of Social Relations* 3(1):15–25.

[2] Activist-traditionist conflict is well illustrated in L. Ling-Chi Wang's "Chinatown in Transition," *The Asian Experience in America*, Asian-American Concern, University of California at Davis, March, 1969.

selves to outsiders as Asians, within their own ranks they self-consciously recognize ethnic differences. This Chinese identity, a powerful factor in social cohesiveness, is strengthened by a history that predates the history of western man. As one traditionist states:

> Our traditions give us the courage to fight the forces of injustice. In America we may be small in numbers but we are proud of our glorious history. We were writing when the white man was still crawling in caves. Truly, we are the more civilized. I know that while my mouth may speak English, my heart will always feel Chinese.

Modernists and activists may use different phraseology to express links with their Chinese past and may choose to publicize their ancestry by emphasizing different aspects of that heritage. Yet pride in ancestors and their accomplishments, in history and in culture, is common to, and shared by, traditionists, modernists, and activists alike.

Regardless of their differences, all Chinese are united by a sense of "family." This familistic spirit, a cultural product of a Confucian ethos, has been strengthened by the more objective realities of Chinese life in America. Early Chinese immigrants, strangers in a strange land, stayed close to their kinsmen and relatives, often living in the same quarters or in adjoining houses. Families often operated shops and restaurants as a unit, drawing upon their members for labor and financing, and living above, or in back of, the family enterprise. Today the family remains a basic unit of Chinese-American life. Moreover, the special feelings reserved for close kin are often extended to both maternal and paternal relatives and include some remotely related affines.[3] Close family friends are often accorded the amenities and sometimes the nomenclature of kinsmen.

Most families celebrate both Chinese (Ch'ing Ming, Moon Festival, New Year's) and American (Thanksgiving, Easter, Christmas) holidays with family dinners. Chinese delicacies like bird's nest soup often share the table wth turkeys and roasts. At these frequent gatherings, ideological differences are temporarily put aside as traditionist grandparents, modernist parents, and their children enjoy feasting and fellowship. As they retell old tales and relive precious moments from the past, they are bound together in the "spirit of family unity." A local activist leader reports:

---

[3] Although a patrilineal group, most Chinese in this community do not exhibit a decided preference for their paternal kinsmen. The recognition of, and behavior toward, relatives appears to be strongly conditioned by personal and idiosyncratic factors.

It may sound strange and sometimes it even puzzles me. How can we get together as a family? Last Sunday we all visited Great-uncle. He is one of the most narrow-minded men I have known and stands for the very things I am against. Yet he is happy that I do so well at school and is proud to be my uncle. As a family I think we share certain feelings that let us relax together. I enjoy getting together. I usually complain about visiting relatives, but when we all get together I don't want to be any place else.

A Chinese communication network is consciously maintained by an informal yet efficient information exchange system which unites the community by cutting across age, sex, generational, and cultural boundaries. This Chinese grapevine, strengthened by long-standing school ties and business friendships, functions through the spreading of news and rumor to maintain a running commentary upon the activities of the Chinese. Stories and gossip about Chinese people and Chinese events travel from mother to daughter to boy friend to peer group to relatives and back again. Thus the effect of Chinese geographic dispersion is minimized and a "community spirit" remains (Weiss 1969:10).

Those individuals who belong to, and participate in, both traditionist and modernist organizations also function to promote unity within the community. Though small in number, no more than 5 per cent, these individuals are often respected spokesmen of their respective associations. They have often achieved monetary success within the Caucasian economic structure yet still wish to maintain a position in the Chinese community. By actively participating in both traditionist and modernist groups, they are aware of the plans and prevailing attitudes of both kinds of organizations and, by functioning as intermediaries, can often prevent conflict situations from arising. One such person reports:

Some of the older men in the family association worried about the civic club being able to handle the details about the festival. They were also concerned about the image they would present. Being a member of both groups, I was able to convince some of the elders that the civic club would make them proud and would not shame their Chinese ancestry. I also helped in the programming of the event and made it a special point to inform the members that the family association had some reservations about the event. I think being able to understand both groups helped to make our festival a success.

Finally, perhaps the most important key to a common Chinese identity must be sought outside of the community itself, for, in the parlance of the Occidental, "all Chinese are alike." Stereotyped images of the "Chinamen" serving in a menial and inferior capacity still remain rooted within Caucasian thought, and attempts on the part of Chinese to move toward the dominant American groups are either rebuffed or only partially satisfied. Racial and cultural barriers continually prevent the Chinese from a full membership in American society, throwing them back among their own people. Thus, out-group hostility often fosters in-group cohesiveness. As long as structural assimilation—the large-scale entry of the Chinese into Caucasian cliques and clubs—remains a myth for most Chinese, and as long as Chinese are categorically distinguished from other Americans, the Chinese community will find it advantageous to act as a cohesive unit (Weiss 1969:13–14).

Underlying the realities of Chinese community life in Valley City is a process of fission and fusion. There are times when internal divisions can split the community into hostile factions. Yet at other times the community acts as a cohesive unit, often with a single spokesman. Both division and union are situational. Whenever there is a need to raise funds, sponsor a pan-community Chinese cultural event, or present a unified front against the dominant society, members of the Chinese community will find it advantageous to combine their resources. Should they ever wish to make their small numbers a significant political force, or should they feel overtly threatened by discrimination or prejudice, they may be expected to act as a single unit. At other times, when threats from outside forces appear to be minimal, or when divergent philosophies cannot be reconciled, the community will fragment and each segment will pursue separate goals.

This ability to coalesce and to fragment, to shift identity and reference group, to join in or withdraw from a common effort, is beneficial for the Chinese minority because it enables them to maintain their ethnic identity and to participate, to varying degrees, in American social life. A single organizational structure, one system to accommodate all Chinese of varying cultural and social persuasions, leaves but two choices—to join or to withdraw. Such was the case during the traditional era and for most of the transitional period.

Today's Chinese communities are made up of a diverse and heterogeneous population. Partially as a response to this diversity, Chinese communities have developed an organizational structure manifesting alternative choices. Chinese who wish to continue to participate actively in their traditionist associations can still do so. Those that find that the traditionist system can no longer meet their needs can enter into a modernist network which caters to their American orientation and yet lets them remain Chinese. Modernist organizations are particularly attractive to marginal men who desire to maintain a bicultural identity. Those young men and women who are satisfied with neither traditionist nor modernist rhetoric and activities can join activist groups.

This tripartite system can also accommodate Chinese who wish to participate in more than one cultural arena, but, perhaps more important, it allows individuals, as they pass through their life cycle from childhood to old age, to retain their ethnic ties while they shift their cultural outlook.

Thus, as the American-born Chinese increase their participation in American life and shift their reference groups, they can nevertheless maintain their Chinese identity. They can continue to be both Chinese and American without sacrificing the psycho-social security that their ethnic identity provides.

Epilogue

Since this research was concluded, Valley City's old Chinatown area has been demolished and replaced by a new Chinatown complex. The city's "new Chinatown" is located in the northwest portion of the central city, a few blocks from the major downtown business district. It was constructed as part of the city's urban renewal project and encompasses an area of two square blocks. The complex was built at two levels, an upper street level surrounding a sunken mall. At street level there are six buildings housing a family association, the tong, the Bank of Hong Kong, a Chinese restaurant, a housing development, and the Confucian Church (community center). While the Confucian Church was built in the 1960's, all other buildings were completed within the past year. Under construction is a ten-story building which will house another family association's headquarters, apartments for the elderly, and professional and business offices. A motel is planned for the one remaining land parcel. At the lower level there is a landscaped pedestrian mall featuring a Chinese garden, another smaller family association building, and a memorial hall to Dr. Sun, Yat-sen, the founder of the Republic of China. There remains much available space for shops and offices but except for a Chinese grocery, most of these spaces were unoccupied.

The F.H.A. sponsored housing development is a modern brick and stone structure with seventy-two apartments. The apartments range from efficiency rooms to three bedroom units and are rent controlled.[1]

---

[1] Efficiency apartments rent for about $80.00/month, the three bedroom units for $130.00. The monthly rent includes all utilities, air-conditioning, cooking range and draperies. All apartments are rented unfurnished. The only restriction for occupancy relates to family income. A single person cannot earn more than $4,500/year while the annual income for two or more people may not exceed $5,400.

259

The apartments are small yet pleasant. The development extends to the lower level where there are three shops located, a men's barber and hairstyling salon, a bail bond service, and a Chinese physician's office. There is no parking within the complex itself and on-street parking is extremely limited. City plans eventually call for parking areas in the near vicinity.

The new Chinatown complex is located near a major business area and is not within walking distance of residential housing, thus if people are to reside permanently in the area they must live within the center itself. Although the housing development has a Chinese name less than half (twenty-eight) of the units are rented to persons of Chinese ancestry. The other units are rented to Caucasians, Mexican-Americans, Negroes and other Asians. The majority of the Chinese residents are elderly and China-born. Because of the F.H.A. restrictions all residents are low-income families. There is also little evidence to suggest that the heterogeneaty of peoples leads to Chinese/non-Chinese primary relationships. Chinese residents continue to interact primarily with other Chinese and while they do not appear to be hostile towards their new neighbors, neither do they appear overly friendly. Overtures of friendship are largely limited to formal greetings in the hallway or within the complex.[2]

There is also little evidence to suggest that the Chinese residents and visitors make extensive use of the facilities. No Chinese have been known to use the bail-bond service and the men's hair salon prices start at $3.00 for a haircut; their other styling services are considerably more expensive. The Chinese physician's office is frequented by non-Asians as much as by Chinese clientelle. The restaurant and a "Chinese smorgy" housed on the street level of an association building attract a predominately Caucasian crowd. The Chinese grocery is the only shop which caters primarily to Chinese customers. The three family associations, the Tong, Confucian Church and the memorial hall are, of course, frequented almost exclusively by elderly China-born males as was the situation for this area before the new construction. The Sun, Yat-sen Memorial Hall is open to visitors during most days from 1–5 P.M. Its one open room contains display replications of dynasty stone and jade art works, Chinese language newspapers and literature, and photographs and exhibits dramatizing the role of Dr. Sun and his movement to liberate China. While the family association and Tong

---

[2] The ten-story building under construction will provide over 300 units for the elderly. Although also F.H.A. sponsored the units will be slightly more expensive than those of the housing development. It is not known how many of the elderly persons will be of Chinese ancestry.

buildings are elaborate and expensive, Chinese in both design and decor, and more spacious than the old facilities, they continue to serve the same functions for the same peoples.

While it is still too early to predict the final relationship of the "new Chinatown" to the Chinese community, a few observations bear notice. The old Chinatown area, while itself not a primary center for the Chinese population, nevertheless supported rooms nearby for elderly men, gaming establishments, and inexpensive eating places. It also housed all of the associational buildings. The new construction enclosing the new Chinatown has significantly altered the area. Gone are the old men's "hotels," eating places, and gaming halls. Furthermore, not all of the traditionist associations have constructed new buildings. Of the nine associations (eight family associations and the Tong) only four have rebuilt in this area. The remaining five associations have relocated within the central city where land and buildings are considerably less expensive. Thus the new Chinatown has spatially divided the traditionist community organizations. Transportation to and from the area and parking facilities are extremely limited thus decreasing the numbers of people who usually frequent the remaining association halls, and although elderly men are present during the day and evening, their numbers are fewer than in times past.

Secondly, because of the new restaurants, the area now attracts many non-Chinese. Once the offices and shops are rented, furnished and operational they will presumably attract more people, fewer of whom however are apt to be Chinese. Modernists hope for the eventual establishment of a "tourist's Chinatown." Yet, the present paucity of tourist attractions within "Chinatown" does not encourage visitors.[3] Many of the office spaces and shops remain empty because business and professional interests are hesitant to locate in this area.

Activists do not generally view the new Chinatown complex as beneficial to the Chinese community at large. They often indicate that the hundreds of thousands of dollars spent on the new buildings could have been put to better use.

Thus, there is little evidence to suggest that the new Chinatown can or will rekindle the spirit of the Chinatowns of years past. It is also doubtful that it will serve as a focus for community integration or establish new ties between traditionist, modernist and activist elements.

[3] The custodian of the Memorial Hall claims that there have been few visitors since the hall opened its doors last year. The Chinese grocery store has one room filled with Chinese "tourist trinkets" but have had few visitors and fewer purchases. As was the practice in the past, the family association doors are not generally open to the public.

It is expected that at the very least it will create another commercial center for the business interests of the greater Valley City community and may serve as a limited but available center for tourists. However, the establishment of this new Chinatown is an indication that the Chinese in Valley City remain proud of their Sinitic heritage and history. The blend of Chinese architecture and cuisine with professional and commercial enterprise reflects the realities of the new Chinese-American world. One traditionist leader commented upon the meaning of the new Chinatown and remarked:

"Well one thing is very certain, that the old ways of living are gone forever. This is a new place and will not bring back the past. It is clear that Chinese and Americans must build together and perhaps this is a good thing after all."

List of References

Abel, Theodora M. and Francis L. K. Hsu 1949 Some aspects of personality of Chinese as revealed by the Rorschach test. *Research Exchange and Journal of Projective Techniques* 12:285–301.

Amyot, J. 1960 The Chinese community in Manila. Unpublished Ph.D. dissertation, Chicago: University of Chicago.

Bancroft, Hubert Howe 1883 History of California (the works of Hubert Howe.

————1890 Bancroft, vols. VII–XXIV). San Francisco: The History Company and A. L. Bancroft Company.

Barnett, Milton L. 1958 Some Cantonese-American problems of status adjustment. *Phylon* 18:420–27.

————1952 Alcohol and culture: a study of drinking in a Chinese-American community. Unpublished Ph.D. dissertation. Ithaca: Cornell University.

Barth, Gunther 1964 Bitter strength: a history of the Chinese in the United States, 1850–1870. Cambridge: Harvard University Press.

Beattie, John 1964 Other cultures; aims, methods and achievements in social anthropology. New York: The Free Press.

Berry, Brewton 1965 Race and ethnic relations. Boston: Houghton Mifflin Company.

Bodde, Derk 1957 China's cultural tradition. New York: Holt, Rinehart and Winston.

Chen, Eugenia V. 1945 Survey of Chinese youth clubs in New York City. Unpublished Master's thesis. Ann Arbor: University of Michigan.

Chen, Ta 1939 Emigrant communities in South China, a study of overseas migration and its influence on standards of living and social change. London: Institute of Pacific Relations.

Chen, Te-Chao 1948   Acculturation of the Chinese in the United States: a Philadelphia study. Unpublished Ph.D. dissertation. Philadelphia: University of Philadelphia.

Chen, Wen-Hui Chung 1952   Changing socio-cultural patterns of the Chinese community in Los Angeles. Unpublished Ph.D. dissertation. Los Angeles: University of Southern California.

Chinn, Thomas W. (Editor) 1969   A history of the Chinese in California, a syllabus. San Francisco: Chinese Historical Society of America.

Chiu, Ping 1963   Chinese labor in California 1850–1880, an economic study. Wisconsin: University of Wisconsin.

Chu, Daniel, and Samuel Chu 1967   Passage to the golden gate: a history of the Chinese in America to 1910. New York: Doubleday and Company, Inc.

Chuan, Hsiao-Kung 1967   The role of the clan and kinship family. In Chinese society under communism. William T. Liu, editor. New York: John Wiley and Sons, Inc. Pp. 33–46.

Coolidge, Mary R. 1909   Chinese immigration. New York: Henry Holt and Company.

Coser, Lewis A. 1956   The functions of social conflict. Illinois: The Free Press of Glencoe.

Cressey, George B. 1963   Asia's land and people. New York: McGraw-Hill, Inc.

Crissman, Lawrence W. 1967   The segmentary structure of urban overseas Chinese communities. *Man* 2:185–204.

Dare, Richard Kock 1959   The economic and social adjustment of San Francisco's Chinese for the past fifty years. Unpublished Master's thesis. Berkeley: University of California.

Eberhard, Wolfram 1962   Economic activities in a Chinese temple in California. *Journal of the American Oriental Society* 82:362–71.

Etzioni, Amitai 1959   The ghetto—a re-evaluation. *Social Forces* 37:255–62.

Fairchild, H. P. 1947   Race and nationality. New York: Ronald Press.

Fang, John T. C. 1961   Yee Fow, the Chinese community in "Valley City". San Francisco: Chinese Publishing House.

Farwell, Williard B. 1885   The Chinese at home and abroad, together with the report of the special committee of the Board of Supervisors of San Francisco on the condition of the Chinese quarter of that city. San Francisco: A. L. Bancroft Company.

Fong, Stanley L. M. 1965   Assimilation of Chinese in America: changes in orientation and social perception. *American Journal of Sociology* LXXI:265–73.

Freedman, Maurice 1966 Chinese lineage and society: Fukien and Kwantung. London: Athlone Press.

——1960 Immigrants and associations: Chinese in 19th century Singapore. *Comparative Studies in Society and History* 3:25–48.

Gallin, Bernard 1967 Chinese peasant values towards the land. In peasant society, a reader. Jack M. Potter, May N. Diaz, and George M. Foster, editors. Boston: Little Brown and Company.

——1960 Matrilateral and affinal relationships of a Taiwanese village. *American Anthropologist* 62:632–42.

Ganz, Herbert 1962 The urban villagers. Illinois: The Free Press of Glencoe.

Glazer, Nathan, and Daniel P. Moynihan 1963 Beyond the melting pot. Cambridge: The Massachusetts Institute of Technology Press.

Gluckman, Max 1955 The judicial process among the Barotse of Northern Rhodesia. New York: The Free Press of Glencoe.

Goffman, Erving, 1967 Interaction ritual: essays on face-to-face behavior. New York: Doubleday and Company.

Goldstein, Sidney, and Calvin Goldscheider 1968 Jewich Americans: three generations in a Jewish community. Englewood Cliffs: Prentice-Hall, Inc.

Gordon, Milton 1967 Assimilation in America: theory and reality. In Minorities in a changing world. Milton Barron, editor. New York: Alfred A. Knopf. Pp. 393–417.

——1964 Assimilation in American life, the role of race, religion, and national origins. New York: Oxford University Press.

Graalfs, Marilyn 1949 A sociometric study of Chinese students in a polytechnic high school. Unpublished Master's thesis.

Grafstein, David I. 1968 A study in intergroup conflict: some consequences of the emergence of an organization in Boston's Chinatown. *Cornell Journal of Social Relations* 3:15–25.

Haynor, Norman, and Charles Reynold 1937 Chinese family life n America. *American Sociological Review* 2:630–37.

Heyer, Virginia 1953 Patterns of social organization in New York City Chinatown. Unpublished Ph.D. dissertation. New York: Columbia University.

Honigmann, John J. 1963 Understanding culture. New York: Harper and Row, Inc.

Hsiao, Kung-Chuan 1960 Imperial control in the nineteenth century. Seattle: University of Washington Press.

Hsu, Francis L. K. 1949 Under the ancestor's shadow. London: Routledge and Kegan Paul, Ltd.

Hu, Chang-Tu 1960 China, its people, its society, its culture. New Haven, HRAF Press.

Hu, Hsien-Chin 1948   The common descent group in China and its functions. New York: Viking Fund Publications in Anthropology, No. 10.

————1944   The Chinese concept of face. *American Anthropologist* 46:45–64.

Ianni, Francis A. J. 1957   Residential and occupational mobility as indices of the acculturation of an ethnic group. *Social Forces* 36:65–72.

Kitano, Harry H. L. 1969   Japanese-Americans: the evolution of a sub-culture. Englewood Cliffs: Prentice-Hall, Inc.

Kroupa, B. 1890   An artist's tour. London: Ward and Downy.

Kulp, Daniel H. 1925   Country life in South China, the sociology of familism. Vol. I, Phenix Village, Kwangtung, China. New York: Teachers College, Columbia University.

Kung, S. W. 1962   Chinese in American life, some aspects of their history, status, problems, and contributions. Seattle: University of Washington Press.

Kwoh, Beulah Ong 1947a   Occupational status of the American-born Chinese college graduate. Unpublished Master's thesis. Chicago: University of Chicago.

————1947b   The occupation of American-born Chinese male college graduates in America. *American Journal of Sociology* 53:192–200.

Lee, Rose Hum 1960   The Chinese in the United States of America. New York: Oxford University Press.

————1949   The decline of Chinatown in the United States. *American Journal of Sociology* 54:422–32.

————1956   The recent immigrant Chinese families of the San Francisco-Oakland area. *Marriage and Family Living* 18:14–24.

Leung, Lincoln 1942   The twain meet. *Common Ground* 2:100–103.

Levy, Marion J. 1967   The role of the family. In Chinese society under Communism. William T. Liu, editor. New York: John Wiley and Sons, Inc. Pp. 67–82.

Lieberson, Stanley 1961a   A societal theory of race and ethnic relations. *American Sociological Review* 26:901–10.

————1961b   The impact of residential segregation on ethnic assimilation. *Social Forces* 40:52–57.

Lin, Yueh-Hwa 1948   The golden wing; a sociological study of Chinese familism. London: Kegan, Paul, Trench, Trubner and Company, Ltd.

Loh, Homer C. 1945   Americans of Chinese ancestry in Philadelphia: cultural conflicts. Unpublished Ph.D. dissertation Philadelphia: University of Pennsylvania.

Lyman, Stanford M. 1969   Strangers in the city: the Chinese on the urban frontier (unpublished monograph).

————1968a Marriage and the family among Chinese immigrants to America 1958–1960. *Phylon* 29:321–30.

————1968b The race relations cycle of Robert E. Park. *Pacific Sociological Review* 2(1):16–22.

————1961 The structure of Chinese society in nineteenth century America. Unpublished Ph.D. dissertation. Berkeley: University of California.

Lyman, Stanford M., W. E. Willmott, and Berching Ho 1964 Rules of a Chinese secret society in British Columbia. *Bulletin of the School of Oriental and African Studies* 28:530–39.

Marden, Charles F., and Gladys Meyer 1968 Minorities in American society. New York: American Book Company.

Murphey, Rhodes 1952 Boston's Chinatown. *Economic Geography* 28:244–55.

Park, Robert E. 1925 Assimilation, social. In Encyclopedia of the social sciences, Vol. II, pp. 281–83.

Reynolds, C. N. 1935 The Chinese tongs. *American Journal of Sociology* 40:612–23.

Siu, Paul C. F. 1952 The sojourner. *American Journal of Sociology* 58:34–44.

Skinner, G. W. 1957 Chinese society in Thailand: an analytical history. Ithaca: Cornell University Press.

————1958 Leadership and power in the Chinese community of Thailand. Ithaca: Cornell University Press.

————1964 Marketing and social structure in rural China. *The Journal of Asian Studies* 24(1):3–43.

Smith, W. C. 1928 Changing personality traits of second-generation Oriental Americans. *American Journal of Sociology* 33:922–29.

Sollenbarger, Richard T. 1968 Chinese-American child-rearing practices and juvenile delinquency. *The Journal of Social Psychology* 74:13–23.

Stephenson, George M. 1926 A history of American immigration 1820–1924. Boston: Ginn and Company.

Sung, Betty Lee 1967 Mountain of gold, the story of the Chinese in America. New York: The Macmillan Company.

Taylor, Robert B. 1969 Cultural ways. Boston: Allyn and Bacon, Inc.

Turner, V. W. 1964 Symbols in Ndembu ritual. In Closed systems and open minds. Max Gluckman and Ely Devons, editors. Chicago: Aldine Publishing Company.

Wang, L. Ling-Chi 1969 Chinatown in transition. In The Asian experience in America. Asian-American concern. Davis: University of California.

Weiss, Melford S. 1970 Selective acculturation and the dating process: the patterning of Chinese-Causacian inter-racial dating. *Journal of Marriage and the Family* 32:273–78.

————1969 Conflict and compromise: the structuring of the Chinese communtiy in America. *Clearing House for Sociological Literature*. CFSL No. 69–6.

————1968b Valley City Chinese community research project: report on Chinese students. *Sacramento State College Community and Service Center Bulletin*.

————1968a Valley City Chinese community research project: report on Chinese students with reference to generational categories. *"Valley State University" Community and Service Center Bulletin*.

Welis, Williams S. 1879 Chinese immigration. New York: Charles Scribner's Sons.

Williams, Lea E. 1960 Overseas Chinese nationalism, the genesis of the pan-Chinese movement in Indonesia. Glencoe: The Free Press.

Willmott, D. E. 1960 The Chinese of Semerang: a changing minority community in Indonesia. Ithaca: Cornell University Press.

Willmott, W. E. 1964 Chinese clan associations in Vancouver. *Man* 49:33–36.

Wirth, Louis 1928 The ghetto. Chicago: University of Chicago Press.

Wolf, Eric R. 1966 Peasants. Englewood Cliffs: Prentice-Hall, Inc.

Wu, C. C. 1928 Chinatowns, a study of symbiosis and assimilation. Unpublished Ph.D. dissertation. University of Chicago.

Yang, C. K. 1961 Religion in Chinese society. Berkeley: University of California Press.

Yuan, D. Y. 1969 Division of labor between native-born and foreign-born Chinese in the United States: a study of their traditional employment. *Phylon* 30:160–69.

————1966 Chinatown and beyond: the Chinese population in metropolitan New York. *Phylon* 27:321–332.

————1963 Voluntary segregation: a study of new Chinatown. *Phylon* 24(3):255–65.

Newspapers

Daily Alta California, October 10, 1854.

East/West, March, 1970.

Valley City Bee, October 10, 1969; January 19, 1971.

Valley City Daily Union, October 19, 1869; January 11, 1872; September 7, 1873; February 23, 1876; February 27, 1876; April 4, 1876; March 4, 1879; May 23, 1881; November 12, 1883; June 6, 1900.

Bulletins

Californians of Japanese, Chinese and Filipino ancestry. State of California, Department of Industrial Relations, Division of Fair Employment Practices. San Francisco: June 1965.

Chinese Business Directory of California—1966. The Overseas Chinese Tourists Society. San Francisco.

City Census Tract Bulletins, 1964–1965. Valley-City.

Department of Finance Bulletin, 1968 and 1969. State of California.

Population and Land Area Bulletin. Valley City Planning Commission, 1969.

Pupil Population Reports, 1963–1969. Valley City Unified School District.